BISON
BOOKS

Trappers Going to Pierre's Hole Fight

OSBORNE RUSSELL'S

JOURNAL OF A TRAPPER

Edited from the original manuscript

in the WILLIAM ROBERTSON COE COLLECTION *of* WESTERN AMERICANA

in the YALE UNIVERSITY LIBRARY;

with a biography of OSBORNE RUSSELL *and maps of his travels*

while a trapper in the ROCKY MOUNTAINS

BY AUBREY L. HAINES

UNIVERSITY OF NEBRASKA PRESS
LINCOLN / LONDON

International Standard Book Number: 0-8032-0897-9 cloth
International Standard Book Number: 0-8032-5166-1
Library of Congress Catalog Card Number: 56–52

First Bison Book printing: October 1965
Most recent printing shown by first digit below:
17   18   19   20

∞

Bison Book edition reprinted from the 1955 edition by arrangement with the Oregon Historical Society.

EDITOR'S PREFACE

The *Journal of a Trapper* is perhaps the best account of the life of a fur trapper in the Rocky Mountains when the trade there was at its peak. It is a factual, unembellished narrative written by one who was not only a trapper but also a keen observer and an able writer. Both of the published editions* have been out of print for some time and unavailable except in a few library reference rooms, so that this valuable source book is neither as well known nor as much used as it should be.

The objective in preparing this edition has been not only to make the journal available to students and readers but also to give it better editorial treatment. The biographical material has been expanded considerably through research into the later life of Osborne Russell, and maps have been added to show his travels while a trapper. The journal and its appendix are presented here just as written by Russell; his arrangement, punctuation, spelling and capitalization have been followed as closely as the difficult chirography allowed. Footnotes and an index have been added to increase the reference value of the work.

Actually, my interest in the *Journal of a Trapper* stems from the need for a footnote. While reading casually in it I came upon a pencilled note, concerning "Twenty-five Yard River," which I found on the margin of a page. Someone had written "Shield's River?" To me it was so apparent that they were the same that I was surprised by the former reader's uncertainty, and, to be sure in my own mind, I took a map and plotted Russell's track over the Yellowstone Plateau, by the courses, distances and landmarks given in his journal. In that area where I had traveled much by car, on horseback and afoot, I found his description checked remarkably well with the country as I knew it.

---

*L. A. York, editor. The 1914 and 1921 editions appeared under the title of *Journal of a trapper, or, Nine years in the Rocky Mountains: 1834-1843.*

Several years later, while taking a course in Pacific Northwest History under Dr. Paul C. Phillips at Montana State University, I mentioned the map I had made of a portion of Osborne Russell's wanderings while a trapper. He suggested that I make a map for the entire period covered by the journal. In that manner the ten maps which appear in this book as "Osborne Russell's Travels" had their beginning. But Dr. Phillips did not let the matter rest there; he also urged me to edit a new edition of the *Journal of a Trapper*, a work which was begun with the proper misgivings.

Of course the editing could not be done adequately without the original manuscript and attempts to locate it were, for a time, unsuccessful. Inquiry was first made of L. A. York, who edited and published the journal previously, but he claimed to have sold the manuscript to Dr. A. S. W. Rosenbach, of Philadelphia, soon after publishing the second edition in 1921. Correspondence with the Rosenbach Company failed to reveal the transaction or any clues to the disposition of the manuscript.

At that point I fortunately told Mr. David C. Duniway, Archivist of the Oregon State Library, of my failure. He reasoned that a resale was made by Dr. Rosenbach to one of the two men then diligently collecting such manuscripts, and a check of the William Robertson Coe Collection of Western Americana in the Yale University Library established the fact that the original manuscript of *Journal of a Trapper* was there. A microfilm of the original manuscript and related papers, made available by the Yale University Library Committee with their kind permission to publish from it, is the basis of this work.

It is my hope that this presentation of Osborne Russell's excellent journal will prove interesting to the casual reader and yet be adequate for the needs of the scholar.

Longmire, Washington.
November 23, 1953.

ACKNOWLEGMENTS

The work of editing the *Journal of a Trapper* was often difficult, but I am sure it would have been infinitely more so, or even impossible, without the generous help of many persons. Dr. Phillips made the suggestion which led me to undertake it in the first place, and his help and encouragement has been vital in bringing it to a conclusion. To Mr. Duniway I owe a debt of gratitude for locating the original manuscript, and also for his assistance in searching the records of the Provisional Government of Oregon. I am also indebted to the Library Committee of Yale University Library for permission to publish from the original manuscript.

The facilities of a number of libraries were used, among which special mention must be made of the Montana State University Library at Missoula; the University of Washington Library at Seattle; the Oregon Historical Society Library at Portland; the Oregon State Library at Salem; the Pacific University Library at Forest Grove, Oregon; and the public libraries of Missoula, Montana; Tacoma, Washington; and Portland, Oregon. In addition, correspondence with the Library of Congress, the Free Library of Philadelphia, and the California State Library at Sacramento, was of material assistance. I must also mention the helpfulness of Superintendent David L. Hieb, of Fort Laramie National Monument, who, by giving me access to unpublished material and through conversations and correspondence, did much to clarify obscure points.

Lastly, among those whose help I acknowledge, is that of my wife Wilma. She has been typist, proof-reader, and consultant, working patiently with micro-films, rough drafts and revisions; and, throughout, her enthusiasm and faith has been that of an author.

INTRODUCTION

The author of *Journal of a Trapper* is not nearly so well known as his priceless book. He was more than a trapper or a mere journalist, for out of the adventurous years he so faithfully records emerged a mature man of high character and good works who should not be forgotten.

Osborne Russell was born June 12, 1814,[1] at the little village of Bowdoinham, Maine, on the estuary of the Kennebec River. He was one of nine children in the family of George G. and Eleanor (Power) Russell; a family which had New Hampshire roots. Osborne's boyhood was probably typical of the Maine farmboy of that day, and there is no doubt the environment was a wholesome one, for, despite the limited schooling which Russell mentions, he developed into an able young man of good morals and sound judgment. According to his great-nephew, L. A. York, Russell ran away to sea at the age of 16 but soon gave up that career by deserting his ship at New York, after which he spent three years in the service of what was called the Northwest Fur Trapping and Trading Company, operating in Wisconsin and Minnesota. Nothing else is known of him until he joined Wyeth's expedition to the Rocky Mountains and the mouth of the Columbia River in 1834.

Nathaniel J. Wyeth had become interested in colonizing the Oregon country, and in the business possibilities there, through the influence of Hall J. Kelley, a one-time Boston school teacher. After years of effort, Kelley succeeded in 1831 in organizing the Oregon Colonization Society, to which Wyeth agreed to attach himself with a company which he would raise. Kelley's plans for an overland expedition to Oregon failed, but Wyeth went ahead and led his party across the country in 1832 along the route which later became the Oregon Trail.

The first expedition was pushed with the resourcefulness characteristic of Wyeth, but inexperience, desertion, sickness and the loss of his supply ship, the *Sultana,* on a South American reef, completely defeated his efforts. Wyeth returned home empty-handed, but with new plans and a contract to deliver $3,000 worth of supplies to Milton Sublette and Thomas Fitzpatrick, of the Rocky Mountain Fur Company, at the rendezvous of 1834. He hoped in that manner to partially finance a second expedition to the Oregon country, where he intended to establish a salmon-fishing and fur-trading enterprise. Wyeth was joined in the venture by three Boston merchants and the Columbia River Fishing and Trading Company was formed.

Again a vessel laden with trade goods and supplies was dispatched to the mouth of the Columbia River, to meet an overland expedition which would, enroute, transport the supplies contracted for by the Rocky Mountain Fur Company. The men of this "second expedition" were recruited on the frontier at St. Louis and Independence, Missouri. Among those who joined at the latter place, was Osborne Russell who agreed to serve the Columbia River Fishing and Trading Company eighteen months for a wage of $250.[2] Thus, he entered the Rocky Mountain fur trade as an inexperienced hand, but he entered it with an enthusiasm which illuminates the opening page of the journal he so fortunately began to keep.

When the overland party arrived at the rendezvous on Ham's Fork of Green River, Wyeth found the Rocky Mountain Fur Company dissolved and a new company formed. As a consequence, the agreement to bring out supplies was not fully honored, so that Wyeth was left with much of the freight on his hands. The decision of the partners of the Rocky Mountain Fur Company to escape their financial obligations through reorganization was the result of a period of fierce competition with the American Fur Company. The brigades of that company were determined interlopers and they hung on the tracks of the Rocky Mountain men with the intention of learning where lay the best trapping grounds, but the latter were as determined to lead the newcomers a fruitless chase. Neither company profited from the struggle and the Rocky Mountain men were brought to the verge of ruin so that they came to the rendezvous without the fur to pay the wages of their men. The easiest way out of financial embarrassment was to default on the contract with Wyeth, who had to alter his plans to rescue his own enterprise.

Accordingly, Wyeth proposed to build a fort on the plains of Snake River and enter into the fur trade with the goods which the Rocky Mountain men did not take. The fort was soon built and named for Henry Hall, one of the partners of the Company, and was left in the care of a garrison of twelve men, among whom was Osborne Russell.

The late summer passed with nothing to ease the monotony of completing the rude post except occasional meat-hunts and the alcohol so freely sold to the men. With the coming of fall a trade was begun with local Indians, but it was not until the spring of 1835 that trapping parties were put into the field. Then they were so poorly managed that many men were lost by desertion. Russell was not one of those but he was no less anxious to leave the service of the Columbia River Fishing and Trading Company.

On receiving his discharge from Wyeth, Russell joined Jim Bridger's brigade of old Rocky Mountain Fur Company men, and he continued with them after the merger which left the American Fur Company in control of the fur trade. However, it was an empty victory for that company as the growing scarcity of beaver and the decline in price resulting from the change in fashion, which substituted the silk hat for that of clipped beaver, combined to make the fur trade less profitable than it had been. It was rumored about the rendezvous of 1838 that the company intended to abandon the trade in the Rocky Mountains, and that great wilderness "fair" was not the carefree gathering it had formerly been. One more rendezvous was held, but Russell was not there; he had become a free-trapper operating out of Fort Hall, which had passed into the hands of the Hudson's Bay Company in 1837.

vii

Like so many of the trappers, Russell was reluctant to give up the old life and he stayed in the mountains trading and trapping in a small way until the great westward migration began. It was an easy life with plenty of leisure to spend with the books he borrowed from Fort Hall; good books sent to that far-away post of the Hudson's Bay Company by Chief Factor John McLoughlin out of his circulating library at Fort Vancouver.

The Rev. George H. Atkinson, whose diary contains a brief biography of Russell,[3] says that out of that reading came a deep religious conviction which changed Russell's life. During the months spent trapping with Elbridge Trask in the country around Gray's Marsh he studied the Bible carefully, became convinced of its truth and came to feel that he had not lived according to its principles. His conversion led him to abandon the life of a "mountain man," and he went to the Willamette Valley with the Elijah White wagon train.

The new life which Osborne Russell began in the Oregon Country was one of great value to that struggling community. At that time the territory north of California and west of the continental divide was occupied jointly by Great Britain and the United States in accordance with the convention of 1818. Neither government took an interest in civil affairs, but left them in the hands of the feudalistic Hudson's Bay Company and the individual settlers. The Canadian settlers, discharged employees of the Company, were satisfied, but the American immigrants felt insecure. As early as 1841 there was recognition of the need for a form of civil government to dispose of the estate of the deceased Ewing Young.[4] Several meetings were held with the objective of electing public officials and drafting a constitution and code of laws. However, the two factions could not agree; so the early meetings accomplished no more than the establishment of legal processes through the election of a supreme judge, with probate powers, and the necessary officers to assist him.

By 1843, the Americans were again pressing for provisional

government. A series of meetings was held, and at the third, at Champoeg, on May 2, 1843, a decision was reached by a narrow majority, to organize a "civil community."[5] Public officers were elected, among them an executive committee of three men and a supreme judge who was destined never to act in that capacity.[6] Osborne Russell was present at the meeting and is listed among those who voted for the organization of a provisional government,[7] but he does not appear to have taken a prominent part.

Soon after that historic meeting, Russell was involved in an accident which turned him toward politics. On June 6, 1843, he lost his right eye while blasting rock in a millrace at Oregon City. During his convalescence he studied law[8] and thus prepared himself for an active part in the affairs of the new government.

The Provisional Government of Oregon became a reality, though a feeble one, at the meeting of July 5, 1843, at which a constitution and code of laws was approved and the elected officers were sworn in. But the chosen judge, Wilson, would not serve, and on October 2nd Osborne Russell was appointed by the Executive Committee to fill the office.[9] On the 30th of the same month he gave G. W. LeBreton a receipt for a copy of the "written laws of Oregon Territory",[10] and a perusal of the trial records and documents of the second term of the Supreme Court leaves no doubt that those laws were applied in a just and dignified manner.[11] The title of "Judge Russell", by which his fellow citizens knew him, was given in recognition of his service on the Oregon bench, rather than for later *pro tempore* Judgeship at a California vigilance trial.[12]

Annual elections were provided for under the organic laws[13] and the first was held on May 14, 1844. The returns show that there were fourteen candidates for election to the executive committee. Of the 591 votes cast, Osborne Russell received 244, Peter G. Stewart 140, Wm. J. Bailey 70.[14] At this election Russell was also a candidate for Supreme Court Judge, but he was defeated in that contest as he ran fourth among six participants.[15]

ix

On May 25, 1844, Osborne Russell and Peter G. Stewart took the oath of office as members of the Executive Committee.[16] The oath is in Russell's handwriting and states with simple dignity, "We and each of us do Solemnly Swear that we will well and truly perform the duties of members of the Executive Committee according to the laws of Oregon Territory according to the best of our skill and judgment." Dr. Bailey took the oath later and he probably did not take an important part in the actions of the committee since most of its documents bear the signatures of Russell and Stewart. This second Executive Committee performed the functions of a governor in an able and dignified manner with no more government than necessary. The salary paid was $100 per annum[17] and it is probable that the duties of office were only of a part-time nature.

The ability and vision of the men at the head of the infant community can be seen in some of their documents. Shortly after taking office the committee framed a message "To the Honorable the Legislative Committee of Oregon Territory . . ." in which the needs of the community were set forth with striking clarity.[18] Again, in their message to the same body on December 16, 1844, the subject of relations with Great Britain was discussed by Russell and Stewart in a manner remarkable for its fairness and restraint.[19] The obvious desire of the authors to avoid friction, which might easily have destroyed the weak beginnings of American government, is evident in the exchange of letters between Dr. McLoughlin and the Executive Committee, regarding the trespass of an American settler upon the Company's lands at Vancouver. Instead of supporting the designs of the immigrant, Russell and Stewart made clear their regrets and stated, ". . . it affords us great pleasure to learn that the offender, after due reflection, desisted from the insolent and rash measure."[20]

But the most important work of the second Executive Committee was the memorial to the United States Congress, June 28, 1845.[21] The defenseless condition of the colony, its pressing needs, and the desire of its citizens for true territorial status under United States sovereignty are made plain. P. H. Burnett expresses his admiration for the members of the Executive Committee, and their statesmanship, in these words: ". . . those intelligent, calm, and faithful American officers . . . admirable men for that position."[22]

The Provisional Government of Oregon, which has been rather facetiously described as "strong without an Army or Navy and rich without taxes," finally was forced to levy upon its citizens in the year 1844.[23] The tax roll shows that the frontier politician, Osborne Russell, was by no means well off. He was listed as having horses valued at $100, and his poll tax was given as sixty-three cents. He had no watch.

One of the revisions of the laws effected by the Legislative Committee in 1844 abolished the Executive Committee of three in favor of a single governor. At the 1845 election Russell was a candidate for the governorship, as were A. L. Lovejoy, George Abernethy and W. J. Bailey; but, at the last moment he and Bailey threw their support to Abernethy, thus assuring his election. Apparently Lovejoy represented the rasher element among the immigrants and so was distasteful to the friends of Russell and Bailey.[24]

Left without office by his defeat in the election, Russell turned to his personal affairs. Although he is included in an 1843 list of settlers in the Willamette Valley,[25] he did not become a "settler" in the fullest sense until he claimed land on the Luckiamute River near the present town of Ledford, in Polk County. His claim was recorded as follows:

"Osborne Russell has this day recorded a land claim in Yam Hill District as follows To Wit: situate and beginning at a fir tree 3 feet in Diameter, standing 800 yards south west of the falls of the north branch of the Lukamyute river, and blazed on the north and east sides, thence running north 600 yards to the stream, thence crossing said stream and running north 1130 yards to three Oaks each 6 inches Diam — standing together on the side of the Mountain, one blazed on the south and another on the east side — thence running nearly east one mile, to an oak tree two feet in Diam — blazed on the west and south sides, standing on a high ridge — thence south 1200 yds to the stream, thence crossing

the stream and running nearly south 560 yds to an Oak tree 12 inches Diam
standing on the side of a ridge, and blazed on the north & west sides—thence
west to the place of beginning, containing 640 acres, said claim is bounded on
the west by Mountaineous forest, on the north by a high spur of Mountain,
which divides the waters of the Lukamyute and LeCreole rivers, on the east,
north of the stream, by a tract of Prairie Land supposed to be claimed, by
Chas Eaton—south of the stream by a tract of prairie claimed and occupied
by Adam Brown and on the south by vacant ridgy Land, and spurs of
Mountain.

"And the Claimant states that he holds the said Claim by personal
occupancy.

"Dated Oct. 23d, 1845.

"Attest
"J. E. Long
"Recorder."[26]

At about this time Russell wrote to his family in Maine. They
had not heard from him after he ran away to sea and believed
him dead. Occasional correspondence continued for a few years
and a number of letters written to his sisters, Eleanor and
Martha, have been preserved.

It was also in the period following his political defeat that
Russell wrote the manuscript of *Journal of a Trapper*. He read
an account of Rocky Mountain life based on a journal kept by
James O. Pattie,[27] and was so impressed by its inaccuracies that
he decided to publish a true version. Accordingly, he prepared
a manuscript from his journal notes and sent it East for publication. In a letter sent in April of 1848 to his sister in Maine,
he stated that he had instructed his agent in New York to forward a copy to her when published.[28] The work did not appear
at that time, which would indicate that the agent could not find
a publisher; however, he did comply with his instructions, inso-
far as he was able, by having the manuscript bound and sent to
Russell's sister.

During 1847 Osborne Russell met the Reverend George H.
Atkinson who apparently was deeply impressed, for his diary
contains a brief but valuable biographical sketch of the Judge.[29]
From it we learn that Russell was reared a Baptist, and that he

joined the church of the Reverend Harvey Clark soon after coming to Oregon City and was a member of that association of Presbyterians and Congregationalists while he remained in Oregon. He avoided noisy religion and enjoyed a retired life, reading and studying as much as his health would allow. The Reverend adds that Russell read French.

In the same year Russell re-entered politics, taking part in the Yamhill Convention as a delegate from Polk County,[30] and election returns in *The Spectator* show that he was elected to represent Polk County in the Territorial Legislature in June of 1848.[31] Russell was also named one of the original Trustees of Pacific University at Forest Grove that September.[32]

News of the discovery of gold in California reached Oregon in 1848, and it drew many of the able-bodied men of the territory to the mines, Russell included. His name appeared on a list presented to the Legislature December 7, 1848, showing ". . . the members who have resigned, or left the territory."[33] According to a letter which Russell wrote his sister from California, he left Oregon in September,[34] though the Polk County census for the spring of 1849 continued to list him as a resident.[35]

After his arrival in California, poor health made it necessary for Russell to engage in merchandising until March of 1849. He then tried mining for a time and was successful enough to enable him to start a boarding house and provision store business in October. His partner in the venture was an old neighbor from Oregon by the name of Gilliam. Russell also served as a judge at the Vigilance trial of three men, whose hanging resulted in the name of "Gallowstown" for what is now known as Placerville.

On April 15, 1850, Russell sold his land claim on the Luckiamute River in Oregon to John H Thessing for five hundred dollars.[36] He may have needed the money to invest in his business or only wished to terminate his absentee ownership. Anyhow, Thessing resold the land to John Thorpe, who appears to have had difficulty establishing his ownership. In a series of letters to General Joseph Lane, who, as first Governor of Oregon

Territory, stood for recognition of land claims made under the Provisional Government and who later worked for passage of a land law while a delegate to Congress, Thorpe pressed for action favorable to his interests. Among the statements made to Lane was one that "... Russell, held the same [his land claim] by personal occupancy, until the 5th day of April, 1850."[37] The falsification probably was a deliberate attempt by Thorpe to validate Russell's claim under the Donation Land Law passed by Congress September 27, 1850.[38] Since the land was sold prior to the passage of that law, there is no doubt Russell acted in good faith, even though his claim did not qualify. From the records of the General Land Office it appears that Thorpe was only allowed to retain 320 acres, or one-half the land he purchased.[39]

Later, Russell and his partner operated two trading vessels between Sacramento and Portland, but the partner absconded with the firm's money and one of the vessels. Russell was ruined financially and is said to have spent the remainder of his life trying to pay off creditors.[40] No evidence has been found to indicate that he ever returned to Oregon.

A letter to his sister indicates that Russell became estranged from his family in the year 1855 because of gossip written home by a relative in California. Also, a misunderstanding with his sister concerning the manuscript he had previously sent her helped to embitter Russell. He had made several inquiries over a period of years to determine if it had reached her, but received no answer. Finally he wrote his other sister, Eleanor, asking her to intercede and stating that he had been offered one thousand dollars for the manuscript.[41] If Russell wrote to his family again, the letter has not been found.

It is probable that Russell lived near Placerville for the remainder of his life. The registration records of El Dorado County list him as a miner residing in Diamond Springs T'p. from 1867 to 1890, and the directory of Sacramento City and County, which then included Amador, El Dorado and Placer Counties, lists him as a resident of Newtown in 1884-85.[42] He never married.

Russell's health was frail after the accident in which he lost his right eye, and his infirmities were frequently mentioned in his letters home. There is no way of knowing how much his life was blighted by that explosion, or how much his usefulness to the community he lived in was reduced because of it. From his handwriting it is evident that he was often under great nervous strain, which may explain his frequent references to "bilious" attacks in later years. He was finally obliged to enter the county hospital at Placerville, May 1, 1884, suffering from what was termed "miner's rheumatism." Toward the last he was paralyzed below the waist[43] and his death occurred August 26, 1892.[44]

Russell's grave, in common with many of that day, is unmarked. His likeness is also lost to us, for what was probably the only picture of him was destroyed by a gang of vandal boys when they wrecked the home of Albert Tozier in Portland.[45] It was brought to Oregon by a cousin who emigrated from Maine. But perhaps the statement of Peter H. Burnett, his good friend and first Governor of California, is enough to remember Osborne Russell by:

"All his comrades agreed he never lost his virtuous habits, but always remained true to his principles ... He is a man of education and refined feelings."[46]

NOTES

1. "Hallowell, Maine, Vital Records," Vol. I (Births), p. 255.

2. Account-books of Fort Hall, 1834-1837, Ledger No. 1, "John Russell in acct Current with the C.R.F. & Trading Co.", pp. 13-14. Although Russell says he joined on April 4, 1834, his wage was computed as beginning on April 19.

3. "Diary of Rev. George H. Atkinson, 1847-58," edited by E. Ruth Rockwood, *Oregon Historical Quarterly*, 40:350f., December, 1939.

4. F. G. Young, "Ewing Young and his estate," *Oregon Historical Quarterly*, 21: (3) 171-316, September, 1920.

5. Frederick V. Holman, "A brief history of the Oregon Provisional Government and what caused its formation," *Oregon Historical Quarterly*, 13: (2) 89-139, June, 1912.

Hon J. Quinn Thornton, "History of the Provisional Government," *Oregon Pioneer Transactions*, 1875:43-96.

6. Oregon Supreme Court Records, "Judges of the Supreme Court of Oregon," (Unpublished biographical data compiled by the clerk of the Supreme Court), c. 1936.

7. Holman, *op. cit.*, p. 114. On the granite shaft erected at the site to commemorate the meeting, Russell's name is given as "Russell Osborne."

8. Atkinson, *op. cit.*, 350f.

9. Papers of the Provisional Government, Document 1369, Archives, Oregon State Library, Salem.

10. Papers of the Provisional Government, Document 837, Archives, Oregon State Library, Salem.

11. Supreme Court record book No. 1, Oregon Territory—1844, Achives, Oregon State Library, Salem, pp. 4-6.

Papers of the Provisional Government, Documents 783 and 847, Archives, Oregon State Library, Salem.

12. Dictionary of American Biography, Vol. 16, 1935, p. 248.

The following item from the Oregon *Spectator* for March 9, 1848, shows that Russell was known by the title of "Judge" during his residence in Oregon:

"A party bound to the United States will rendezvous on the North fork of the Luciamute, near Judge Russell's, from the 25th of March to the 1st of April, and then start by way of the 'Southern Route.' Persons wishing further information, may apply to D. M. Judd, at Wm. Savage's Salem, or to J. Neall at Judge Russell's on the Luckiamute."

Also, the Griffin records at Pacific University, Forest Grove, Oregon, list "Judge Russell" among the "Subscribers to the *American and Unionist* in account with J. S. Griffin, June 1848," p. 12.

13. LaFayette Grover, *The Oregon archives ...*, (Salem, Oregon; Asahel Bush, public printer, 1853) , p. 29.

14. J. Henry Brown, *Brown's political history of Oregon,* Vol. I, (Portland, Oregon: Wiley B. Allen, publisher, 1892) , p. 155.

15. Brown, *op. cit.,* p. 155.

16. Papers of the Provisional Government, Document 920, Archives, Oregon State Library, Salem.

"Sketches of Oregon, No. 2, The process of government," in *The* (Oregon) *Spectator,* June 24, 1847, 2:2.

17. Brown, *op. cit.,* p. 156.

18. Hubert Howe Bancroft, *History of Oregon, 1834-1848,* Vol. I; *Bancroft's Works,* Vol. XXIX, (San Francisco: The History Company, 1886) , p. 430.

19. W. D. Fenton, "The winning of the Oregon country," *Oregon Historical Quarterly,* 6: (4) 361, December, 1905.

Papers of the Provisional Government, Document 12220, Archives, Oregon State Library, Salem.

20. Peter H. Burnett, "Recollections and opinions of an old pioneer," Chap. V, *Oregon Historical Quarterly,* 5: (3) 297-99, September, 1904.

21. Papers of the Provisional Government, Document 1521, Archives, Oregon State Library, Salem.

Fenton, *op. cit.,* pp. 359f.

22. Burnett, *op. cit.,* pp. 299, 302.

23. Leslie M. Scott, "First taxes in Oregon, 1844," *Oregon Historical Quarterly,* 31: (1) 21, March, 1930.

24. Bancroft, *op. cit.,* pp. 427 f., 471 f.

25. Hon. J. W. Nesmith, "List of settlers in Oregon country in fall of 1843," *Oregon Pioneer Transactions,* 1875:54.

26. Oregon land claim record, 1845-6, Book 4 (This is the first book and contains the index from another book) , Office of the Secretary of State, Salem, Oregon, p. 37.

27. James Ohio Pattie, *The personal narrative of James O. Pattie,* of Kentucky, edited by Timothy Flint, (Cincinnati, Ohio, 1833) .

28. Letter to Martha A. Russell, April 3, 1848, (original now in the William Robertson Coe Collection of Western Americana) , Yale University Library, New Haven, Connecticut.

29. Atkinson, *op. cit.,* pp. 350-51.

30. Editorial in *The* (Oregon) *Spectator,* November 25, 1847, 2:3.

31. *Ibid.* June 15, 1848, 2:2, and July 27, 1848, 2:6.

32. Tualatin Academy, Secretary's record book, 1848, (Minute book No. 1) , Pacific University, Forest Grove, Oregon, p. 1.

James R. Robertson, "Origin of Pacific University," prepared from University records and other sources, *Oregon Historical Quarterly*, 6: (2) 116f., June, 1905.

33. Provisional Government of Oregon, Fee Record Book, (Resignations, etc., 1848), Archives, Oregon State Library, Salem, p. 14.

Grover, *op. cit.*, pp. 257f.

34. Letter to Mrs. Eleanor Read, November 10, 1849, (Original now in the William Robertson Coe Collection of Western Americana), Yale University Library, New Haven, Connecticut.

35. Papers of the Provisional Government, Document 1079, (Census book for Polk County for the spring of 1849), Archives, Oregon State Library, Salem.

36. Letters from John Thorpe to Gen. Joseph Lane, July 23, 1851; November 22, 1841; and January 7, 1854 (originals now in the Oregon Historical Society Library), Portland, Oregon.

37. *Ibid.*, November 7, 1851.

38. National Resources Board, *Certain aspects of the land problems and government land policies*, Section V, (Washington, D. C.: Government Printing Office, 1935), p. 61.

39. "Oregon City donation land certificate file in the National Archives," (File microcopy FM145-Claim of John Thorpe), Archives, Oregon State Library, Salem.

40. Publisher's note, *Journal of a trapper . . .*, Edited by L. A. York, (Boise, Idaho: Syms-York Company, 1914), p. 104.

41. Letter to Mrs. Eleanor Read, August 26, 1855, (Original now in the William Robertson Coe Collection of Western Americana), Yale University Library, New Haven, Connecticut.

42. Correspondence with the California State Library, Sacramento, California, 1951.

43. Caroline C. Dobbs, *Men of Champoeg*, (Portland, Oregon: Metropolitan Press, 1932), p. 47.

York, *loc. cit.*

44. Death notice in the *Placerville Mountain Democrat*, September 4, 1892, 1:3.

"Death Notice.

"Russell — at the County Hospital, August 26, 1892, Osborn Russel (Judge), a native of Maine, aged 78 years."

45. Letter from Albert Tozier to Harriet C. Long, April 1936, regarding portraits of Alanson Beers, David Hill, Osborne Russell and Dr. W. J. Bailey, Archives, Oregon State Library, Salem.

46. Burnett, *op. cit.*, pp. 161f.

Journal of a Trapper

Or

Nine Years Residence among the

Rocky Mountains

Between the years of 1834 and 1843

Comprising

A general description of the Country, Climate,
Rivers, Lakes, Mountains, etc The nature and habits
of Animals, Manners and Customs of Indians and a Complete
view of the life led by a Hunter in those regions

By

Osborne Russell

I envy no man that knows more than myself
and pity them that know less: Sir T. Brown.

PREFACE

Reader, if you are in search of the travels of a Classical and Scientific tourist, please to lay this Volume down, and pass on, for this simply informs you what a Trapper has seen and experienced. But if you wish to peruse a Hunter's rambles among the wild regions of the Rocky Mountains, please to read this, and forgive the authors foibles and imperfections, considering as you pass along that he has been chiefly educated in Nature's School under that rigid tutor experience, and you will also bear in mind the author does not hold himself responsible for the correctness of statements made otherwise than from observation.

THE AUTHOR.

JOURNAL OF A TRAPPER

During the years 1834 to 1843

At the town of Independence Missouri on the 4th of April 1834 I joined an expedition fitted out for the Rocky Mountains and Mouth of the Columbia River, by a Company formed in Boston under the name and style of the Columbia River Fishing and Trading Company. The same firm has fitted out a Brig of two hundred tons burthen, freighted with the nessesary assortment of merchandise for the Salmon and Fur Trade, with orders to sail to the mouth of the Columbia River, whilst the land party, under the direction of Mr. Nathaniel J. Wyeth, should proceed across the Rocky Mountains and unite with the Brig's Company in establishing a Post on the Columbia near the Pacific. Our party consisted of forty men engaged in the service accompanied by Mess Nutall and Townsend[1] [?] Botanists and Ornithologists with two attendants; likewise Rev's Jason and Daniel Lee Methodist Missionaries with four attendants on their way to establish a Mission in Oregon: which brot. our numbers (including six independent Trappers) to fifty Eight men. From the 23 to the 27th of April we were engaged in arranging our packs and moving to a place about 4 Miles from Independence. On the morning of the 28th we were all equipped and mounted hunter like: about forty men leading two loaded horses each were marched out in double file with joyous hearts enlivened by anticipated prospects: led by Mr. Wyeth a persevering adventurer and lover of Enterprise whilst the remainder of the party with twenty head of extra horses and as many cattle to supply emergencies brot. up the rear under the direction of Capt. Joseph Thing[2] an eminent navigator and fearless son of Neptune who had been employed by the Company in Boston to accompany the party and measure the route across the Rocky Mountains by Astronomical observation

We travelled slowly thru the beautiful verdant and widely ex-

1

tended prairie untill about 2 clk P.M. and encamped at a small grove of timber near a spring 29th We took up our march and travelled across a large and beautifully undulating prairie intersected by small streams skirted with timber intermingled with shrubbery untill the 3d of May when we arrived at the Caw or Kanzas River near the residence of the U S agent for those Indians.[3]

The Caw or Kanzas Indians are the most filthy indolent and degraded sett of human beings I ever saw. They live in small oval huts 4 or 5 feet high formed of willow branches and covered with Deer Elk or Buffaloe skins. On the 4th of May we crossed the River and on the 5th resumed our march into the interior, travelling over beautiful rolling prairies and Encamping on small streams at night untill the 10th when we arrived at the River Platte.[4]

We followed up this River to the forks, then forded the South fork and travelled up the north untill the 1st day of June when we arrived at Laramy's fork of Platte;[5] where is the first perceptible commencement of the Rocky Mountains we crossed this fork and travelled up the main River untill night and encamped. The next day we left the River and travelled across the Black hills[6] nearly paralell with the general course of the Platte untill the 9th of June when we came to the River again and crossed it at a place called the Red Butes[7] (high mountains of Red Rock from which the River issues). The next day we left the River on our left hand and traveled a northwest direction, and stopped at night on a small spring branch nearly destitute of wood or shrubbery. The next day we arrived at a stream running [in]to the Platte called Sweet Water,[8] this we ascended to a rocky mountainous country untill the 15th of June then left it and crossed the divide between waters of the Atlantic and Pacific Oceans:[9] and encamped on Sandy Creek a branch running into Green River which flows into the Colorado of the West. The next day moved down Sandy WNW direction and arrived at Green river on the 18th of June.[10]

Here we found some white Hunters who informed us that the grand rendezvous of Whites and Indians would be on a small western branch of the River about 20 miles distant, in a South West direction. Next day June 20th we arrived at the destined place.[11] Here we met with two companies of Trappers and Traders: One is a branch of the "American Fur Company," under the direction of Mess Dripps and Fonanell:[12] The other is called the "Rocky Mountain Fur Company" The names of the partners are Thomas Fitzpatrick, Milton Sublett and James Bridger. The two companies consist of about six hundred men, including men engaged in the service, White, Half Breed and Indian Fur Trappers. This stream is called Ham's fork of Green River. The face of the adjacent country is very mountaneous and broken except in the small alluvial bottoms along the streams, it abounds with Buffaloe, Antelope, Elk and Bear, and some few Deer along the Rivers. Here Mr Wyeth disposed of a part of his loads to the Rocky Mountain Fur Company and on *on* the 2d of July we renewed our march towards the Columbia River. After leaving Ham's Fork we took across a high range of hills in a NW direction and fell on to a stream called Bear River which emptied [in]to the Big Salt Lake. This is a beautiful country. the river which is about [20] yards wide runs through large fertile bottoms bordered by rolling ridges which gradually ascended [?] on each side of the river to the high ranges [of] dark and lofty mountains upon whose tops the snow remains nearly the year round. We travelled down this river N West about 15 miles and [cn]camped opposite a Lake of fresh water about 60 miles in circumference which outlets into the river on the west side.[13] Along the west border of this Lake the country is generally smooth ascending gradually into the interior and terminates in a high range of mountains which nearly surrounds the Lake approaching close to the shore on the East. The next day (the 7th) we travelled down this river and on the 9th encamped at a place called the Sheep Rock so called from a point of the mountain terminating at the river bank in a perpen-

dicular high rock:[14] the river curves around the foot of this rock
and forms a half circle which brings its course to the S.W. from
whence it runs in the same direction to the Salt Lake about 80
miles distant. The Sheep occupy this prominent elevation (which
overlooks the surrounding country to a great extent) at all seasons of the year.

On the right hand or East side of the river about 2 miles above
the rock is 5 or 6 mineral Springs[15] some of which have precisely
the taste of soda water when taken up and drank immediately
others have a sour, sulperous taste: none of them have any outlet but boil and bubble in small holes a few inches from the surface
of the ground. This place which now looks so lonely, visited only
by the rambling Trapper or solitary Savage will doubtless at no
distant day be a resort for thousands of the gay and fashionable
world, as well as Invalids and spectators. The country immediately adjacent seems to have all undergone volcanic action at
some remote period the evidences of which, however still remains
in the deep and frightful chasms which may be found in the rocks,
throughout this portion of country which could only have been
formed by some terrible convulsion of nature. The ground about
these springs is very strongly impregnated with Sal Soda There
is also large beds of clay in the vicinity of a snowy whiteness
which is much used by the Indians for cleansing their clothes and
skins, it not being any inferior to soap for cleansing woollens or
skins dressed after the Indian fashion. On the 11th (July) we left
Bear river and crossed low ridges of broken country for about 15
miles in a N East direction and fell on to a stream which runs into
Snake river called Black Foot. Here we met with Capt. B. L.
Bonnenvill[16] with a party of 10 or 12 men. He was on his way to
the Columbia and was employed killing and drying Buffaloe meat
for the journey. The next day we travelled in a west direction
over a rough mountaneous country about 25 miles and the day
following after travelling about 20 miles in the same direction we
emerged from the mountain into the great valley of Snake River

on the 16th — We crossed the valley and reached the river in about 25 miles travel West. Here Mr. Wyeth concluded to stop[17] build a Fort & deposit the remainder of his merchandise: leaving a few men to protect them and trade with the Snake and Bonnack Indians. On the 18th we commenced the Fort which was a stockade 80 ft square built of Cotton wood trees set on end sunk 2½ feet in the ground and standing about 15 feet above with two bastions 8 ft square at the opposite angles. On the 4th of August the Fort was completed. And on the 5th the "Stars and Stripes" were unfurled to the breeze at Sunrise in the center of a savage and uncivilized country over an American Trading Post.[18]

The next day Mr Wyeth departed for the mouth of the Columbia River with all the party excepting twelve men (myself included) [19] who were stationed at the Fort. I now began to experience the difficulties attending a mountaineer we being all raw hands excepting the man who had charge of the Fort and a Mullattoe: the two latter having but very little experience in hunting game with the Rifle: and altho the country abounded with game still it wanted experience to kill it.

On the 12th of August myself and 3 others (the Mullattoe included) started from the Fort to hunt Buffaloe. We proceeded up the stream running into Snake River near the Fort called Ross's fork[20] in an East direction about 25 miles, crossed a low mountain in the same direction about 5 miles and fell on to a stream called Portneuf: [21] here we found several large bands of Buffaloe we went to a small spring and encamped. I now prepared myself for the first time in my life to kill meat for my supper with a Rifle. I had an elegant one but had little experience in useing it, I however approached the band of Buffaloe crawling on my hands and knees within about 80 yards of them then raised my body erect took aim and shot at a Bull: at the crack of the gun the Buffaloe all ran off excepting the Bull which I had wounded, I then reloaded and shot as fast as I could untill I had driven 25 bullets at, in and about him which was all that I had in my bullet pouch whilst the Bull still stood apparently riveted to the spot I watched him anxiously for half an hour in hopes of seeing him fall, but to no purpose, I was obliged to give it up as a bad job and retreat to our encampment without meat: but the Mullattoe had better luck he had killed a fat cow whilst shooting 15 bullets at the band. The next day we succeeded in killing another cow and two Bulls, we butchered them took the meat and returned to the Fort. On the 20th of August we started again to hunt meat: we left the Fort and travelled abot 6 miles when we discovered a Grizzly Bear digging and eating roots in a piece of marshy ground near a large bunch of willows. The Mullattoe approached within 100 yards and shot him thro. the left shoulder he gave a hideous growl and sprang into the thicket. The Mullattoe then said "let him go he is a dangerous varmint" but not being acquainted with the nature of these animals I determined on making another trial, and persuaded the Mullatto to assist me we walked round the bunch of willows where *where* the Bear lay keeping close together, with our Rifles ready cocked and presented towards the bushes untill near the place where he had entered, when we heard a sullen growl about 10 ft from us, which was instantly followed by a spring of the Bear toward us; his enormous jaws extended and eyes flashing fire. Oh Heavens! was ever anything so hideous? We could not retain sufficient presence of mind to shoot at him but took to our heels separating as we ran the Bear taking after me, finding I could out run him he left and turned to the other who wheeled about and discharged his Rifle covering the Bear with smoke and fire the ball however missing him he turned and bounding toward me—I could go no further without jumping into a large quagmire which hemmed me on three sides, I was obliged to turn about and face him he came within about 10 paces of me then suddenly stopped and raised his ponderous body erect, his mouth wide open, gazing at me with a beastly laugh at this moment I pulled trigger and I knew not what else to do and hardly knew that I did this but it

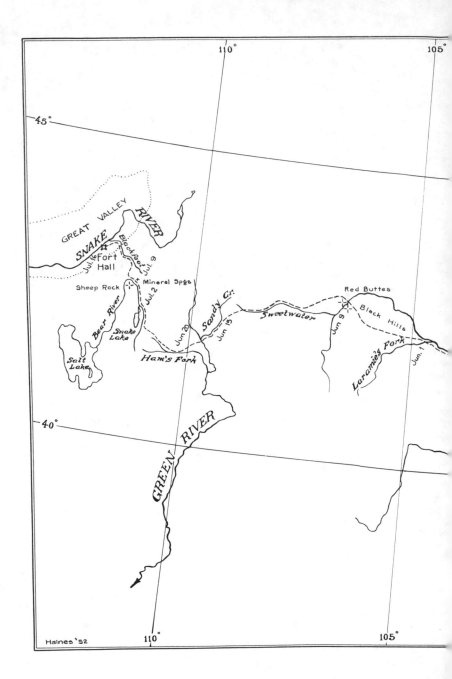

GREAT VALLEY

SNAKE RIVER

Blackfoot

Jul 16 Fort Hall Jul 9

Sheep Rock Jul 2 Mineral Spgs

Bear River

Snake Lake

Salt Lake

Jun 20 Sandy Cr. Jun 15 Sweetwater Jun 9 Red Buttes Black Hills

Ham's Fork

Laramie's Fork Jun 1

GREEN RIVER

Haines '52   110°   105°

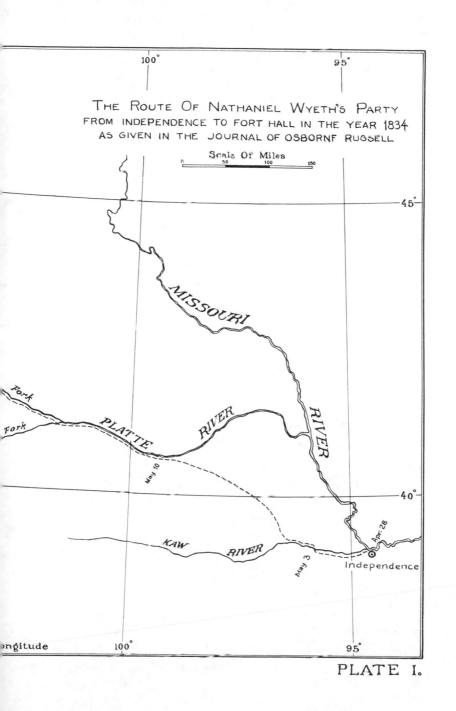

THE ROUTE OF NATHANIEL WYETH'S PARTY
FROM INDEPENDENCE TO FORT HALL IN THE YEAR 1834
AS GIVEN IN THE JOURNAL OF OSBORNE RUSSELL

Scale Of Miles

PLATE I.

accidentally happened that my Rifle was pointed towards the Bear when I pulled and the ball piercing his heart, he gave one bound from me uttered a deathly howl and fell dead: but I trembled as if I had an ague fit[22] for half an hour after, we butchered him as he was very fat packed the meat and skin on our horses and returned to the Fort with the trophies of our bravery, but I secretly determined in my own mind never to molest another wounded Grizzly Bear in a marsh or thicket. On the 26th of Septr. our stock of provisions beginning to get short 4 men started again to hunt buffaloe; as I had been out several times in succession I concluded to stay in the Fort awhile and [let] others try it. This is the most lonely and dreary place I think I ever saw; not a human face to be seen excepting the men about the Fort. The country very smoky and the weather sultry and hot. On the 1st day of Octr. our hunters arrived with news which caused some little excitement among us. they had discovered a village of Indians on Blackfoot Creek about 25 miles from the Fort in a north East direction, consisting of about 60 Lodges. They had rode Green horn like into the Village without any ceremony or knowledge of the friendly or hostile disposition of the Indians, neither could they inform us to what Nation they belonged. It happened however that they were Snake[23] friendly to the Whites and treated our men in a hospitable manner—After remaining all night with them three of the Indians accompanied our hunters to the Fort: From these we gathered (thro. the Mullatto who could speak a little of their language) much desired information. The next day myself and the Mullatto started to the Village where we arrived about sun half an hour high we were conducted to the chiefs Lodge where we dismounted and [were] cheerfully saluted by the chief who was called by the Whites "Iron wristbands" and by the Indians "Pah-da-her-wak-un-dah" or the hiding bear. Our horses were taken to grass and we followed him into his Lodge when he soon ordered supper to be prepared for us. He seemed very much pleased when we told him the Whites had built a trading post on Snake River.

He said the Village would go to the Fort in three or four days to trade. We left them next morning loaded with as much fat dried Buffaloe meat as our horses could carry which had been given as a gratuity: we were accompanied on our return to the Fort by six of the men. On the 10th the Village arrived and pitched their Lodges within about 200 yards of the Fort. I now commenced learning the Snake Language and progressed so far in a short time that I was able to understand most of their words employed in matters of trade. Octr 20th a Village of Bonnaks[24] consisting of 250 Lodges arrived at the Fort from these we traded a considerable quantity of furs, a large supply of dried meat, Deer, Elk and Sheep skins etc.— In the meantime we were employed building small log houses and making other nessary preparations for the approaching winter.

Novr. 5th Some White hunters arrived at the Fort who had been defeated by the Blackfeet Indians on Ham's Fork of Green River. One of them had his arm broken by a fusee ball[25] but by the salutary relief which he obtained from the Fort he was soon enabled to return to his avocations. 16th Two more White men arrived and reported that Capt. Bonneville had returned from the lower country and was passing within 30 miles of the Fort on his way to Green River. 20th four Whites more arrived and reported that a party of the Rocky Mountain Fur Company consisting of 60 men under the direction of one of the Partners (Mr. Bridger) were at the forks of Snake River about 60 miles above the Fort where they intended to pass the winter. We were also informed that the two Fur Companies had formed a coalition.[26] Decr. 15th The ground still bare but frozen and the weather very cold. 24th Capt. Thing arrived from the Mouth of the Columbia with 10 men fetching supplies for the Fort. Times now began to have a different appearance. the Whites and Indians were very numerous in the valley all came to pass the winter on Snake

River. On the 20th of Jany 12 of Mr Bridger's men left his camp and came to the Fort to get employment They immediately made an engagement with Capt. Thing to form a party for hunting and trapping On the 15 of March the party was fitted out consisting of 10 trappers and 7 Camp keepers (myself being one of the latter) under the direction of Mr. Joseph Gale[27] a native of the City of Washington. Mch. 25th we left the Fort and travelled about 6 miles N.E.[28] and encamped on a stream running into the river about 12 Miles below the Fort, called Port neuf. The next day we followed up this stream in an Easterly direction about 15 miles here we found the snow very deep from this we took a south course in the direction of Bear River our animals being so poor and the traveling so bad we had to make short marches and reached Bear River on the 1st day of April. The place where we struck the River is called Cache Valley[29] so called from its having been formerly a place of deposit for the Fur Traders. The country on the north and west side of the river is somewhat broken uneven and covered with wild Sage. The snow had disappeared only upon the South sides of the hills. On the South and East sides of the river lay the valley but it appeared very white and the river nearly overflowing its banks insomuch that it was very difficult crossing: and should we have been able to have crossed, the snow would have prevented us gaining the foot of the mountain on the East side of the valley. This place being entirely destitute of game we had to live chiefly upon roots for ten days. On the 11th of April we swam the river with our horses and baggage and pushed our way thru. the snow accross the Valley to the foot of the mountain: here we found the ground bare and dry. But we had to stay another night without supper. About 4 oclk the next day the meat of two fat Grizzly Bear was brought into Camp. Our Camp Kettles had not been greased for some time: as we were continually boiling thistle roots in them during the day: but now four of them containing about 3 gallons each were soon filled with fat bear meat cut in very small pieces

and hung over a fire which all hands were employed in keeping
up with the utmost impatience: An old experienced hand who
stood six feet six and was never in a hurry about anything was
selected by a unanimous vote to say when the stew (as we called
it) was done but I thought with my comrades that it took a longer
time to cook than any meal I ever saw prepared, and after repeated appeals to his long and hungry Stewardship by all hands
he at length consented that it might be seasoned with salt and
pepper and dished out to cool. But it had not much time for cool-
ing before we commenced operations: and all pronounced it the
best meal they had ever eaten as a matter of course where men
had been starving. The next morning I took a walk up a smooth
spur of the mountain to look at the country. This valley commences about 30 miles below the Soda Springs the river running
west of south enters the valley thro. a deep cut in the high hills:
after winding its way thro. the North and West borders of the
Valley: turns due West and runs thro. a deep Kanyon of perpendicular rocks on its way to the Salt Lake. The valley lies in a
sort of semi circle or rather an oblong. On the South and East of
about 20 miles in length by 5 in diameter and nearly surrounded
by high and rugged mountains from which flow large numbers of
small streams crossing the valley and emptying into the river.
There are large quantities of Beaver and Otter living in these
streams but the snow melting raises the water so high that our
Trappers made but slow progress in catching them. We stopped
in this valley until the 20th of April then moved to the South East
extremity and made an attempt to cross the mountain. The next
day we travelled up a stream called Rush Creek[30] in an East
direction thro. a deep gorge in the mountain for about 12 miles
which then widened about a mile into a smooth and rolling country here we staid the following day we then took a N E course
over the divide and travelled about 12 Miles thro. Snow two or
three feet deep and in many places drifts to the depth of 6 or 8
ft. deep. At night we encamped on a small dry spot of ground on

the South side of a steep mountain where there was little or no vegetation excepting wild sage.

Sometime after we had stopped it was disclosed that one man was missing a young English Shoemaker from Bristol, we found he had been seen last dismounted and stopping to drink at a small branch at some distance before we entered snow. On the following morning I was ordered to go back in search of him. I started on the snow which was frozen hard enough to bear me and my horse. I went to the place where he was last seen and found his trail which I followed on to a high mountain when I lost it among the rocks. I then built a large fire shot my gun several times and after hunting till near sunset without hopes of finding him I gave it up and went to the edge of the snow and stopped for the night. The next morning I started at day light in a gallop on the snow traversing Mountain and Valley smoothed up with snow so hard frozen that a galloping horse scarcely left a foot print: About noon I arrived on a high ridge which over looked the Snake Lake[31] and the Valley South West of it which had been apparently clear of snow for some length of time. At the Southern extremity of the Lake lay the Camp about 2 miles distant NE of me. I descended the Mountain and entered the Camp. On the 27th of April we travelled down the West side of the Lake to the outlet into Bear river. here we found about 300 Lodges of Snake Indians: we encamped at the village and staid 3 days, in the meantime our Trappers were engaged hunting Beaver in the river and small streams We then crossed the river and ascended a branch called Thoma's Fork[32] in a north direction about 10 Mls. the next day we started across the Mountain in a North direction and after travelling about 5 Mls. we discovered a large Grizzly Bear about 200 yards ahead of us: one of our hunters approached and shot him dead on the spot. We all rode up and dismounted to butcher him: he was an enormous animal a hideous brute a savage looking beast. On removing the skin we found the fat on his back measured six inches deep. He had probably not left his winter quarters more than 2 hours as we saw his [tracks] on the snow where he had just left the thick forest of pines on the side of the Mountain. We put the meat on our pack animals and travelled up the Mountain about 5 miles and encamped. The next morning we started about 2 hours before day and crossed the Mountain on the snow which was frozen hard enough to bear our animals and at 10 oclk AM we found ourselves travelling down a beautiful green vale which led us to the Valley on Salt River where we encamped about 2 oclk P.M

This river derives its name from the numerous salt springs found on its branches it runs thro. the middle of a smooth valley about 40 miles long and 10 wide emptying its waters into Lewis fork of Snake River its course being almost due North. This is a beautiful valley covered with green grass and herbage surrounded by towering mountains covered with snow spotted with groves of tall spruce pines which from their vast elevation resemble small twigs half imersed in the snow, whilst thousands of Buffaloe carelessly feeding *feeding* in the green vales contribut to the wild and romantic Splendor of the Surrounding Scenery. On the 10th of May we moved down the river about 12 miles to a stream running into it on the west side called Scotts Fork.[33] Here are some fine Salt Springs the Salt forms on the pebbles by evaporation to the depth of 5 or 6 inches in a short time after the snow has dissappeared 11th May After gathering a Supply of Salt we travelled down the river about 15 miles and encamped near the mouth of a stream on the west side called Gardners Fork.[34] Here we met with Mr. Bridger and his party who informed us that the country around and below was much infested with Blackfeet. they had had several skirmishes with them in which they had lost a number of horses and traps and one young man had been wounded in the shoulder by a ball from a fusee. Upon the receipt of this information our leader concluded to shape his course towards the Fort. On the 14th of May we ascended Gardners fork about 15 mls. thro. a deep gorge in the high craggy mountain May 15 travelled up this stream West abt. 10 Mls. when the country opened into a valley ten miles long and 2 wide. Here we left Gardners fork which turns almost due North into the high mountain with the bend of it just cutting the north end of this valley, we travelled South about 3 miles and encamped on Blackfoot which runs into Snake river after a course of about 100 mls. Here the snow was very deep over nearly the whole plain which was surrounded by high mountains. 16th we travelled down Blackfoot which runs South West accross the Valley then turns West and runs into a deep cut in the mountain upwards of a thousand feet above *above* the bed of the stream[35] the entrance of which seems barely wide enough to admit its waters. We travelled thro this Kanyon for about 10 miles when it opened into a large plain extending to the Sheep Rock on Bear river which appeared to be about 40 mls distant to the South West. There Black foot makes a sweeping curve to the South West then gradually turning to the North enters a narrow gorge of basaltic rock[36] thro. which it rushes with impetuosity for about 15 Mls. then emerges into the great plain of Snake River 17th we travelled down this stream about 15 Mls and stopped to kill and dry Buffaloe meat sufficient to load our loose horses. On the 22d We moved down 10 mls. where we found thousands of Buffaloe Bulls and killed a great number of them as the Cows were very poor at this season of the year. May 30th We travelled down to the Plains and on the day following arrived at the Fort after travelling about 30 Mls in a South W. direction. On arriving at the Fort we learned that Capt. Thing had started in April with 12 men for the purpose of establishing a trading post on a branch of Salmon River: but had been defeated by the Blackfeet with the total loss of his outfit excepting his men and horses.

On the 10th of June a small party belonging to the Hudsons Bay Company arrived from Fort Vancouver on the Columbia River under the direction of Mr F. Ermatinger[37] accompanied by Capt. Wm. Stewart[38] an English half pay Officer who had passed the winter at Vancouver and was on a tour of pleasure in the Rocky Mountains. On the 12th they left Fort Hall and started for the grand rendezvous on Green River. We now began to make preperations for what the Trappers termed the "Fall Hunt" and all being ready on the 15th we started. Our party (under our former leader) consisted of 24 men 14 Trappers and 10 Camp Keepers It was the intention of our leader to proceed to the Yellow Stone Lake and hunt the country which lay in the vicinity of our route: from thence proceed to the head waters of the Missouri and Snake Rivers on our return back to Fort Hall where it was intended we should arrive about the middle of Octr. next We travelled to the mouth of Blackfoot Creek about 10 mls. 16th Up Blackfoot abt. 15 Mls. 17th Followed up this stream abt. 10 mls. farther then left it to our right and took a N E cours thro. the dry plains covered with wild sage and sand hills about 15 mls. to the foot of the mountain and encamped at a small spring which sinks in the plain soon after leaving the mountain. Here we Killed a couple of fine Bulls and took some of the best meat. 18th We crossed a low Mountain in an East direction about 12 mls. and encamped on a stream called Gray's Creek,[39] which empties into Snake River abt. 40 mls. above Fort Hall 19th Travelled East over a rough broken Mountaneous country about 12 mls. and encamped on a small branch of the same stream. This country affords no timber excepting the quaking Asp which grows in small scrubby groves in the nooks and ravines among the hills 20th we left the waters of Gray's Creek and crossed a low place in the mountain in an East direction fell on to a small stream running into Lewis' fork — distance 10 mls. 21st travelled East following this stream to the mouth about 15 mls which [was] about 30 mls. below the mouth of Salt River. Here we were obliged to cross Lewis fork which is about 300 yds. wide and might be forded at a low stage of water, but at present was almost overflowing its banks and running at the rate of about 6 mls per hour. We commenced making a boat by sewing two raw Bulls hides

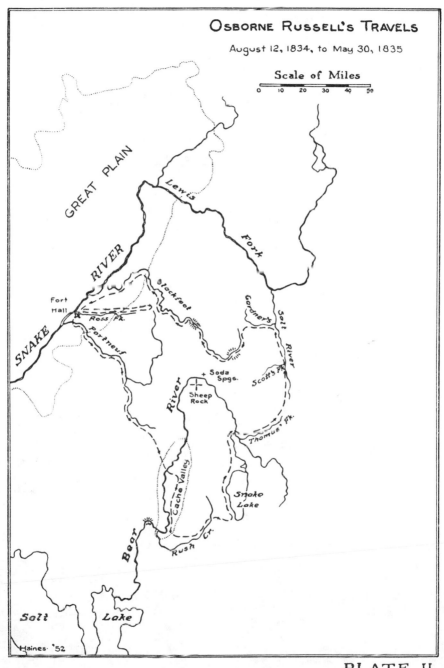

OSBORNE RUSSELL'S TRAVELS

August 12, 1834, to May 30, 1835

Scale of Miles

0   10   20   30   40   50

GREAT PLAIN

Lewis Fork

SNAKE RIVER

Fort Hall

Ross Fk.

Blackfoot

Gardner's

Salt River

Portneuf

River

+ Soda Spgs.

Sheep Rock

Scott's Fk.

Thomas' Fk.

Cache Valley

Snake Lake

Bear

Rush Cr.

Salt Lake

Haines '52

PLATE II.

together[40] which we stretched over a frame formed of green willow branches and then dried it gradually over a slow fire during
the night 22d Our boat being completed we commenced crossing
our equippage and while 5 of us were employed at this a young
man by the name of Abram Patterson attempted to cross on horse
back in spite of all the advice and entreaty of those present his
wild and rash temper got the better of his reason and after a
desperate struggle to reach the opposite bank he abandoned his
horse made a few springs and sunk to rise no more—he was a
native of Penna. about 23 years of age.[41] We succeeded in crossing our baggage and encamped on the East side for the night.
Lewis' fork at this place is timbered with large Cotton wood trees
along the banks on both sides On the East lies a valley about 28
miles long and 3 or 4 wide in an oblong shape half enclosed by a
range of towering mountains which approach the river at each
extremity of the valley.[42] 23d We crossed the North point of the
valley and ascended a small stream about 15 mls. NE where we
encamped among the mountains thickly covered with tall pines
intermingled with fallen timber 24th Crossed the mountain 12
mls. East course and descended into the South W. extremity of
a valley called Pierre's hole[43] where we staid the next day. This
valley lies north & South in an oblong form abt. 30 mls long and
10 wide surrounded except on the Nth. by wild and rugged Mountains: the East range resembles Mountains piled on Mountains
and capped with three spiral peaks which pierce the cloud. These
peaks bear the French name of Tetons or Teats[44]—The Snake
Indians call them the hoary headed Fathers. This is a beautiful
valley consisting of a Smooth plain intersected by small streams
and thickly clothed with grass and herbage and abounds with
Buffaloe Elk Deer antelope etc 27th We travelled to the north
end of the valley and encamped on one of the numerous branches
which unite at the Northern extremity and forms a stream called
Pierre's fork[45] which discharges its waters into Henry's fork of
Snake River. The stream on which we encamped flows directly

from the central Teton and is narrowly skirted with Cottonwood trees closely intermingled with underbrush, on both sides. We were encamped on the South Side in a place partially clear of brush under the shade of the large Cottonwoods 28th abt 9 oclk AM we were arouse by an alarm of "Indians" we ran to our horses, All was confusion—each one trying to catch his horses. We succeeded in driving them into Camp where we caught all but 6 which escaped into the Prarie: in the meantime the Indians appeared before our camp to the number of 60 of which 15 or 20 were mounted on horse back & the remainder on foot—all being entirely naked armed with fusees, bows, arrows etc They immediately caught the horses which had escaped from us and commenced riding to and fro within gunshot of our Camp with all the speed their horses were capable of producing without shooting a single gun for about 20 minutes brandishing their war weapons and yelling at the top of their voices; Some had Scalps suspended on small poles which they waved in the air. Others had pieces of scarlet cloth with one end fastened round head while the other trailed after them. After Securing my horses I took my gun examined the priming set the breech on the ground and hand on the Muzzle with my arms folded gazing at the novelty of this scene for some minutes quite unconscious of danger until the whistling of balls about my ears gave me to understand that these were something more than mere pictures of imagination and gave me assurance that these living Centaurs were a little more dangerous than those I had been accustomed to see portrayed on canvass—

The first gun was fired by one of our party which was taken as a signal for attack on both sides but the well directed fire from our Rifles soon compelled them to retire from the front and take to the brush behind us: where they had the advantage until 7 or 8 of our men glided into the brush and concealing themselves until their left wing approached within about 30 ft of them before they shot a gun they then raised and attacked them in the flank the

Indians did not stop to return the fire, but retreated thro. the brush as fast as possible dragging their wounded along with them and leaving their dead on the spot. In the meantime myself and the remainder of our party were closely engaged with the centre and right. I took the advantage of a large tree which stood near the edge of the brush between the Indians and our horses: They approached until the smoke of our guns met. I kept a large German horse pistol loaded by me in case they should make a charge when my gun was empty. When I first stationed myself at the tree I placed a hat on some twigs which grew at the foot of it and would put it in motion by Kicking the twig with my foot in order that they might shoot at the hat and give me a better chance at their heads but I soon found this sport was no joke for the poor horses behind me were killed and wounded by the balls intended for me. The Indians stood the fight for about 2 hours then retreated thro the brush with a dismal lamentation. We then began to look about to find what damage they had done us: One of our comrades was found under the side of an old root wounded by balls in 3 places in the right and one in the left leg below the knee no bones having been broken. another had received a slight wound in the groin. We lost 3 horses killed on the spot and several more wounded but not so bad as to be unable to travel.

Towards night some of our men followed down the stream about a mile and found the place where they had stopped and laid their wounded comrades on the ground in a circle the blood was still standing congealed in 9 places where they had apparently been dressing the wounds. 29th Staid at the same place fearing no further attempt by the same party of Indians 30th Travelled up the main branch abt. 10 mls. July 1st Travelled to the SE extremity of the valley and encamped for the night Our wounded comrade suffered very much in riding altho. everything was done which lay in our power to ease his sufferings: A pallet was made upon the best gaited horse belonging to the party for him to ride on and one man appointed to lead the animal 2d Crossed the Teton mountain in an east direction[46]—about 15 mls. the ascent was very steep and rugged covered with tall pines but the descent was somewhat smoother.

Here we again fell on to Lewis' fork which runs in a Southern direction thro. a valley about 80 mls long then turning to the West thro. a narrow cut in the mountain to the mouth of Salt River about 30 miles. This Valley is called "Jackson Hole"[47] it is generally from 5 to 15 mls wide: the Southern part where the river enters the mountain is hilly and uneven but the Northern portion is wide smooth and comparatively even the whole being covered with wild sage and Surrounded by high and rugged mountains upon whose summits the snow remains during the hottest months in Summer. The alluvial bottoms along the river and streams inter sect it thro. the valley produce a luxuriant growth of vegetation among which wild flax and a species of onion are abundant. The great altitude of this place however connected with the cold descending from the mountains at night I think would be a serious obstruction to growth of most Kinds of cultivated grains. This valley like all other parts of the country abounds with game.

Here we again attempted to cross Lewis' fork with a Bull skin boat July 4th Our boat being completed we loaded it with baggage and crossed to the other side but on returning we ran it into some brush when it instantly filled and sunk but without further accident than the loss of the boat we had already forded half the distance accross the river upon horse back and were now upon a other shore We now commenced making a raft of logs that had other shore. We now commenced making a raft of logs that had drifted on the Island on this when completed we put the remainder of our equipments about 2 oclk P.M and 10 of us started with it for the other side but we no sooner reached the rapid current than our raft (which was constructed of large timber) became unmanageable and all efforts to reach either side were vaine and fearing lest We should run on to the dreadful rapids to which we were fast approaching we abandoned the raft and committed ourselves to the mercy of the current. We being all tolerable good swimmers excepting myself, I would fain have called for help but at this critical period every one had to Shift for himself fortunately I scrambled to the shore among the last swimmers. We were now on the side from whence we started without a single article of bedding except an old cloth tent whilst the rain poured incessantly. Fortunately we had built a large fire previous to our departure on the raft which was still burning

I now began to reflect on the miserable condition of myself and those around me, without clothing provisions or fire arms and drenched to the skin with the rain

I thought of those who were perhaps at this moment Celebrating the anniversary of our Independence in my Native Land or seated around tables loaded with the richest dainties that a rich independent and enlightened country could afford or perhaps collected in the gay Saloon relating the heroic deeds of our ancestors or joining in the nimble dance forgetful of cares and toils whilst here presented a group of human beings crouched round a fire which the rain was fast diminishing meditating on their deplorable condition not knowing at what moment we might be aroused by the shrill war cry of the hostile Savages with which the country was infested whilst not an article for defense excepting our butcher Knives remained in our possession—

The night at length came on and we lay down to await the events of the morrow day light appeared and we started down along the shore in hopes of finding something that might get loose from the raft and drift upon the beach—We had not gone a mile when we discovered the raft lodged on a gravel bar which projected from the Island where it had been driven by the current—we hastened thro. the water waist deep to the spot where to our great surprise and satisfaction we found everything safe upon the raft in the same manner we had left it. we also discovered that the river could with some difficulty be forded on horseback at this place. Accordingly we had our horses driven accross to us packed them up mounted and crossed without further accident and the day being fair we spent the remainder of it in and the following day in drying our equippage 7th Left the river followed up a stream called the "Grosvent fork"[48] in an East direction about 2 Mils this stream was very high and rapid in fording it we lost 2 Rifles 8th we followed the stream thro. the mountain east passing thro. narrow defiles over rocky precipices and deep gulches for 15 mls. 9th travelled up the stream about 10 Mls east then turned up a left hand fork about 8 Mls N E and encamped among the high rough mountains thickly covered with pine timber. There was not a man in the party who had ever been at this place or at the Yellow Stone Lake where we intended to go but our leader had received information respecting the route from some person at the Fort and had written the direction on a piece of paper which he carried with him They directed us to go from the place where now were due North but he said the directions must be wrong as he could discover no passage thro. the mountains to the North of us. 10th We took a narrow defile which led us in an East direction about 12 mls. on to a Stream running S.E.: This we followed down about six miles when the defile opened into a beautiful valley about 15 mls. in circumference thro. which the Stream ran in the direction above stated and entered the mountain on the East side. Here a dispute arose about the part of country we were in. Our Leader maintained that this was a branch of the Yellow Stone River but some of the Trappers had been in this valley before and knew it to be a branch of wind River[49] pointed out their old encampments and the Beaver lodges where they had been trapping 2 years previous. But our man at the helm was inflexible, he commanded the party and had a right to call the streams by what names he pleased and as a matter of course this was called the Yellow Stone. Three of the party however called it Wind River and left us but not

before one of them had given our Charge d'affairs a sound drub-
bing about some small matters of little importance to any one but
themselves—11th We left the stream and crossed the valley in a
N E direction ascended a high point of mountain thickly covered
with pines then descended over cliffs and crags crossing deep
gulches among the dark forests of pines and logs until about noon
when we came into a smooth grassy spot about a mile in circumference watered by a small rivulet which fell from the rocks above
[passed] thro. the valley and fell into a chasm on the SE side
among the pines. On the North and West were towering rocks
several thousand feet high which seem to overhang this little
vale—Thousands of mountain Sheep were scattered up and down
feeding on the short grass which grew among the cliffs and
crevices: some so high that it required a telescope to see them.
Our wounded companion suffered severely by this day's travel
and our director concluded to remain at this place the next day.
He now began to think that these were not the waters of the
Yellow Stone as all the branches ran SE. Finally he gave it up
and openly declared he could form no distinct idea what part of
the country we were in. 12th Myself and another had orders to
mount 2 of the best mules and ascend the mountain to see if we
could discover any pass to the N West of us. We left the campt and
travelled in a North direction about 2 Mls. then turning to our
left around a high point of perpendicular rock entered a narrow
glen which led N West up the Mountain thro. this we directed
our course ascending over the loose fragments of rock which had
fallen from the dark threatning precipices that seemed suspended
in the air above us on either side for about 5 Mls. when the ascent
became so steep that we were obliged to dismount and lead our
Mules After climbing about a mile further we came to large
banks of snow 8 or 10 ft. deep and so hard that we were compelled
to cut steps with our butcher knives to place our feet in whilst
our Mules followed in the same track. These places were from 50
to 200 yards accross and so steep that we had to use both hands

and feet Dog like in climbing over them We succeeded in reaching what we at first supposed to be the Summit when another peak appeared in view completely shrouded with Snow dotted here and there with a few dwarfish weather beaten Cedars. We now seated ourselves for a few minutes to rest our wearied limbs and gaze on surrounding objects near us on either hand the large bands of Mountain Sheep carelessly feeding upon the short grass and herbage which grew among the Crags and Cliffs whilst Crowds of little lambs were nimbly Skipping and playing upon the banks of snow. After resting ourselves a short time we resumed our march over the snow leaving the Mules behind. We reached the highest Summit in about a miles travel. On the top of this elevation is a flat place of about a quarter of a mile in circumference. On the West and North of us [was] one vast pile of huge mountains crowned with snow[50] but none appeared so high as the one on which we stood. On the South and East nothing could be seen in the distance but the dense blue atmosphere. We did not prolong our [stay] at this place for the north wind blew keen and cold as the month of January in a Northern Climate. We hurried down to where we had left the mules in order to descend to a more temperate climate before the night came on. Our next object was to find a place to descend with our Mules it being impossible to retrace our steps without the greatest danger. After hunting around Sometime we at length found a place on the NE side where we concluded to try it. We drove our mules on to the snow which being hard and slippery their feet tripped and after sliding about 300 [sic] they arrived in a smooth green spot at the foot of the declevity. We then let ourselves down by cutting steps with our butcher knives and the breeches of our guns. After travelling down out of the snow we encamped on a smooth green spot and turned our mules loose to feed At Sunset we built a large fire, eat supper and laid down to sleep. The next morning at daybreak I arose and kindled a fire and seeing the mules grazing at a short distance I filled my tobacco pipe and

sat down to Smoke, presently I cast my eyes down the mountain
and discovered 2 Indians approaching within 200 yards of us
I immediately aroused my companion who was still sleeping, we
grasped our guns and presented them upon the intruders upon
our Solitude, they quickly accosted us in the Snake tongue saying
they were Shoshonies[51] and friends to the whites, I invited them
to approach and sit down then gave them some meat and tobacco,
they seemed astonished to find us here with Mules saying they
knew of but one place where they thought mules or horses could
ascend the mountain and that was in a NE direction. The small
stream which was formed by the melting of the snow above us
after running past where we sat rushed down a fearful chasm and
was lost in spray. After our visitors had eaten and smoked we
began to question them concerning their families and the country
around them. They said their families were some distance below
in a North Direction and that there was a large lake[52] beyond all
the snowy peaks in sight to the N. W. they also pointed out the
place where we could desend the mountain and told us that this
stream ran down thro. the mountain and united with a larger
stream[53]—which after running a long distance North turned toward the rising of the sun into a large plain where there was plenty
of Buffaloe and Crow Indians. After getting this desired information we left these two sons of the wilderness to hunt their sheep
and we to hunt our camp as we could. We travelled over a high
point of rocks chiefly composed of Granite and coars Sand Stone.
In many places we saw large quantities of petrifaction, nearly
whole trees broken in pieces from one to three feet long completely petrified. We also saw imense pieces of rock on the top
of the mountain composed of coarse sand pebbles and Sea Shells
of various kinds and sizes. After crossing the Summit we fell into
a defile which led a winding course down the mountain. Near the
foot of this defile we found a stone jar which would contain 3
gallons neatly cut from a piece of granite well shaped and smooth

After travelling all day over broken rocks fallen timber and rough country we arrived at the camp about dark—

14th We raised Camp and travelled N NE over rough craggy spurs about 15 Mls. and encamped in a narrow Glen between two enormous peaks of rocks. As we were passing along over a spur of the mountain we came to a place from which the earth had slide at some previous period and left the steep inclined ledge bare and difficult to cross: our horses were obliged to place their feet in the small holes and fissures in the rock to keep themselves from sliding off an unfortunate pack horse however missed his footing and slid down the declevity to near the brink of a deep and frightful kanyon thro. which the Cataract madly dashed some hundred feet below fortunately his foot caught in some roots which projected from a crevice in rock and arrested his terrible cours until we could attach ropes to him and drag him from his perilous situation. 15th We followed the windings of the Glen East as far as we could ride and then all dismounted and walked except the wounded man who rode until the mountain became so steep his horse could carry him no longer we then assisted him from his horse and carried or pushed him to the top of the divide over the snow—

In the meantime it commenced snowing very hard—After gaining the Summit we unloaded our animals and rushed them on to the Snow on the other side which being hard they went helter skelter down to a warmer climate and were arrested by a smooth grassy spot. We then [?] lowered the wounded man down by cords and put our saddles and baggage together on the Snow jumped on the top and started slowly at first but the velocity soon increased until we brought up tumbling heels over head on a grassy bench in a more moderate climate. Now we were down; but whether we could get out was a question yet to be Solved. Tremendous towering mountains of rocks Surrounded us excepting on the SE—where a small stream ran from the snow into a dismal chasm below. But for my part I was well contented for an eye could scarcely be cast in any direction around above or below without seeing the fat sheep gazing at us with anxious curiosity or lazily feeding among the rocks and scrubby pines. The bench where we encamped contained about 500 acres nearly level. 16th We staid at this place as our wounded comrade had suffered severely the day before. Some went down the stream to hunt a passage while others went to hunt Sheep. Being in Camp about 10 ock I heard the faint report of a rifle overhead I looked up and saw a sheep tumbling down the rocks which stopped close to where I stood but the man who shot it had to travel 3 or 4 miles before he could descend with safety to the Camp. The Sheep were all very fat so that this could be called no other than high living both as regarded altitude of position and rich provisions. 17th Travelled down the stream thro. difficult and dangerous passage about 10 mls. where we struck another branch on the left This we ascended due North about 8 mls and encamped on another green Spot near the Snow at the head of the Glen 18th We ascended the Mountain at the head of this branch and crossed the divide and descended another branch (which ran in a North direction) about 8 mls. and encamped in an enormous gorge 19th Travelled about 15 mls. down stream and encamped in the edge of a plain 20th Travelled down to the two forks of this stream about 5 mls. and stopped for the night. Here some of the Trappers knew the country. This stream is called Stinking River[54] a branch of the Bighorn which after running about 40 mls thro. the big plain enters the above river about 15 mls. above the lower Bighorn Mountain. It takes its name from several hot Springs about 5 miles below the forks producing a sulphurous stench which is often carried by the wind to the distance of 5 or 6 Mls. Here are also large quarries of gypsum almost transparent of the finest quality and also appearances of Lead with large rich beds of Iron and bituminous coal We stopped at this place and rested our animals until the 23d By this time our wounded comrade had recovered so far as to be able to hobble about on crutches.

24th We took up the right hand fork in a NW direction about 15 mls thro. a rugged defile in the mountain. 25th Travelled about 18 mls in the same direction still following the stream which ran very rapid down thro. the dense piles of mountains which are formed of Granite Slate and Sand Stone covered with pines where there is sufficient soil to support them 26th followed the stream almost due Nth. about 8 mls. and encamped where we staid the next day 28th We crossed the mountain in a West direction thro. the thick pines and fallen timber about 12 mls and encamped in a small prairie about a mile in circumference Thro. this valley ran a small stream in a North direction which all agreed in believing to be a branch of the Yellow Stone.[55] 29th We descended the stream about 15 mls thro. the dense forest and at length came to a beautiful valley about 8 Mls. long and 3 or 4 wide[56] surrounded by dark and lofty mountains. The stream after running thro. the center in a NW direction rushed down a tremendous canyon of basaltic rock apparently just wide enough to admit its waters. The banks of the stream in the valley were low and skirted in many places with beautiful Cotton wood groves

Here we found a few Snake Indians[57] comprising 6 men 7 women and 8 or 10 children who were the only Inhabitants of this lonely and secluded spot. They were all neatly clothed in dressed deer and Sheep skins of the best quality and seemed to be perfectly contented and happy. They were rather surprised at our approach and retreated to the heights where they might have a view of us without apprehending any danger, but having persuaded them of our pacific intentions we then succeeded in getting them to encamp with us. Their personal property consisted of one old butcher Knife nearly worn to the back two old shattered fusees which had long since become useless for want of ammunition a Small Stone pot and about 30 dogs on which they carried their skins, clothing, provisions etc on their hunting excursions. They were well armed with bows and arrows pointed with obsidian The bows were beautifully wrought from

Osborne Russell's "Secluded Valley" is this valley of the Lamar River in present Yellowstone National Park. *(Photo courtesy of Aubrey L. Haines)*

Sheep, Buffaloe and Elk horns secured with Deer and Elk sinews and ornamented with porcupine quills and generally about 3 feet long. We obtained a large number of Elk Deer and Sheep skins from them of the finest quality and three large neatly dressed Panther Skins in return for awls axes kettles tobacco ammunition etc. They would throw the skins at our feet and say "give us whatever you please for them and we are satisfied We can get plenty of Skins but we do not often see the Tibuboes" (or People of the Sun They said there had been a great many beaver on the branches of this stream but they had killed nearly all of them and being ignorant of the value of fur had singed it off with fire in order to drip the meat more conveniently. They had seen some whites some years previous who had passed thro. the valley and lft a horse behind but he had died during the first winter. They are never at a loss for fire which they produce by the friction of two pieces of wood which are rubbed together with a quick and steady motion One of them drew a map of the country around us on a white Elk Skin with a piece of Charcoal after which he explained the direction of the different passes, streams etc From them we discovered that it was about one days travel in a SW direction to the outlet or northern extremity of the Yellow Stone Lake, but the route from his description being difficult and Beaver comparatively scarce our leader gave out the idea of going to it this season as our horses were much jaded and their feet badly worn. Our Geographer also told us that this stream united with the Yellow Stone after leaving this Valley half a days travel in a west direction. The river then ran a long distance thro a tremendous cut in the mountain in the same direction and emerged into a large plain the extent of which was beyond his geographical knowledge or conception 30th We stopped at this place and for my own part I almost wished I could spend the remainder of my days in a place like this where happiness and contentment seemed to reign in wild romantic splendor surrounded by majestic battlements which seemed to support the heavens and shut out all hostile instruders. 21st We left the valley and descended the stream by a narrow difficult path winding among the huge fragments of basaltic rock for about 12 Mls when the trail came to an end and the towering rocks seemed to overhang the river on either side forbidding further progress of man or beast and obliged us to halt for the night. About dark some of our Trappers came to camp and reported one of their Comrades to be lost or met with some serious accident The next day we concluded to stop at this place for the lost man and four men went in search of him and returned at night without any tidings of him whatever It was then agreed that either his gun had bursted and killed him or his horse had fallen with him over some tremendous precipice. He was a man about 55 years of age and of 30 years experience as a hunter Our leader concluded that further search was useless in this rocky pathless and pine covered country Aug. 2d we forded the Yellow Stone with some difficulty to the South side.[58] The river at this place is about 200 yds wide and nearly swimming to horses. a short distance below it rushes down a chasm with a dreadful roar echoing among the Mountains. After crossing we took up a steep and narrow defile in a South direction and on gaining the Summit in about 3 mls we found the country to open South and West of us into rolling prarie hills. We descended the mountain and encamped on a small stream running West 3d Travelled about 25 Mls. due West the route broken and uneven in the latter part of the day and some places thickly covered with pines. encamped at inght in a valley called "Gardnr's hole"[59] This Valley is about 40 mls in circumference surrounded except on the North and West by low piney Mountains On the West is a high narrow range of mountains running North and South dividing the waters of the Yellow Stone from those of Gallatin fork of the Missouri. We stopped in this Valley until the 20th The Trappers being continually employed in hunting and trapping beaver. 21st we crossed the mountains thro. a defile in a west direction and fell on to a small branch of the Gallatin Here we encamped on a small clear spot and killed the fattest Elk I ever saw. It was a large Buck the fat on his rump measured seven inches thick he had 14 spikes or branches on the left horn and 12 on the right. 22d after we had started in the morning five of our party (4 Trappers and one Camp [Keeper] secretly dropped behind with their pack and riding horses and took a different direction forming a party of their own, but they could not be much blamed for leaving—as our fractious leader was continually wrangling with the Trappers by endeavoring to exercise his authority tyranically. we followed down this branch to the Gallatin about 10 mls. West encamped and staid the next day 24th Down the Gallatin N NW the river running between two high ranges of mountains skirted along its banks by a narrow valley. 25th left the defile and took up the Gallatin an East direction crossed the mountain and fell on to a stream running into the Yellow Stone and finding no beaver returned to the Gallatin the next day by the route we had come. 28th up the Gallatin to the place where we had struck it on the 22d 29th Took up the stream a South course about 10 mls. then left it to the left hand and proceeded about 4 mls South thro. a low pass and fell on to a branch of the Madison fork of the Missouri running south this we followed down about six miles further and encamped where we staid next day This pass is formed by the minor ranges of hills or spurs on the two high ranges of mountains on either side of us which approach towards each other and terminate in a low defile completely covered with pines except along the stream where small praries may be found thickly clothed with grass forming beautiful encampment 31st Travelled SW down the stream about 10 Mls. when we came to the "burnt hole"[60] a prarie Valley about 80 mls in circumference surrouned by low spurs of pine covered mountains which are the sources of great number of streams which by uniting in this valley form the Madison fork Septr 1st Travelled down the stream about 12 Mls NW and encamped during a heavy snow storm This stream after leaving the valley enters a gorge in the mountain in a NW direction. 2d We stopped in the entrance of this gorge[61] until the 8th Travelled down about 15 mls. where the country opened into a large plain thro. which the stream turned in a sweeping curve due North 9th Crossed the Valley in a west direction travelled up a small branch and encamped about 3 miles from the river in a place with high bluffs on each side of us we had been encamped about an hour when fourteen white Trappers came to us in full gallop they were of Mr. Bridgers party who was encamped at Henry's Lake about 20 mls in a South direction and expected to arrive at the Madison the next day his party consisted of 60 white men and about 20 flathead Indians. The trappers remained with us during the night telling Mountain "Yarns" and the news from the States. Early next morning 8 of them started down the stream to set Traps on the main Fork but returned in about an hour closely pursued by about 80 Blackfeet.[62] We immediately secured our horses in a yard previously mad for the purpose and prepared ourselves for battle. In the meantime the Indians had gained the bluffs and commenced shooting into the camp from both sides. The bluff on the East side was very steep and rocky covered with tall pines the foot approaching within 40 yds of us. On the west the bluffs were covered with thick groves of quaking asps: from these hights they poured fusee balls without mercy or even damage except killing our animals who were exposed to their fire. In the meantime we concealed ourselves in the thicket around the camp to await a nearer approach, but they were too much afraid of our rifles to come near enough for us [to] use Ammunition— We lay almost silently about 3 hours when finding they could not arouse us to action by their long shots they commenced setting fire to the dry grass and rubbish with which we were surrounded: the wind blowing brisk from the South in a few moments the fire was converted into one circle of flame and smoke which united over our heads. This was the most horrid position I was ever placed in death seemed almost inevitable but we did not despair but all hands began immediately to remove the rubbish around the encampment and setting fire to it to act against the flames that were hovering over our heads: this plan proved successful beyond our expectations Scarce half an hour had elapsed when the fire had passed around us and driven our enemies from their position. At length we saw an Indian whom we supposed to be the Chief standing on a high point of rock and give the signal for retiring which was done by taking hold of the opposite corners of his robe lifting it up and striking it 3 times on the ground. The cracking of guns then ceased and the party moved off in silence.[63] They had killed two horses and one mule on the spot and five more were badly wounded. It was about 4 oclk in the afternoon when the firing ceased. We then saddled and packed our remaining animals and started for Mr. Bridger's camp, which we found on the Madison at the place where we had left it. Our party was now so disabled from the previous desertion of Men and loss of animals that our leader concluded to travel with Mr Bridger until we should arrive at the forks of Snake river where the latter intended to pass the winter. On the 11th Myself with 5 others returned to the battle ground to get some traps which had been set for beaver on the stream above our encampment whilst the main camp was to travel down the river about 5 mls. and stop the remainder of the day to await our return We went for the traps and returned to the camp about [?] olk. P.M. 12th At sunrise an alarm of "Blackfeet!" echoed thro. the Camp. In a moment all were under arms and enquiring "where are they" when 'twas replied "On the hills to the West": I cast a glance along the high range of hills which projected toward the river from the mountain and discovered them standing on a line *on a line* on a ridge in their center stood a small pole and from it waved an American flag displaying a wish to make peace about 30 of us walked up within about 300 yards of their line when they made a signal for us to halt and send two men to meet the same number of theirs and treat for peace. Two of the whites who could speak the Blackfoot language were appointed to negotiate while the respective lines sat upon the ground to await the event. After talking and smoking for half an hour the negotiators separated and returned to their respective parties Our reported them to be a party of Pagans[64] a small tribe of the Blackfeet who desired to make peace with the whites and for that purpose had procured the flag from an American trading post[65] on the Missouri they were 45 [in] number well armed and equipped. We gave them a general invitation to our Camp which they accepted with a great deal of reluctance when they were informed of the battle on the 10th but arriving at the Camp and receiving friendly treatment their fears in a manner subsided. After smoking several rounds of the big pipe the Chief began to relate his adventures. He said he had been in several battles with the whites and some of the party were at the battle in "Pierre's hole" on the 28th of June last[66] in which there was four Indians killed on the spot and eight died of their wounds on the way to the village but he denied having any knowledge of the late battle, but said there was several parties of the Blood Indians[67] lurking about the mountains around us They stopped with us until nearly night and all left except one who concluded to remain. 13th We left the Madison Fork with Mr Bridger's Camp and ascended a small branch in a West direction thro. the mountains about 20 Mls. and encamped on the divide After we had encamped a Frenchman started down the mountain to set his traps for beaver contrary to the advice and persuasion of his comrades he had gone but a few miles when he was fired upon by a party of Blackfeet killed and scalped. 14th Travelled down the mountain about 15 Mls NW. and encamped on a stream called "Stinking Creek"[68] which runs into the Jefferson fork of the Missouri. After we had encamped some trappers ascended the stream but were driven back by the Blackfeet Others went below and shared the same fate from another party but escaped to the camp unhurt 15 Moved down this stream about 12 Mls Nth. This part of the country is comprised of high bald hills on either side of the stream which terminate in rough pine covered mountains. 16 Travelled down the stream NW about 8 Mls The Valley opened wider as we descended and large numbers of Buffaloe were scattered over the plains and among the hills 17th Down abt. 10 Mls NW. the mountain on the West descends to a sloping spur from thence to a plain 18 We did not raise camp and about noon some Flathead Indians arrived and told us their village was on a branch of the Jefferson called Beaver Head Creek[69] about 30 mls in a west direction The next day we went to their village, which consisted of 180 lodges of Flatheads and Pend Oreilles (or hanging ears) [70] Here we found a trading party belonging to the Hudsons Bay Co They were under the direction of Mr. Francis Ermatinger who was endeavoring to trade every Beaver skin as fast as they were taken from the water by the Indians. 20th the whole Cavalcade moved "en mass" up the stream about 12 Mls SW. and encamped with another Village of the same tribes consisting of 130 lodges. From this place is a large plain slightly undulating extending nearly to the junction of the three forks of the Missouri The Flatheads are a brave friendly generous and hospitable tribe strictly honest with a mixture of pride which exalts them far above the rude appellation of Savages when contrasted with the tribes around them. They boast of never injuring the whites and consider it a disgrace to their tribe if they are not treated like brothers whilst in company with them. Larceny, Fornication, and adultery are severely punished. Their Chiefs are obeyed with a reverence due to their station and rank. 23d We left the Village in company with Mr. Bridger and his party and travelled SE accross the plain about 6 Mls. to the foot of the hills and encamped at a spring. 24th Travelled about 18 mls SE over high rolling hills beautifully clothed with bunch grass—25th Travelled in the same direction 12 Mls and encamped in a smooth valley about 80 Mls in circumference surrounded on the North & East by a high range of mountains at the NE extremity is a marshy lake[71]

about 12 Mls. in circumference from this flows the head stream of
the Jefferson fork of the Missouri which curves to the SW thro.
the valley and enters the low mountain on the west thro. a narrow cut still continuing the curve encircling a large portion of
country previous to its arrival at the junction 26 Crossed the
valley about 16 Mls. and encamped on the East side. This Valley
as a Mountaineer would say was full of Buffaloe when we entered it and large numbers of which were killed by our hunters
we repeatedly saw signs of Blackfeet about us to waylay the
Trappers. 27th We stopped at this place to feast on fat Buffaloe
28th Crossed the Mountain SE about 12 Mls. and encamped on
"Camas Creek"[72] at the NW extremity of the great plain of
Snake River Here the leader of our party desired me to go to
Fort Hall and get some horses to assist them to the Fort as we
were dependent on Mr Bridger for animals to move camp 30th
After getting the nessary information from our leader I started
contrary to the advice and remonstrances of Mr. Bridger and his
men rather than be impeached of cowardice by our austocratical
director. I travelled according to his directions South untill dark
amid thousands of Buffaloe. The route was very rocky and my
horses feet (he not being shod) were worn nearly to the quick
which caused him to limp very much. After travelling about 30
Mls. I lay down and slept soundly during the night. The next
morning I arose and proceeded on my journey down the stream
about 9 oclk I came to where it formed a lake[73] where it sank
in the dry sandy plain from this I took a SE course as directed
towards a high Bute which stood in the almost barren plain by
passing to the East of this Bute I was informed that it was about
25 Mls to Snake River

In this direction I travelled untill about two hours after dark
my horse had been previously wounded by a ball in the loins and
tho. nearly recovered before I started yet travelling over the
rocks and gravel with tender feet and his wound together had
nearly exhausted him. I turned him loose among the rocks and

wild Sage and laid myself down to meditate on the follies of myself and others: In about two hours I fell asleep to dream of cool
spring rich frosts and cool shades In the morning I arose and
looked around me my horse was near by me picking the scanty
blades of sunburned grass which grew among the sage. On surveying the place I found I could go no further in a South or East
direction as there lay before me a range of broken basaltic rock
which appeared to extend for 5 or 6 miles on either hand and 5 or
6 Mls wide thrown together promiscuously in such a manner
that it was impossible for a horse to cross them. The Bute stood
to the SW about 10 Mls. which I was informed was about half
the distance from "Camas Lake" to Snake river. I now found
that either from ignorance or some other motive less pure our
Leader had given me directions entirely false and came to the
conclusion to put no further confidence in what he had told me,
but return to the Lake I had left as it was the nearest water I
knew of this point being settled I saddled my horse and started
on foot leading him by the bridle and travelled all day in the
direction of the Lake over the hot sand and gravel. After daylight disappeared I took a star for my guide but it led me South
of the Lake where I came on to several large bands of Buffaloe
who would start on my near approach and run in all directions
It was near midnight when I laid down to rest I had plenty of
provisions but could not eat Water! Water was the object of my
wishes travelling for two long [days] in the hot burning sun without water is by no means a pleasant way of passing the time
I soon fell asleep and dreamed again of bathing in the cool rivulets issuing from the snow topped Mountains. About an hour
before day I was awakened by the howling of wolves who had
formed a complete circle within 30 paces of me and my horse
at the flashing of my pistol however they soon dispersed. At daylight I discovered some willows about 3 miles distant to the West
where large numbers of Buffaloe had assembled apparently for
water In two hours I had dispersed the Brutes and lay by the

water side. After drinking and bathing for half an hour I travelled up the stream[74] about a mile and lay down among some willows to sleep in the shade whilst my horse was carelessly grazing among the bushes The next day being the 4th I lay all day and watched the Buffaloe which were feeding in immense bands all about me 5th I arose in the morning at sunrise and looking to the SW I discovered the dust arising in a defile which led thro. the mountain about 5 Mls distant The Buffaloe were carelessly feeding all over the plain as far as the eye could reach. I watched the motions of the dust for a few minutes when I saw a body of men on horse back pouring out of the defile among the Buffaloe. In a few minutes the dust raised to the heavens The whole mass of Buffaloe became agitated producing a sound resembling distant thunder. At length an Indian pursued a Cow close to me running alongside of her he let slip an arrow and she fell. I immediately recognized him to be a Bonnack with whom I was acquainted. On discovering myself he came to me and saluted me in Snake which I answered in the Same tongue. He told me the Village would come and encamp where I was. In the meantime he pulled off some of his Clothing and hung it on a Stick as a signal for the place where his squaw should set his lodge he then said he had killed three fat cows but would kill one more and stop. So saying he wheeled his foaming charger and the next moment disappeared in the cloud of dust. In about a half an hour the Old Chief came up with the village and invited me to stop with him which I accepted. While the squaws were putting up and stretching their lodges I walked out with the Chief on to a small hillock to view the field of slaughter the cloud of dust had passed away and the prarie was covered with the slain upwards of a Thousand Cows were killed without burning one single grain of gun powder. The Village consisted of 332 lodges and averaged six persons young and old to each lodge They were just returned from the salmon fishing to feast on fat Buffaloe. After the lodges were pitched I returned [to] the village This

Chief is called "Aiken-lo-ruckkup" (or the tongue cut with a flint) he is the brother of the celebrated horn chief who was killed in a battle with the Blackfeet some years ago: and it is related by the Bonnaks without the least scruple that he was killed by a piece of Antclope [horn] the only manner in which he could [be] taken as he was protected by a Supernatural power from all other harm. My worthy host spared no pains to make my situation as comfortable as his circumstances would permit. The next morning I took a walk thro. the Village and found there was fifteen lodges of Snakes with whom I had formed an acquaintance the year before. On my first entering the Village I was informed that two white Trappers belonging to Mr. Wyeths party had been lately killed by the Bonnaks in the lower country and that the two Indians who had killed or caused them to be killed were then in this village. The Old Chief had pointed them out to me as we walked thro. the village and asked me what the white men would do about it I told him they would hang them if they caught them at the Fort He said it was good that they deserved death for said he "I believe they have murdered the two white men to get their property and lost it all in gambling" for continued he "ill gained wealth often flies away and does the owner no good. "But" said he "you need not be under any apprehensions of danger whilst you stop with the village." The squaws were employed cutting and drying meat for two days at the end of which the ground on which the village stood seemed covered with meat scaffolds bending beneath their rich loads of fat Buffaloe meat 13th My horse being somewhat recruited I left the Village with a good supply of boiled Buffaloe tongues prepared by my land lady and the necessary directions and precautions from the Old Chief. I travelled due east about 25 Mls which brot. me to the forks of Snake River[75] when approaching to the waters I discovered fresh human footprints. I immediately turned my horse and rode out from the river about a quarter of a mile intending to travel parralel with the river in order to avoid any straggling party of Blackfeet which might be secreted in the timber growing along the banks

I had not gone far when I discovered three Indians on horse back running a Bull towards me: I jumped my horse into a ravine out of sight and crawled up among [the] high Sage to watch their movements as they approached nearer to me I saw they were Snakes and showed myself to them. They left the Bull and galloped up to me after the usual salutation I followed them to their Village which was on the East bank of the river. The Village consisted of 15 lodges under the direction of a chief called "Comb Daughter" by the Snakes and by the whites the "Lame Chief." He welcomed me to this lodge in the utmost good humor and jocular manner [I] had ever experienced among Indians and I was sufficiently acquainted with the Snake language to repay his jokes in his own coin without hesitation. I passed the time very agreeably for six days among those simple but well fed and good humored Savages. On the 19th learning that Bridger was approaching the forks and the party of hunters to which I had belonged had passed down the river towards the Fort I mounted my horse—started down the river and arrived at the Fort next day about noon the distance being about 60 Mls S.S.W. When I arrived the party had given up all hopes of ever seeing me again and had already fancied my lifeless body lying on the plains after having been scalped by the savages. The time for which myself and all of Mr. Wyeth's men were engaged had recently expired so that now I was independent of the world and no longer to be termed a "Greenhorn" At least I determined not to be so green as to bind myself to an arbitrary Rocky Mountain Chieftain to be kicked over hill and dale at his pleasure. Novr. 15th Capt. Thing arrived from the Columbia with supplies for the Fort. In the meantime the men about the Fort were doing nothing and I was lending them a hand until Mr. Wyeth should arrive and give us our discharge. Decr. 20th Mr. Wyeth arrived when I bid adieu to the "Columbia River Fishing and Trading Company"

OSBORNE RUSSELL'S TRAVELS

June 15, 1835, to December 20, 1835

Scale of Miles

0   10   20   30   40   50

RIVER

YELLOWSTONE

Jefferson Fk.

Beaverhead Cr.

Stinking Creek

Madison Fk.

Gallatin Fk.

Gardners Hole

Burnt Hole

Henry's Lake

Yellowstone Lake

Stinking River

Fork

Camas Creek

Henry's

Pierre's Fork

Pierre's Hole

Lewis'

TETONS

Jackson's Hole

Crescent Fk.

Wind River

RIVER

SNAKE

Grays Creek

Fork

Blackfoot

Portneuf

Mutton Hill

Winter Quarters 1835-36

Haines '52

PLATE III.

and started in company with 15 of my old Messmates to pass
the winter at a place called "Mutton Hill"[76] on Port Neuf, about
40 Mls. SE from Fort Hall. Mr Wyeth had brot. a new recruit of
Sailors and Sandwich Islanders to supply our places at the Fort.
We lived on fat mutton until the snow drove us from the Mountain in Feby. Our party then dispersing I joined Mr. Bridgers
Company who were passing the winter on Blackfoot Creek about
15 Mls. from the Fort where we staid until the latter part of
March. Mr. Bridger's men lived very poor and it was their own
fault for the valley was crowded with fat Cows when they arrived
in Novr. but instead of approaching and killing their meat for
the winter they began to Kill by running on horse back which
had driven the Buffaloe all over the Mountain to the head of the
Missouri and the snow falling deep they could not return during
the winter They killed plenty of Bulls but they were so poor
that their meat was perfectly blue yet this was their only article
of food as bread or vegetables were out of the question in the
Rocky Mountains except a few kinds of roots of spontaneous
growth which the Indians dig and prepare for food. It would
doubtless be amusing to a disinter[est]ed spectator to witness the
process of cooking poor Bull meat as practiced by this camp
during the winter of 1835-6 On going thro. the camp at any time
in the day heaps of ashes might be seen with the fire burning on
the summit and an independent looking individual who is termed
a Camp Keeper sitting with a "two year old club" in his hand
watching the pile with as much seeming impatience as Philoctete
did the burning of Hercules[77] at length poking over the ashes
with his club he rolls out a ponderous mass of Bull beef and
hitting it a rap with his club it bounds 5 or 6 feet from the
ground like a huge ball of gum elastic: this operation frequently
repeated divests [it] of the ashes adhering to it and prepares it
for carving He then drops his club and draws his butcher knife
calling to his comrades "Come Major, Judge, Squire, Dollar
Pike, Cotton, and Gabe[78] wont you take a lunch of Simon?"

each of whom acts according to the dictates of his appetite in accepting or refusing the invitation. I have often witnessed these Philosophical and independent dignitaries collected round a Bulls ham just torn from a pile of embers goodhumoredly observing as they hacked the hugh slices from the lean mass that this was tough eating but that it was tougher where there was none and consoling themselves with a promise to make the fat cows suffer before the year rolled round. The camp remained on Blackfoot untill the latter part of March, when the Winter broke up and we commenced travelling and hunting Beaver. We left winter quarters on the 28th and travelled along the foot of the mountain in a north direction to Lewis' fork and ascended it SE to the mouth of Muddy Creek where we arrived on the 7th of April. Here Mr. Bridger ordered a party of 12 Trappers to branch off to the right and hunt the head waters of Grays and Blackfoot creeks. I was included in the number and felt anxious to try my skill in Trapping 10th We set off leaving the main camp to proceed leisurely to Salt [River] Valley and from thence to the mouth of Thomo's fork of Bear river where we were instructed to meet them. We ascended Muddy and crossed the Mountain on to Grays creek here we found the snow disappearing very fast and the streams so much swollen that we made but slow progress in taking Beaver We traversed the numerous branches of this stream to and fro setting traps when the water would permit until the 25th of April when we left the waters of Grays creek and travelled about 40 Mls in a SW direction from where we had struck it, crossed a low mountain about 8 Mls and fell on to Blackfoot This we ascended two days and hunted until the 5th of May wen three of our party were waylaid and fired upon by a party of Blackfeet whilst ascending the stream thro. a Kanyon one of them was slightly wounded in the side by a fusee ball and all escaped to the Camp and reported the Indians to be about 25 in number 7th of May we left Blackfoot and crossed the Mountain SW thro. deep snow and thick pines [and] at night fell into the valley on Bear river and encamped about 25 Mls above the Soda springs 8th Travelled up Bear river to Thomos fork where we found the main Camp likewise Mr. A Dripps and his party, consisting of about 60 whites and nearly as many half breeds who were encamped with 400 lodges of Snakes and Bonnaks and 100 lodges of Nez Perces and flatheads 9th We all camped together in the beautiful plain on Bear River above the mouth of Smith's fork[79] 11th The whole company of Indians and whites left Bear river and travelled to Ham's fork, excepting Mr Dripps and a small party who went round to Blacks fork of Green river to get some furs and other articles deposited there in the ground After reaching Ham's fork the Indians concluded to separate in different directions as we were in too large a body and had too many horses to thrive long together They were instructed to be at the mouth of horse creek on Green River about the 1st of July as we expected supplies from the U S about that time. We laid about on the branches of Green river until the 28th of June when we arrived at the destined place of Rendezvous[80] On the 1st of July Mr. Wyeth arrived from the mouth of the Columbia on his way to the U S with a small party of men 3d The outfit arrived from St. Louis consisting of 40 men having 20 horse carts drawn by mules and loaded with supplies for the ensueing year They were accompanied by Dr Marcus Whitman and lady Mr H H Spaulding and lady and Mr. W H Gray Presbyterian missionaries on their way to the Columbia to establish a mission among the Indians in that quarter. The two ladies were gazed upon with wonder and astonishment by the rude Savages they being the first white women ever seen by these Indians and the first that had ever penetrated into these wild and rocky regions. We remained at the rendezvous until the 16 of July and then began to branch off into parties for the fall hunt in different directions. Mr Bridgers party were destined as usual for the Blackfoot country it contained most of the American trappers and amounted to 60 men. I started with a party of 15

Trappers and 2 Camp Keepers ordered by Mr Bridger to proceed to the Yellow Stone lake and there await his arrival with the remainder of his party. July 24th we set off and travelled up Green river 25 [miles] in a North direction 25th Up Green river 15 Mls in the same direction, then left it to our right and took up a small branch still keeping a Nth. course. The course of the river where we left it turns abruptly to the East and heads in a high craggy mountain covered with snow about 30 Mls distant. This mountain is a spur of the Wind river range and is commonly called the "Sweetwater Mountain"[81] as that stream heads in its southern termination—

After leaving the river we travelled about 4 Mls to the head of the branch and encamped in a smooth grassy plain on the divide between Green and Snake Rivers which head within 200 paces of each other at this place 26th Travelled North about 15 Mls. descending a small stream thro. a rough mountaneous country covered with pine trees and underbrush and encamped on the Gros vent fork. 27th We descended the Gros vent fork to "Jacksons hole" about 20 Mls. general course West. 28th We followed Lewis' fork thro. the Valley crossing several large streams coming in from the East we then left the valley and followed the river about 5 Mls. thro. a piece of rough piney country and came to Jacksons Lake which is formed by the river. We encamped at the outlet at a small prarie about a mile in circumference. This lake is about 25 Mls long and 3 wide lying Nth & South bordered on the east by pine swamps and marshes extending from 1 to 2 Mls from the Lake to the spurs of the Mountain On the SW. stands the 3 Tetons whose dark frightful forms rising abruptly from the Lake and towering above the clouds casts a gloomy shade upon the waters beneath whilst the water rushes in torrents down the awful precipices from the snow by which they are crowned The high range of Mountains on the west after leaving the Tetons slope gradually to the Nth and spread into low piney mountains. This place like all other

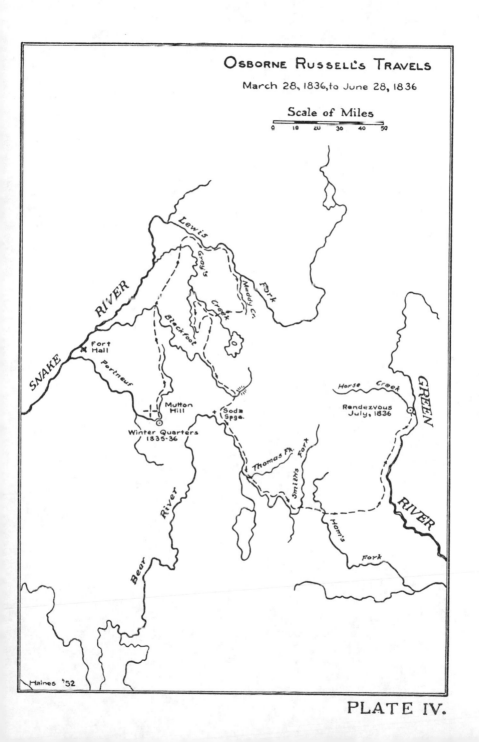

OSBORNE RUSSELL'S TRAVELS

March 28, 1836, to June 28, 1836

Scale of Miles

0   10   20   30   40   50

Lewis

Gray's

Muddy Cr.

Fork

RIVER

Blackfoot

Creek

SNAKE

Fort Hall

Portneuf

Mutton Hill

Soda Spgs.

Winter Quarters 1835-36

Horse Creek

Rendezvous July, 1836

GREEN

Thomas Fk.

Smith's Fork

River

Harris Fork

Bear

Fork

RIVER

Haines '52

PLATE IV.

marshes and swamps among the mountains is infested with in-
numerable swarms of horse flies and musketoes to the great
annoyance of man and beast during the day but the cold air
descending from the mountains at night compells them to seek
shelter among the leaves and grass at an early hour. Game is
plenty and the river and lake abounds with fish. After hunting
the streams and marshes about this lake we left it, on the 7th
of August and travelled down Lewis' fork about 4 Mls to the
second stream running into it on the east side below the Lake.[82]
This we ascended about 12 Mls East and encamped among the
pines close to where it emerged from a deep kanyon in the mountain 8th We took accross a high spur thickly covered with pines
intermingled with brush and fallen timber in a NE direction for
about 12 Mls where we fell into a small valley on a left hand
branch of the stream we had left 9th We took up this branch due
North about 10 Mls. when it turning short to the right we left it
and ascended a narrow Glen keeping a Nth course sometimes
travelling thro. thick pines and then crossing small green spots
thro. which little streams were running from the remaining
banks of snow lying among the pines in the shade of the mountains for about 6 Mls when we came to a smooth prarie about 2
Mls long and half a Ml. wide lying east and west surrounded by
pines. On the South side about midway of the prarie stands a
high snowy peak from whence issues a Stream of water which
after entering the plain it divides equally one half running West
and the other East thus bidding adieu to each other one bound
for the Pacific and the other for the Atlantic ocean.[83] Here a
trout of 12 inches in length may cross the mountains in safety.
Poets have sung of the "meeting of the waters" and fish climbing cataracts but the "parting of the waters and fish crossing
mountains" I believe remains unsung as yet by all except the
solitary Trapper who sits under the shade of a spreading pine
whistling blank-verse and beating time to the tune with a whip
on his trap sack whilst musing on the parting advice of these

waters. 10th We took down the East branch and followed it about 8 Mls to the Yellow Stone river which is about 80 yds wide and at the shallowest place nearly swimming to our horses. To this place it comes from a deep gorge in the mountains enters a valley lying Nth & South about 15 Ms. long and 3 wide[84] thro. which it winds its way slowly to the Nth. thro swamps and marshes and calmly reposes in the bosom of the Yellow Stone Lake. The South extremity of this valley is smooth and thickly clothed with high meadow grass surrounded by high craggy mountains topped with snow. We stopped at this place trapping until the 3d of August, when we travelled down [to] the lake to the inlet or southern extremity. 16th Mr. Bridger came up with the remainder of the party 18th The whole camp moved down the East shore of the Lake thro. thick pines and fallen timber about 18 Mls. and encamped in a small prarie 19th Continued down the shore to the Outlet about 20 Mls. and encamped in a beautiful plain which extends along the Northern extremity of the Lake.[85] This valley is interspersed with scattering groves of tall pines forming shady retreats for the numerous Elk and Deer during the heat of the day. The Lake is about 100 Mls. in circumference bordered on the East by high ranges of Mountains whose spurs terminate at the shore and on the west by a low bed of piney mountains its greatest width is about 15 Mls lying in an oblong form south to north or rather in the shape of a crescent. Near where we encamped were several hot springs which boil perpetually. Near these was an opening in the ground about 8 inches in diameter from which hot steam issues continually with a noise similar to that made by the steam issuing from a safety valve of an engine and can be heard 5 or 6 Mls distant I should think the steam issued with sufficient force to work an engine of 30 horse power. We encamped about 3 ock. PM. and after resting our horses about an hour seven of us were ordered to go and hunt some streams running into the Yillow Stone some distance below the Lake. We startid from the Camp in an East direction

crossed the plain and entered the pines and after travelling about
an hour thro. dense forests we fell into a broken tract of country
which seemed to be all on fire at some distance below the surface.
It being very difficult to get around this place we concluded to
follow an Elk Trail accross it for about half a mile the treading
of our horses sounded like travelling on a plank platform covering an imense cavity in the earth whilst the hot water and steam
were spouting and hissing around us in all directions. As we were
walking and leading our horses accross this place the horse that
was before me broke thro. the crust with one hind foot and the
blue steam rushed forth from the hole. The whole place was
covered with a crust of Limestone[86] of a dazzling whiteness
formed by the overflowing of the boiling water. Shortly after
leaving this resemblance of the infernal regions we killed a fat
buck Elk and camped at Sunset in a smooth grassy spot between
two high shaggy ridges watered by a small stream which came
tumbling down the gorge behind us. As we had passed the
infernal regions we thought as a matter of course these must be
a commencement of the Elysian fields and accordingly commenced preparing a feast. A large fire was soon blazing encircled
with sides of Elk ribs and meat cut in slices supported on sticks
down which the grease ran in torrents The repast being over the
jovial tale goes round the circle the peals of loud laughter break
upon the stillness of the night which after being mimicked in the
echo from rock to rock it dies away in the solitary [gloom]. Every
tale puts an auditor in mind of something similar to it but under
different circumstances which being told the "laughing part"
gives rise to increasing merriment and furnishes more subjects
for good jokes and witty sayings such as Swift never dreamed of
Thus the evening passed with eating drinking and stories enlivened with witty humor until near Midnight all being wrapped
in their blankets lying around the fire gradually falling to sleep
one by one until the last tale is "encored" by the snoring of the
drowsy audience The Speaker takes the hint breaks off the sub-

ject and wrapping his blanket more closely about him soon joins
the snoring party — The light of the fire being supersed by that
of the Moon just rising from behind the Eastern Mountain a
sullen gloom is cast over the remaining fragments of the feast
and all is silent except the occasional howling of the solitary wolf
on the neighboring mountain whose senses are attracted by the
flavors of roasted meat but fearing to approach nearer he sits
upon a rock and bewails his calamities in piteous moans which
are re-echoed among the Mountains. Aug 20th Took over a high
rugged mountain about 12 Mls NE and fell into the Secluded
Valley of which I have described in my last years journal.[87] Here
we found some of those independent and happy Natives of whom
I gave a description we traded some Beaver and dressed Skins
from them and hunted the streams running into the valley for
several days There is something in the wild romantic scenery of
this valley which I cannot nor will I, attempt to describe but the
impressions made upon my mind while gazing from a high eminence on the surrounding landscape one evening as the sun was
gently gliding behind the western mountain and casting its
gigantic shadows accross the vale were such as time can never
efface from my memory but as I am neither Poet Painter or
Romance writer I must content myself to be what I am a humble
journalist and leave this beautiful Vale in obscurity until visited
by some more skillful admirer of the beauties of nature who may
chance to stroll this way at some future period 25th left the
Valley and travelled down to the Yellow Stone and crossed it at
the ford 26th Crossed the Mountain in a SW[88] direction and fell
on to Gardners fork. Here myself and another set some traps
and stopped for the night whilst the remainder of the party went
in different directions to hunt setting 27th Crossed the mountain SW to "Gardners hole" where we found the main camp.
28th Camp left "Gardners hole" and travelled North to the Yellow Stone about 20 Mls. 29th The whole party followed the river
out of the mountain in to the great Yellow Stone plain distance

Gardner's Hole, this mountain valley in present Yellowstone National Park, was a favorite resort of the trappers. (*Photo courtesy of Aubrey L. Haines*)

about 12 Mls. The Trappers then scattered out in small parties of from 2 to 5 in number leaving Mr. Bridger with 25 Camp Keepers to travel slowly down the river. Myself and another travelled down the river about 40 Mls NE to a branch called "25 Yard river"[89] This we ascended about 25 Mls in a Nth direction where we remained trapping several days The country lying on this stream is mostly comprised of high rolling ridges thickly clothed with grass and herbage and crowded with imense bands of Buffaloe intermingled with bands of antelope Sepr. 1st We returned to the Camp which we found at the mouth of this stream where we found also 10 Delaware Indians who had joined the camp in order to hunt Beaver with greater security. 2d Travelled down the Yellow Stone river about 20 Mls. This is a beautiful country the large plains widely extending on either side of the river intersected with streams and occasional low spurs of Mountains whilst thousands of Buffaloe may be seen in almost every direction and Deer Elk and Grizzly bear are abundant. The latter are more numerous than in any other part of the mountains. Owing to the vast quantities of cherries plums and other wild fruits which this section of country affords In going to visit my traps a distance of 3 or 4 mils early in the morning I have frequently seen 7 or 8 standing about the clumps of Cherry bushes on their hind legs gathering cherries with surprising dexterity not even deigning to turn their Grizzly heads to gaze at the passing trapper but merely casting a sidelong glance at him without altering their position 3d I left the camp on the Yellow Stone and started accross a low and somewhat broken tract of country in a SE direction to a stream called the Rosebud[90] accompanied by another Trapper 5th The Camp came to us on the Rosebud and the next day passed on in the same direction. Whilst myself and comrade stopped behind to trap 7th We overtook the camp on a stream called Rocky fork[91] a branch of Clarks fork of the Yellow Stone when we arrived at camp we were told the sad news of the death of a french Trapper named

Bodah, who had been waylaid and killed by a party of Blackfeet while setting his traps and one of the Delawares had been shot thro the hip by the rifle of one of his comrades going off accidentally and several war parties of Blackfeet had been seen scouting about the country. We had been in camp but a few minutes when two trappers rode up whom we called "Major Meek" and "Dave Crow"[92] The former was riding a white Indian pony, a tall Virginian who had been in the mountains some 12 years on dismounting some blood was discovered which had apparently been running down his horses neck and dried on the hair. He was immediately asked where he had been and what was the news? "News! exclaimed he "I have been, me and Dave over on to Priors fork[93] to set our traps and found old Benj Johnson's boys[94] there just walking up and down them are streams with their hands on their hips gathering plums, they gave me a tilt and turned me a somerset or two shot my horse "Too Shebit" in the neck and sent us heels over head in a pile together but we raised arunnin Gabe do you know where Prior leaves the cut bluffs going up it? Yes, replied Bridger. Well after you get out of the hills on the right hand fork there is scrubby box elders about 3 miles along the Creek up to where a little right hand spring branch puts in with lots and slivers of Plum trees about the mouth of it and some old beaver dams at the mouth on the main Creek? Well sir we went up there and set yesterday morning I set two traps right below the mouth of that little branch and in them old dams and Dave set his down the creek apiece, so after we had got our traps set we cruised round and eat plums a while, the best plums I ever saw is there" the trees are loaded and breaking down to the ground with the finest kind as large as Pheasants eggs and sweet as sugar the'l almost melt in yo mouth no wonder them rascally Savages like that place so well— Well sir after we had eat what plums we wanted me and Dave took down the creek and staid all night on a little branch in the hills and this morning started to our traps we came up to Dave's traps and in the first there was a 4 year old "spade" the next was false lickt went to the next and it had cut a foot and none of the rest disturbed, we then went up to mine to the mouth of the branch I rode on 5 or 6 steps ahead of Dave and just as I got opposite the first trap I heard a rustling in the bushes within about 5 steps of me I looked round and pop pop pop went the guns covering me with smoke so close that I could see the blanket wads coming out of the muzzles Well sir I wheeled and a ball struck Too shebit in the neck and just touched the bone and we pitched heels overhead but too shebit raised runnin and I on his back and the savages jist squattin and grabbin at me but I raised a fog for about half a mile till I overtook Dave" The foregoing story was corroborated by "Dave" a small inoffensive man who had come to the Rocky Mountains with Gen. Ashley some 15 years ago and remained ever since: an excellent hunter and a good trapper The next day we moved down the stream to its junction with Clarks fork within about 3 Mls of the Yellowstone On the following morning two men went to set traps down on the river and as they were hunting along the brushy banks for places to set a party of sixty Blackfeet surrounded them drove them into the river and shot after them as they were swimming accross on their horses One by the name of Howell[95] was shot by two fusee balls thro. the chest the other escaped unhurt. Howell rode within half a mile of camp fell and was brought in on a litter he lived about 20 hours and expired in the greatest agony imaginable—about an hour after he was brought in 20 Whites and Delawares went to scour the brush along the river and fight the Blackfeet Having found them they drove them on to an Island and fought them till dark. The loss on our side during the battle was a Nez percey Indian killed and one White slightly wounded in the shoulder. The Blackfeet who were fortified on the Island drew off in the night secreting their dead and carrying off their wounded The next day we interred the remains of poor Howell at the foot of a large Cottonwood tree and called the place "Howells encampment" as a compliment to his memory 11th We travelled on to Priors Fork and struck it where the Majors traps were setting distance 25 Mls Couse SE— 12th Stopped at this place and gathered plums 13th Travelled East 12 Mls to the left hand fork of Prior. 14th The snow fell all day and on the 15th it was 15 inches deep 16th We returned to the west fork of Prior and stopped the next day 18th The snow being gone we returned to Clarks Fork 19th Seven of us left the Camp and travelled to Rock fork near the mountain distance about 25 Mls course SW. We all kept together and set our traps on Rocky fork near the Mountain. We had been here five days when a party of Crow Indians came to us consisting of 49 warriors. They were on their way to the Blackfoot village to steal horses, they staid with us two nights and then went to the camp which had come on to this stream about 20 Mls below us. 28th Another party of Crows came to us consisting of 110 warriors. We went with them to the Camp which we found about 10 mls below. They remained with the camp the next day and then left for the Blackfoot village which they said was at the three forks of the Missouri. 30th We travelled with the Camp west on to the Rosebud Octr 1st The trappers scattered out in every direction to hunt Beaver on the branches of the "Rosebud" and continued to the 10th when we followed the Camp down the Yellow Stone where Mr. Bridger had concluded to pass the winter. The small streams being frozen trapping was suspended and all collected to winters quarters where were Thousands of fat Buffaloe feeding in the plains and we had nothing to do but slay and eat Octr. 25 The weather becoming fine and warm some of the trappers started again to hunt Beaver Myself and another started to Priors fork and set our traps on the East branch where we staid six days We then crossed a broken piece of country about 12 Mls NE and fell on to a stream running NE into the Big horn called "Bovy's fork"[96] Here we set traps and staid 10 dys. This section of country is very uneven and broken but abounds with Buffaloe Elk Deer and Bear. Among other spontaneous productions of this country are hops which grow in great abundance and of a superior quality. [On] Thousands of acres along the small branches the trees and shrubbery are completely entangled in the vines 11th The weather [commenced] cold the streams froze over again and we started for Camp which we found on Clarks fork about a mile above "Howells encampment" The Camp stopped at this place until Christmas then moved down about 4 Mls onto the Yellowstone. The bottoms along these rivers are heavily timbered with sweet cottonwood and our horses and mules are very fond of the bark which we strip from the limbs and give them every night as the Buffaloe have entirely destroyed the grass throughout this part of the country We passed away the time very agreeably our only employment being to feed our horses kill Buffaloe and eat that is to say the Trappers The camp keepers' business in winter quarters is to guard the horses cook and keep fires. We all had snug lodges made of dressed Buffaloe skins in the center of which we built a fire and generally comprised about six men to the lodge The long winter evenings were passed away by collecting in some of the most spacious lodges and entering into debates arguments or spinning long yarns until midnight in perfect good humour and I for one will cheerfully confess that I have derived no little benefit from the frequent arguments and debates held in what we termed The Rocky Mountain College and I doubt not but some of my comrades who considered themselves Classical Scholars have had some little added to their wisdom in these assemblies however rude they might appear On the 28th of Jany myself and six more trappers concluded to take a cruise of 5 or 6 days after Buffaloe The snow was about 4 inches deep and the weather clear and cold we took seven loose animals to pack meat and travelled up Clarks fork about 12 Mls killed a cow and encamped The next morning we started across towards Rock fork and had gone about 3 Mls over the smooth plain gradually ascending to a range of hills which divides Clarks fork from Rock We were riding carelessly along with our rifles lying carelessly before us on our saddles when we came to a deep narrow gulch made by the water running from the hills in the Spring Season when behold! the earth seemed teeming with naked Savages A quick volley of fusees a shower of balls and a cloud of smoke clearly bespoke their nation tribe manners and customs and mode of warfare: A ball broke the right arm of one man[97] and he dropped his rifle which a savage immediately caught up and shot after us as we wheeled and scampered away out of the reach of their guns. There was about 80 Indians who had secreted themselves until we rode within 15 feet of them They got a rifle clear gain and we had one man wounded and lost a Rifle so they had so much the advantage and we were obliged to go to Camp and study out some plan to get even as by the two or three last skirmishes we had fell in this rebt. A few days afterwards a party of 20 were discovered crossing the plain to the river about 6 Mls below us 20 men immediately mounted and set off and arrived at the place just as they had entered the timber — they ran into some old rotten Indian forts formed of small poles in a conical shape The whites immediately surrounded and opened fire upon them which was kept up until darkness and the severity of the weather compelled them to retire We had one man wounded slightly thro. the hip and one Delaware[98] was shot by a poisoned ball in the leg which lodged under the knee cap he lived four days and expired. On examining the battle ground next day we found that three or four at least had been killed and put under the Ice in the river seven or 8 had been badly wounded which they dragged away on trains[99] to their village. We found that the old forts were not bullet proof in any place our rifle balls had whistled thro. them nearly every shot and blood and brains lay scattered about inside on the shattered fragments of rotton wood. Feby. 22d Mr Bridger according to his usual custom took his telescope &

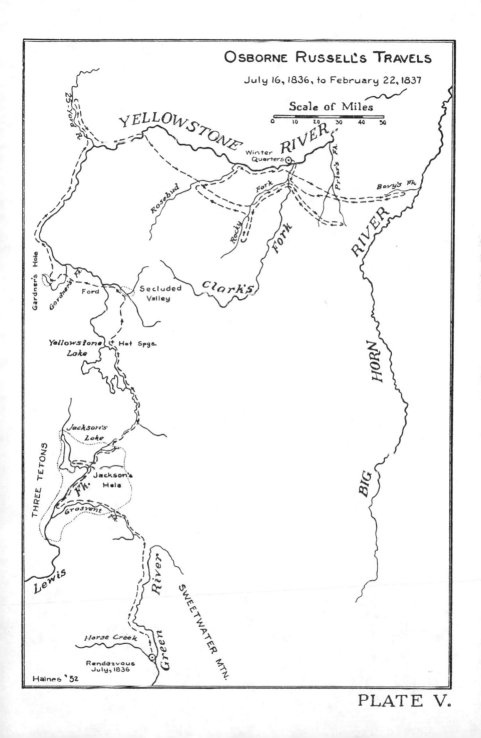

OSBORNE RUSSELL'S TRAVELS

July 16, 1836, to February 22, 1837

Scale of Miles

0   10   20   30   40   50

YELLOWSTONE   RIVER

Winter Quarters

Prior's Fk.

Bovy's Fk.

Rosebud

Rocky

Fork

Fork

RIVER

Gardner's Hole

Gardner's Fk.

Ford

Secluded Valley

Clark's

HORN

Yellowstone Lake

Hot Spgs.

BIG

Jackson's Lake

THREE TETONS

Jackson's Hole

Fk.

Grosvent Fk.

Lewis

Green River

SWEETWATER MTN.

Horse Creek

Rendezvous July, 1836

Green River

Haines '52

PLATE V.

mounted a high bluff near the encampment[100] to look out for "squalls" as he termed it about 1 ock PM he returned appearing somewhat alarmed and on being asked the cause, He said the great plain below was alive with savages who were coming accross the hills to the timber about 10 Mls below us. From this place the river runs in a NE direction bearing E. On the Nth and West side is a plain from 6 to 10 Mls wide bordered by rough broken hills and clay bluffs on the S and E the river runs along the foot of a high range of steep bluffs intersected by deep ravines and gulches. Along the river are large bottoms covered with large cottonwood timber and clear of underbrush. All hands commenced to build a breast work round the camp, which was constructed of Logs and brush piled horizontally 6 feet high around the camp enclosing about 250 feet square

This being completed at dark a double guard was mounted and all remained quiet but it was a bitter Cold night. I mounted guard from 9 till 12 oclk the weather was clear the stars shone with an unusual lustre and the trees cracked like pistols about 10 oclk the northern lights commenced streaming up darting flashing rushing to and fro like the movements of an army at length the shooting and flashing died away and gradually turned to a deep blood red spreading over one half of the sky. This awful and sublime phenomenon (if I may be alowed to mingle such terms) lasted near two hours then gradually disappeared—and being relieved by the morning guard I went to bed and slept soundly till Sunrise. The next day we were engaged strengthening the fortress by cutting timber from 12 to 18 inches in diameter standing them inside on end leaning them on the breastwork close to gether. This was completed about noon. About 2 oclk. Mr. Bridger and six men mounted and went to reconnoiter the enemy but returned soon after with the intelligence of their being encamped about 3 Miles below on the river and there was a multitude of them on foot. 24th The night passed without any disturbance and we began to fear we should not

have a fight after *after* all our trouble. About sunrise one solitary
Savage crept up behind the trees and shot about 200 yds at Mr
Bridger's Cook as he was gathering wood outside the fort Then
scampered off without doing any damage

A Spaniard[101] was ordered on to the bluff to look out and found
an Indian in the observatory built on the top who waited until
the Spaniard approached the Indian then raised and the Spaniard wheeled and took to his heels the Indian shot and the ball
struck him in the heel as he made a 50 foot leap down the bluff
and slid down the snow to the bottom. In about half an hour the
word was passed that they were coming on the Ice and presently
they appeared coming round a bend of the river in close columns
within about 400 yards They then turned off to the right into the
plain and called a halt. The Chief who wore a white blanket
came forward a few steps and gave us the signal that he should
not fight but return to his village They then turned and took
a NW Course accross the Plain toward the 3 forks of the
Missouri. We came to a conclusion after numerous conjectures
that the wonderful appearance of the heavens a few nights previous connected with our strong fortification had caused them to
abandon the ground without an attack which is very probable as
all Indians are very superstitious We supposed on examining
their Camp next day that [their] numbers must have been about
eleven hundred who had started from their village with the
determination of rubbing us from the face of the earth but that
the Great spirit had shown them that their side of the heavens
was bloody whilst ours was Clear and Serene. 28th Feby we left
our winter quarters on the Yellow Stone and Started for the Big
horn the snow being 6 inches deep on an average we travelled
slowly and reached it in eight days at the mouth of "Bovy fork"
about 15 Mls below the lower Big horn mountain and then began to Slay and eat but we slayed so much faster than we eat
that our meat scaffolds groand under the weight of fat buffaloe
meat We remained here amusing ourselves with playing ball

hoping wrestling running foot races etc until the 14th of March
when we discovered the Crow village moving down the Big horn
toward us[102] immediately all sports were ended Some mounted
horses to meet them others fortified camp ready for battle in
case there should be a misunderstanding between us The scouting party soon returned with some of the Chiefs accompanied by
an American who was trading with them in the employ of the
American Fur Company. The Chiefs after smoking and looking
about some time returned to their village which had encamped
about 3 mls above on the river. The next morning they came
and encamped within 300 yds of us. Their Village contained 200
lodges and about 200 warriors. The Crows are a proud haughty
insolent Tribe whenever their party is the strongest but if the
case is reversed they are equally cowardly and submissive. This
Village is called "Long hair's band" after their chief whose hair
is eleven fcct six inches long done up in an enormous queue about
18 inches long and six inches thick hanging down his back he
is about 80 years of age and seems to be afflicted with the Dropsy
the only case of the kind I have ever known among the Mountain Indians. The village staid with us until the 25 of March
and then moved down the river about 6 mls. We left the Big
horn on the 1st of April and started on the Spring hunt. On the
3d up Bovy's fork 20mls. 4th Up the same 10 mls. After we had
encamped four Delawares who were cruising about in the hills
hunting buffaloe fell in with a party of 10 or 12 Blackfeet killed
one on the spot and wounded several more. The Blackfeet then
took to their heels and left the victorious Delawares without loss
except one horse being slightly wounded in the neck 10th We
arrived at "Howells encampment" at the mouth of Rocky fork.
The whole country here was filled with Buffaloe driven this way
by the Crow Village 11th We raised a Cache of Beaver and other
articles which had been deposited in the ground in Novr. last.
14 A party of 12 Trappers and two Camp Keepers started to
trap the "Muscle Shell" river[103] which heads in the mountain

near "25 Yard river" and runs into the Missouri on the South side above the mouth of the Yellow Stone. Myself and three others travelled up Rocky fork about 20 mls but found so much Snow and ice that we could not set our traps for Beaver. We found a large cave on the SE side of a perpendicular rock. in this we encamped six days during which we made great havoc among the Buffaloe On the 23d the camp moved up to our Cave and the next day I went up the stream about 12 mls and set my traps and saw signs of several war parties of Blackfeet who were scouting about the country 26th I was cruising with another Trapper thro. the timber and brush above where we had set our traps when on a sudden we came within 10 steps of two Black-foot Forts and saw the smoke ascending from the tops as we saw no individuals we entered and found the Indians had been gone about half an hour. 28th The party arrived from the Muscle Shell having been defeated and lost one Trapper and nearly all their horses and traps by the Blackfeet May 1st All being col-lected we left Rocky fork close to the Mountain and took round the foot in an east direction and encamped at a spring where we staid the next day, the Blackfeet still continued dogging at our heels to steal now and then a horse which might get loose in the night. There is a proverb among Mountaineers "That It is better to count ribs than tracks" That is to say it is better to fasten a horse at night untill you can count his ribs with poverty than turn him loose to fatten and count his tracks after an Indian has stolen him 3d Travelled on to Clarks fork 12 Mls SE and the next day up the same 15 mls South 5th Travelled to a small branch running into Stinking river, South direction 15 mls 6th we encamped on Stinking river about 15 mls below the forks distance about 12 mls course SE. 7th We travelled from the river about 20 mls in a South direction and encamped at a Spring 8th to the "Gray Bull fork"[104] of the Big horn 9th to the Medi-cine lodge fork[105] 12 mls South 10th to the middle fork of the "Medicine lodge" 8 mls 11th to the South fork of the Medicine lodge 8 mls South. Here we staid two days 14th Travelled SE to a small spring at the foot of the upper Big horn mountain distance 13 mls The 15 travelled to the top of the Big horn mountain and encamped on the divide The country over which we have travelled since we left "Stinking" [is] much broken by spurs of Mountains and deep gullies entirely destitute of timber except along the banks of the streams 16th Travelled down the Mountain on the South side and encamped on a small branch of Wind river This river loses its name whilst passing thro. the upper Big horn mountain From thence it takes the name of the Big horn derived from the vast numbers of Mountain Sheep or Big horn inhabiting the mountains thro. which it passes. 17th Over broken country South about 15 mls 18th Encamped on the river after a march of 10 ms. South. 19th The camp intending to stop here several days I started with a raw Son of Erin to hunt Beaver on the head branches of the river. We travelled up west about 25 Mls to what is called the "red rock"[106] Killed a sheep and encamped for the night where several branches of the river united 20th We took up a large branch about 15 ms NW and found the water overflowing the banks of all the branches so much that it was impossible to catch Beaver We then altered our Course NE accross the country in order to examine the small branches on our right but finding all our efforts to trap useless and discovering that a war party consisting of 80 Blackfeet were in pursuit of us we returned to the camp by a different route on the 23 24th Travelled with the Camp to the north fork of "Popo azia" or "[?] river"[107] one of the principal branches of Wind river distance 12 mls course South 25 to the middle fork of the same stream 8 mls distance 26th To the Oil Spring[108] on the South fork of "Popo-azia" This spring produces about one Gallon per hour of pure Oil of Coal or rather Coal Tar the scent of which is often carried on the wind 5 or 6 mls. The Oil issues from the ground within 30 feet of the stream and runs off slowly into the water Camp stopped here eight days We set fire to the spring when there was 2 or 3 Bbls. of oil on the ground about it, it burnt very quick and clear but produced a dense column of thick black smoke the oil above ground being consumed the fire soon went out. This is a beautiful country thickly clothed with grass intermingled with flowers of every hue. On the west rises the Wind River range of Mountains abruptly from the smooth rolling hills until crowned with Snow above the Clouds On the East stretches away the Great Wind River plain and terminates at a low range of Mountains rising between Wind and Powder Rivers

Buffaloe Elk and Sheep are abundant. Beds of Iron and Coal are frequently found in this part of the country June 5th We left the Oil Spring and took over a point of Mountain about 15 mls SW and encamped on a small spring branch 6th Crossed the Spurs of Mountains due west 12 mls and encamped on a branch of Sweet water 7th Travelled west about 15 mls and encamped on "little Sandy" a branch of Green River 8th Travelled North up the Valley about 18 mls. and encamped on a stream called the New fork[109] of Green river where we staid the next day 10th Travelled west to the Main river about 25 mls and struck the river about 12 mls below the mouth of horse creek Here we found the hunting Parties all assembled waiting for the arrival of Supplies from the States. Here presented what might be termed a mixed multitude The whites were chiefly Americans and Canadian French with some Dutch, Scotch, Irish, English, halfbreed, and full blood Indians, of nearly every tribe in the Rocky Mountains. Some were gambling at Cards some playing the Indian game of hand and others horse racing while here and there could be seen small groups collected under shady trees relating the events of the past year all in good Spirits and health for Sickness is a Stranger seldom met with in these regions. Sheep Elk Deer Buffaloe and Bear Skins mostly supply the Mountaineers with clothing bedding and lodges while the meat of the same animals supplies them with food. They have not the misfortune to get any of the luxuries from the civilized world but once a year and then in such small quantities that they last but a few days. We had not remained in this quiet manner long before something new arose for our amusement The Bonnak Indians had for several years lived with the whites on terms partly hostile frequently stealing horses and traps and in one instance killed two White Trappers. They had taken some horses and traps from a party of French trappers who were hunting Bear river in April last, and they were now impudent enough to come with the village of 60 lodges and encamp within 3 mls of us in order to trade with the whites as usual still having the stolen property in their possession and refusing to give it up On the 15 of June 4 or 5 whites an two Nez Percey Indians went to their Village and took the stolen horses (whilst the men were out hunting buffaloe) and returned with them to our camp. About 3 oclk PM of the same day 30 Bonnaks came riding at full gallop up to the Camp—armed with their war weapons. They rode into the midst and demanded the horses. which the Nez percey had taken, saying they did not wish to fight with the whites. But the Nez percey who were only Six in number gave the horses to the whites for protection which we were bound to do as they were numbered among our Trappers and far from their own tribe. Some of the Bonnacks on seeing this started to leave the Camp one of them as he passed me observed that he did not come to fight Whites but another a fierce looking Savage who still stopped behind called out to the others saying "we came to get horses or blood and let us do it" I was standing near the Speaker and understood what he said I immediately gave the whites warning to be in readiness for an attack nearly all the men in camp were under arms Mr. Bridger was holding one of the stolen horses by the bridle when one of the Bonnaks rushed thro. the crowd seized the bridle and attempted to drag it from Mr Bridger by force without heeding the cocked rifles that surrounded him any more than if they had been so many reeds in the hands of Children. He was a brave Indian but his bravery proved fatal to himself, for the moment he seized the bridle two rifle balls whistled thro. his body. the others wheeled to run but 12 of them were shot from their horses before they were out of the reach of Rifles. We then mounted horses and pursued them destroyed and plundered their village and followed and fought them three days when they begged us to let them go and promised to be good Indians in future. We granted their request and returned to our Camp satisfied that the best way to negotiate and settle disputes with hostile Indians is with the rifle: for that is the only pen that can write a treaty which they will not forget[110] Two days after we left them three white trappers ignorant of what had taken place went into their village and were treated in the most friendly manner The Indians said however they had been fighting with the Blackfeet. July 5th[111] a party arrived from the States with supplies The cavalcade consisting of 45 men and 20 Carts drawn by Mules under the direction of Mr. Thomas Fitzpatrick accompanied by Capt. Wm. Stewart on another tour to the Rocky Mountains. Joy now beamed in every countenance Some received letters from their friends and relations Some received the public papers and news of the day others consoled themselves with the idea of getting a blanket a Cotton Shirt or a few pints of Coffee and sugar to sweeten it just by way of a treat gratis that is to say by paying 2,000 percent on the first cost by way of accommodation for instance Sugar 2$ pr pint Coffee the same Blankets 20$ each Tobacco 2$ pr pound alcohol 4$ pr pint and Common Cotton Shirts 5$ each etc And in return paid 4 or 5$ pr pound for Beaver. In a few days the bustle began to subside. the furs were done up in packs ready for transportation to the States and parties were formed for hunting the ensuing year One party consisting of 110 men were destined for the Blackfoot Country under the direction of L B Fontanelle as commander and James Bridger Pilot

I started with five others to hunt the head waters of the

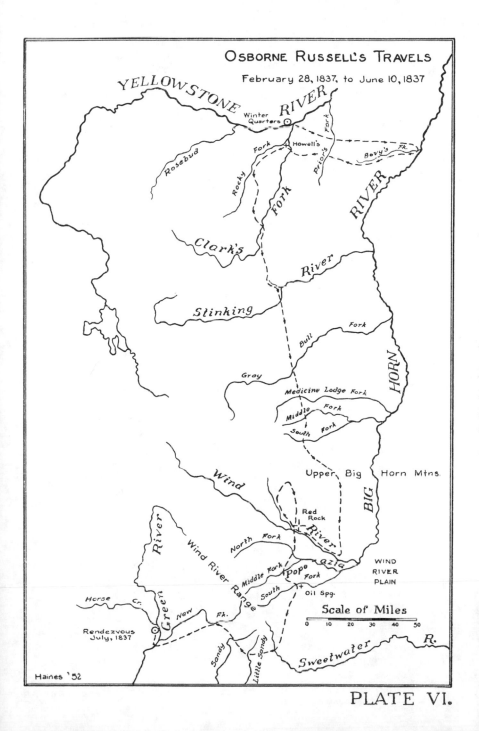

OSBORNE RUSSELL'S TRAVELS

February 28, 1837, to June 10, 1837

YELLOWSTONE RIVER

Winter Quarters

Howell's

Rocky Fork

Prior's Fork

Bovy's Fk.

Rosebud

Fork

Clark's

River

BIG HORN RIVER

Stinking

Bull Fork

Gray

Medicine Lodge Fork

Middle Fork

South Fork

BIG HORN

Upper Big Horn Mtns.

Wind

Red Rock

North Fork

River

Azia

Middle Fork

Popo Fork

WIND RIVER PLAIN

South

River

Green

Oil Spg.

Horse Cr.

New Fk.

Rendezvous July, 1837

Scale of Miles

0   10   20   30   40   50

Sandy

Little Sandy

Sweetwater R.

Haines '52

PLATE VI.

Yellowstone Missouri and Big horn rivers a portion of country I was particularly fond of hunting On the 20th of July we left the Rendezvous and travelled up Green River about 10 mls. 21st We travelled up green river till noon when we discovered a trail of 8 or 10 Blackfeet and a Buffaloe fresh killed and butched with the meat tied up in small bundles on the ground which they had left on seeing us approach and run into the bushes, we supposing them to be a small scouting party tied their bundles of meat on to our saddles and still kept on our route but had not gone far before we discovered them secreted among some willows growing a long a branch which crossed our trail I was ahead leading the party when I discovered them we stopped and one of my comrades whose name was [William] Allen began to arrange the load on his pack mule in the meantime I reined my horse to the left and rode onto a small hillock near by and casting a glance towards the bushes which were about 150 yds distant I saw two guns pointed at me I instantly wheeled my horse but to no purpose the two balls struck him one in the loins and the other in the shoulder which dropped him under me the Indians at the Sametime jumped out of the bushes 60 or 70 in number and ran toward us shooting and yelling I jumped on a horse behind one of My comrades and we scampered away towards the Rendezvous where we arrived at dark. 25th The parties started and we travelled with Mr Fontanelle's party up Green River 10 mls intending to keep in their company 5 or 6 days and then branch off to our first intended route 26th We travelled 20 mls NW accross a low range of hills and encamped in a valley lying on a branch of Lewis fork called "Jackson's little hole."[112] 27th We travelled down this Stream 18 mls NW This stream runs thro. a tremendous mountain in a deep narrow Kanyon of rock.[113] The trail runs along the Cliffs from 50 to 200 feet above its bed and is so narrow in many places that only one horse can pass at a time for several hundred yards and one false step would precipitate him into the Chasm *into the Chasm* below after leaving the Kanyon we encamped at a small spring in "Jacksons big hole" near the Southern extremity 28th travelled up the Valley North 15 mls. encamped killed some Buffaloe and Staid next day 30th I left the Camp in company with two trappers and one Camp Keeper we received instructions from Mr. Fontanele to meet the Camp at the mouth of Clarks fork of the Yellow Stone on the 15th of the ensuing Octr where they expected to pass the winter but he said if he should conclude to change his winter quarters he would cause a tree to be marked at Howells grave and bury a letter in the ground at the foot of it containing directions for finding the camp after bidding adieu to the Camp we travelled North till near sunset and encamped about 40 mls from the main party 31st We travelled to the fork 5 mls below Jacksons Lake and ascended it in the same direction I had done the year before and encamped about 15 mls from the Valley Aug. 1st we reached the dividing spring about 4 oclk P.M. and stopped for the night 2d We encamped at the inlet of the YellowStone Lake 3d Travelled down the East Shore of the Lake and stopped for the night near the outlet at the steam spring 4th We took our course ENE and after travelling all day over rugged mountains thickly covered with pines and underbrush we encamped at night about 10 mls Nth[114] of the secluded valley on the stream which runs thro it after we had encamped we Killed a Dear which came in good time as we had eaten the last of our provisions the night previous at the Yellowstone Lake and the flies and musketoes were so bad and the underbrush so thick that we had not killed anything during the day 5th We travelled up a left hand branch of this Stream NE 15 mls thro the thick pines and brush untill near the head where we encamped in a beautiful valley about 2 Mls in circumference[115] almost encircled with huge Mountains whose tops were covered with snow from which small rivulets were issueing clear as Crystal and uniting in the smooth grassy vale formed the stream we had ascended. We concluded to spend the next day at this place as there was no flies or musktoos for tho warm and pleasant in the day the nights were too cold for them to survive. The next day after eating a light breakfast of roasted venison I shouldered my rifle and ascended the highest mountain on foot. I reached the snow in about an hour when seating myself upon a huge fragment of Granite and having full view of the country around Me in a few moments was almost lost in contemplation. This said I is not a place where heroes' deeds of Chivalry have been atchieved in days of yore neither is a place of which bards have sung until the world knows the precise posture of every tree rock and [?] or the winding turn of every streamlet. But on the contrary those stupendous rocks whose surface is formed into irregular benches rising one above another from the vale to the snow dotted here and there with low pines and covered with green herbages intermingled with flowers with the scattered flocks of Sheep and Elk carelessly feeding or thoughtlessly reposing beneath the shade having Providence for their founder and preserver and Nature for Shepherd Gardner and Historian. In viewing scenes like this the imagination of one unskilled in Science wanders to the days of the Patriarchs and after numerous conjecturings returns without any final decision wonder is put to the test but having no proof for its argument a doubt still remains but supposition steps forward and taking the place of Knowledge in a few words solves the mysteries of ages Centuries and Eras after including in such a train of reflections for about two hours I descended to the camp where I found my companions had killed a fat Buck Elk during my abscence and some of the choisest parts of it were supported on sticks around the fire. My ramble had sharpened my appetite and the delicious savor of roasted meat soon rid my brains of romantic ideas. My comrades were men who never troubled themselves about vain and frivolous notions as they called them with them every country was pretty when there was weather and as to beauty of nature or arts it was all a "humbug" as one of them (an Englishman) often expressed it. "Talk of a fine Country" said he "and beautiful places in these mountains if you want to see a beautiful place" said he "go to Hingland and see the Duke of Rutlands Castle" "Aye" says a son of Erin who sat opposite with an Elk rib in one hand and a butcher knife in the other while the sweat rolling from his face mingled in the channels of greas which ran from the corners of his mouth, "Aye an ye would see a pretty place gow to old Ireland and take a walk in Lord Farnhams domain" that is the place where ye can see "plisure" Arrah an I were upon that same ground this day Id fill my body wid good ould whisky "Yes" said the back woods hunter on my left, as he cast away his bone and smoothed down his long auburn hair with his greasy hand, "Yes you English and Irish are always talking about your fine Countries but if they are so mighty fine" (said he with an oath) "why do so many of you run off and leave them and come to America to get a living" from this the conversation turned to an argument in which the Hunter came off victorious driving his opponents from the field. 7th of Aug. we travelled up the mountain in a South direction and fell into a smooth grassy defile about 200 paces wide which led thro. between two high peaks of rocks. In this place we fell in with a large band of Sheep killed two Ewes packed the best meat on our horses and proceeded down the defile which led us on to the headwaters of "Stinking River" about 50 mls from where it enters the plain We travelled down this stream about 10 mls South and encamped where we saw some signs of Snake Indians who inhabited these wilds. The next morning I arose about day break and went in search of Our horses which had been turned loose to feed during the night I soon found all but 3 and after hunting sometime I discovered a trail made in the dew on the grass where an Indian had been crawling on his belly and soon found where he had caught the horses. Two of us then mounted mules and followed the trail in a west direction up a steep piney mountain until 10 ock when we lost the trail among the rocks and were obliged to give up the pursuit, we then returned to Camp. We then packed our remaining animals and travelled down the stream abot 10 miles 9th We left the main Stream and ascended a small branch in a SSW direction about 8 mls up a steep ascent and encamped in a smooth grassy spot near the head[116] where we concluded to stop the next day and hunt Beaver Early the next morning a few of the "Mountain Snakes" came to our camp consisting of 3 men and 5 or 6 women and children One of them told me he knew the Indians who had stolen our horses that they lived in the mountains between Stinking river and Clarks fork and said that he would go and try to get them After trading some Beaver and Sheep Skins from them talking smoking etc about an hour I mounted my Mule with 6 traps and my rifle and one of my comrades did the same and we started to hunt Beaver. We left the camp in a SW direction and travelled abot 8 mls over a high craggy mountain then desended into a small circular Valley about a mile in circumference which was completely covered with logs shattered fragments of trees and splinters 4 or 5 ft deep. There had been trees 2 and 3 feet in diameter broken off within 2 ft of the ground and shivered into pieces small enough for a kitchen fireplace This in all probability was the effect of an avalanche About 2 years previous as the tall pines had been completely cleared for the space of 400 yds wide and more than 2 Mls up the steep side of the mountain. Finding no Beaver on the branches of this stream[117] we returned to Camp at Sunset Our Camp Keeper had prepared an elegant supper of Grizzly Bear meat and Mutton nicely stewed and seasoned with pepper and salt which as the mountain phrase goes "is not bad to take" upon an empty Stomach after a hard days riding and climbing over mountains & rocks Aug 11th We returned to the river and travelled up about 4 Mls. Then left it and travelled up a branch in a due west[118] direction about 6 Mls. Killed a couple of fat Doe Elk and encamped. 12th Myself and Allen (which was the name of the backwoodsman) started to hunt the small streams in the mountains to the West of us leaving the Englishman (who was the other trapper) to set traps about the camp we hunted the branches of this stream then crossed the divide[119] to the waters of the Yellowstone Lake where we found the whole country swarming with Elk we killed a fat Buck for supper and encamped for the night the next day Allen shot a Grizzly Bear and bursted the percussion tube of his rifle which obliged us to return to our comrades on the 13th and make another tube. The next day we returned to Stinking river and travelled up about 10 Mls above where we first struck it 15th It rained and snowed all day and we stopped in camp 16th Took a NE course up the Mountain and reached the divide about noon then descended in a direction nearly East and encamped in a valley on the head of Clarks fork This valley is a prarie about 30 Mls in circumference completely surrounded by high mountains.[120] The Stream after passing SE falls into a tremendous kanyon just wide enough to admit its waters between rocks from 3 to 500 ft perpendicular height extending about 12 Mls to the great plain 18th we moved up the stream to the head of the valley and encamped. Here the stream is formed of two forks nearly equal in size The right hand fork falls into the left from off a bench upwards of 700 feet high nearly perpendicular. The view of it at the distance of 8 or 10 Mls resembles a bank of snow. 19th travelled up the left branch about 10 Mls NW thro. thick pines and fallen timber then leaving the stream to our right turned into a defile which led us on to the waters of the Yellowstone[121] in about 8 Mls. where we stopped set traps for beaver and staid next day. 21st We travelled down this stream (which runs west thro. a high range of mountains) about 25 Mls 22d Travelled down the stream 15 Mls West and encamped in the Secluded Valley where we staid two days 25th Travelled down the Valley to the Nth and crossed a low spur about 4 Mls Nth and fell on to a stream[122] running into the one we had left he[re] we set traps and staid until the 2d of Septr. 3d Travelled over a high rugged mountain about 20 Mls NW

and encamped in a beautiful Valley on a small stream running
into the one we had left in the morning 4th Travelled 15 Mls
NW over a high piney mountain and encamped on a stream[123]
running South into the Yellowstone where we staid and trapped
until the 13th We then travelled up the stream NE about 8 Mls
14 Travelled up the Stream 12 Mls in the same direction 15
We crossed the divide of the main range North towards the Big
plains. We found the snow belly deep to our horses after leaving
the snow we travelled about 8 Mls north and encamped on the
head branch of the Cross Creek[124] running North into the Yellowstone about 12 Mls below the Mouth of "25 Yard" river
Here a circumstance occurred which furnished the subject for a
good joke upon our green Irish camp keeper The Englishman
had stopped for the night on the mountain to hunt Sheep whilst
we descended to the stream and encamped in a prarie about
2 Mls in circumference. It was the commencement of the rutting
season with the Elk when the Bucks frequently utter a loud cry
resembling a shrill whistle especially when they see anything of
a strange appearance. We had made our beds at night on a little
bench between two small dry gullies. The weather was clear and
the moon shone brightly abot 10 at night when I supposed my
comrades fast asleep an Elk blew his shrill whistle within about
100 yards of us. I took my gun slipped silently into the gully
and crept towards the place where I heard the sound but I soon
found he had been frightened by the horses and ran off up the
Mountain. On turning back I met Allen who hearing the Elk had
started to get a shot at him in the same manner I had done without speaking a word. We went back to Camp but our Camp
keeper was no where to be found. We searched the bushes high
and low ever and anon calling for "Conn" but no "Conn" answered at length Allen cruising thro the brush tumbled over a
pile of rubbish when lo! Conn was beneath nearly frightened out
of his wits "Arrah! an is it you Allen" Said he trembling as if an
ague fit was shaking him "but I thought the whole world was

full of the spalpeens of savages And where are they gone?"—
It was near an hour before we could Satisfy him of his mistake
and I dare say his slumbers were by no means soft or smooth
during the remainder of the night 16th The Englishman arrived
and we travelled down this stream about 10 Mls when we staid
the next day as it snowed very hard 18 Travelled down about
20 Mls and on the 19 came to the plains in about 10 Mls Travel
where we encamped Here we found the country filled with buffaloe as usual 20th We shaped our Course NE and travelled
about 25 Mls accross the Spurs of the mountain fell onto the
Nth. fork of the "Rosebud" where we staid the next day as it
rained 22d We travelled South along the foot of the Mountain
20 Mls keeping among the low Spurs which project into the
plain in order to prevent being discovered by any straggling
parties of Blackfeet which might chance to be lurking about the
country, the plains below us were crowded with Buffaloe which
we were careful not to disturb for fear of being discovered We
stopped and Set our traps on the small branches of the "Rosebud" until the 11th of Octr. then travelled to Rocky fork and
went up it into the Mountain and encamped. On the 13th Myself
and Allen started to hunt Mr. Fontanells party leaving our
Comrades in the Mountain to await our return We travelled
down Rocky fork all day amid crowds of Buffaloe and encamped
after dark near the mouth. The next morning we went to "Howells encampment" but found no tree marked neither had the
earth been disturbed since we had closed it upon the remains
of the unfortunate Howell We now sat down and consulted upon
the best course to pursue As Winter was approaching we could
not think of stopping in this country where parties of Blackfeet
were ranging at all seasons of the year. After a few moments
deliberation we came to the conclusion and I wrote a note enclosed it in a Buffaloe horn buried it at the foot of the tree and
then marked the tree with my hatchet This being done we
mounted our Mules and started back to the mountain Travelled

about 6 Mls stopped and killed a cow. As we were lying within about 60 paces of the band which contained about 300 cows Allen made an observation which I shall never forget Said he I have been watching these cows some time and I can see but one that is poor enough to Kill" for said he it is a shame to kill one of those large fat Cows merely for two mens suppers" So saying he leveled his rifle on the poorest and brot. her down. She was a heifer about 3 years old and but an inch of fat on the back. After cooking and eating we proceeded on our journey until sometime after dark when we found ourselves on a sudden in the midst of an immense band of Buffaloe who getting the scent of us ran helter skelter around us in every direction rushing to and fro like the waves of the ocean, approaching sometimes within 10 ft. of us We stood still for we dare not retreat or advance until this storm of brutes took a general course and rolled away with a noise like distant thunder and then we hurried on thro. egyptian darkness a few 100 paces when we found a bunch of willows where we concluded to stop for the night rather than risk our lives any further among such whirlwinds of beef 15 We reached the Camp about 10 oclk AM. We staid on Rocky fork and its branches trapping until the 27th of Octr. when we concluded to go to a small fork running into Wind river on the east side above the upper Big horn mountain and there pass the winter, unless we should hear from the main party 28th we travelled to Clarks fork and the next day to Stinking river ESE direction 30th we crossed Stinking and travelled in the same direction over a broken barren tract of country about 25 Mls whilst the rain poured all day in torrents. About sun an hour high we stopped and the weather cleared up We encamped for the night in a small ravine where was some watter standing in a puddle but no wood but a lone green Cottonwood tree which had supported a Bald Eagles nest probably more than half a century 31st We travelled over ground similar to that of the day before shaping our course more Easterly until night Novr.

1st After travelling about 10 Mls we reached Bighorn river and stopped and commenced setting traps. The river at this place is bordered with heavy Cottonwood timber with little or no under brush beneath. Towards night a party of Crow Indians came to us on foot armed as if going to war after smoking and eating they told us they were on their way to the Snaks to Steal horses and intended to stay all night with us and leave the next morning. They told us the village to which they belonged was nearly a days travel below on the river and that "Long hair's" village was on Wind river above the mountain but could give us no information of Mr. Fontanell or his party They were very insolent and saucy saying that we had no right in their country and intimated they could take everything from us if they wished. The next morning after eating breakfast they said if we would give them some tobacco and ammunition they would leave us so we divided our little stock with them They then persisted in having all and when we refused telling them we could not spare it one of them seized the sack which contained it while another grasped the Englishmans rifle we immediately wrenched them out of their hands and told them if they got more they should fight for it. During the Scuffle they had all presented their arms but when we gained possession of the rifle and the sack they put down their arms and told us with an envious Savage laugh they were only joking but we were too well acquainted with the Crows to relish such capers as mere jokes and wished to get out of their power the easiest way possible as their Villages were on either side of us. We then packed up our horses and forded the river and travelled up about 6 Mls and encamped at the same time the Indians were mounted on our pack horses and riding animals [trailing] us and the remainder on foot except one who returned towards the Village crying. After we had stopped they made a sort of Shelter as it looked likely for rain and at night ordered us to go into it and sleep but we bluntly refused and removed our baggage about 30 paces from them. Sitting down reclining against it one of them had taken the only Blanket I possessed off my riding Saddle and put an old worn out coat in its place with a hint that exchanging was not robbing They laid down in their shelter and continued to sing their noisy and uncouth war songs until near midnight when they ceased and all became Silent The night was dark with a sprinkling rain we lay without hearing any disturbance until daybreak when we began to look around but could find neither Indians or horses tho. we soon found their trail going down the river we then set about burning our saddles robes etc and cacheing our Beaver in the ground intending after making a few deposits and bon fires to Shoulder our rifles and travel to Fort William at the mouth of Larameys fork of the Platte Our Saddles Epishemores[125] ropes etc were scarcely consumed when we saw 5 or 6 Indians on horseback coming towards us at full gallop and presently 15 or 20 more appeared following them They rode up alighted from their horses and asked for tobacco to smoke we gave them some they formed a circle and sat down I was not acquainted with any of them except the Chief who was called the "Little Soldier" he spoke to me in the Snake language and said he wished me to smoke with them but the manner in which they had formed the ring and placed their war weapons excited Suspicion and Allen immediately declined as he had lived with the Crows two winters he said he knew that thieving and treachery were two of the greatest virtues the Nation could boast of and we quickly resolved to leave them at all hazards So we shouldered our rifles and those who had blankets took them and began to travel The Indians looked at us with pretended astonishment and asked what was the matter. Allen told them that he was aware that they wanted to rob us and were laying a plan to do it with out danger to themselves but said he "if you follow or molest us we will besmear the ground with blood and guts of Crow Indians' and do not speak to me more' said he for I despise the odious jargon of your Nation So saying he wheeled around and we marched away in a South direction towards the mountain. We had not gone far before two of them came after us we stopped and turned around when one of them stopped within 300 paces of us while the other (who was the chief) advanced slowly unarmed When he came up he addressed me in the Snake language for knowing the disposition of Allen he did not wish to trifle with his own life so much as to begin a conversation with him in his own language taking me by the hand as he spoke he said my friends you are very foolish you do not know how bad my heart feels to think you have been robbed by men belonging to my village but they are not men they are Dogs who took your animals. The first I knew of your being in this country about midnight a young man came to the village crying and told me of their intention. I immediately mounted my horse and hastened to your assistance, but arrived too late but if you will go with me I will get your animals and give you some Saddles and robes and fit you out as well as I can you can then stay with me until the Blanket Chief comes (the name they gave Mr Bridger) I interpreted what he had said to my comrades, but they said tell him we will not go to the Crow Village we will not trust our lives among them. When I told him this he replied I am very sorry, what shall I say to the Blanket Chief? how can I hold up my head when I shall meet him? and what shall I do with the things you have left behind? I told him to give them *to give them* to the Blanket Chief he then turned and left us slowly and sadly but I am well aware that a Crow Indian can express great sorrow for me and at the sametime be laying a plan to rob me or secretly take my life. After he had left us we travelled on toward the Mountain about 10 Mls. stopped killed a Cow and eat supper and then travelled until about Midnight when it being dark and cloudy we stopped and kindled a fire with Sage and weeds which we gathered about us and sat down to wait for daylight. Sleep was far from us our minds were so absorbed in the reflections on the past that few

were the words that passed among us during the night A Short
time after we stopped it commenced snowing very fast and we
were obliged to hover over our little fire to keep it from being extinguished. The day at length appeared and we proceeded on our
journey toward the mountain while it still continued to snow
as we began to ascend the Mountain the snow grew deeper and
about noon was up to our knees. We travelled on until Sun
about an hour high and stopped at some scrubby cedars and
willows which grew around a Spring. After scraping away the
snow we built a fire broke some cedar boughs spread them on
the ground and laid down weary and hungry but we had meat
nough with us for supper. Three of us Myself Allen and Greenberry[126] had been more or less inured to the hardships of a hunters life but our camp keeper John Conn could not relish the
manner in which he was treated in a country that boasted so
much its freedom and independence and often wished himself
back on the Shamrock Shore. Myself and Allen had one blanket
between us the others had a blanket each. The wind blew cold
and the snow drifted along the brow of the mountain around us
when we arose in the morning our fire had gone out the snow
was 3 inches deep on our covering and it still kept snowing.
Allen killed a black tailed Deer close by and we concluded to
stop all day at this place Novr 6th Sun rose clear and we started
up the mountain keeping on the ridges where the wind had
driven off the snow and arrived at the top about 10 oclk a.m.
From this elevation we could see the Wind river plains which
were dry and dusty whilst we were in snow up to the Middle.
We killed some sheep which were in large numbers about us
Cooked some of the best meat over a slow fire packed it on our
backs and proceeded down the mountain South and slept on bare
ground that night Novr. 7th We arose and found ourselves much
refreshed by our nights rest. We travelled nearly E all day
ascending a gradual smooth slope of country which lies between
Wind and Powder Rivers and stopped at night on the divide

where we found the snow about 2 inches deep and hard and the weather cold and windy whilst not a stick of wood or a drop of water were to be found within 10 Mls of us. We found a placed washed out by the water in the Spring of the year as the only shelter we could find from the wind and digging down the dry earth scattered some branches of Sage upon it to lie upon. I then went in search of rock in order to heat it and melt snow in my hat but I could not find so much as a pebble so we kindled a little fire of sage and sat down with a piece of Mutton in one hand and a piece of snow in the other eating meat and snow in this manner mad out our suppers and laid down to shake tremble and suffer with the cold till day light when we started and travelled as fast as our wearied limbs would permit in the same direction we had travelled the day before descending a gradual slope towards the head of powder river until near night when finding some water standing in a puddle with large quantities of dry sage about it we killed a Bull near by taking his skin for a bed and some of the best meat for supper passed the night very comfortable We were now in sight of the red Butes on the river Platte—which appeared about 40 ms distant SE The next morning we found the weather foggy with sleet and snow falling I tried to persuade my comrades to stop until it should clear away urging the probability of our steering a wrong course as we could not see more than 200 paces but they concluded we could travel by the wind and after making several objections to travelling by Such an uncertain guide to no purpose I gave up the argument and we started and travelled about ESE for 3 hours as we supposed then stopped a short time and built a fire of Sage while it still continued to snow and rain alternately. and seeing no signs of the weather clearing we started again and went on till near Night when the Sun coming out we found that instead of travelling ESE our course had been NNE and we were as far from the Platte as we were in the Morning with the Country around us very broken intersected with deep ravines and gullies We saw some Bulls 3 or 4 Mls ahead and Started for them After the Sun hat set it clouded up and began to rain. We reached the Bulls about an hour after dark Allen crawled close to them shot and killed one took off the skin and some of the meat whilst myself and the others were groping around in the dark hunting a few bits of Sage and weeds to make a fire and after repeated unsuccessful exertions we at last kindled a blaze. We had plenty of water under over and all around us but could not find a stick for fuel bigger than a mans thumb. We sat down round the fire with each holding a piece of beef over it on a stick with one hand while the other was employed in keeping up the blaze by feeding it with wet sage and weeds until the meat was warmed thro. when it was devoured with an observation that "Bull Meat was dry eating when cooked too much." After supper (if I may be allowed to disgrace the term by applying it to such a Wolfish feast) we spread the Bull skin down in the mud in the dryest place we could find and laid down upon it. Our fire was immediately put out by the rain and all was Egyptian darkness. We lay tolerably comfortable whilst the skin retained its animal warmth and remained above the surface but the mud being soft the weight of our bodies sunk it by degrees below the water level which ran under us on the skin but we concluded it was best to lie still and keep the water warm that was about us for if we stirred we let in the cold water and if we removed our bed we were more likely to find a worse instead of a better place as it rained very hard all night. At daylight we arose bid adieu to our uncomfortable lodgins and left as fast as our legs would carry us thro. the mud and water and after travelling about 12 Mls South course we stopped killed a bull and took breakfast. After eating we travelled south untill sunset The weather was clear and cold but we found plenty of dry sage to make a fire and dry weeds for a bed 11th the ground was frozen hard in the morning and the winds blew cold from the North. We travelled til about noon when we fell in with large bands of Buffaloe and seeing the red

Butes about 5 or 6 ms ahead we killed two fat cows and took as much of the Meat as we could conveniently carry and travelled to the Platte where we arrived about the middle of the afternoon weary and fatigued. Here we had plenty of wood water meat and dry grass to sleep on, and taking everything into consideration we thought ourselves comfortably situated—comfortably I say for mountaineers not for those who never repose on anything but a bed of down or sit or recline on anything harder than Silken cushions for such would spurn at the idea of a Hunter's talking about comfort and happiness but experience is the best Teacher hunger good Sauce and I really think to be acquainted with misery contributes to the enjoyment of happiness and to know ones self greatly facilitates the Knowledge of Mankind—One thing I often console myself with and that is the earth will lie as hard upon the Monarch as it will on a Hunter and I have no assurance that it will lie upon me at all, my bones may in a few years or perhaps days be bleaching on the plains in these regions like many of my occupation without a friend to turn even a turf upon them after a hungry wolf has finished his feast. 12th The sun rose clear and warm and we found ourselves much refreshed by our nights rest. We travelled down the river about 5 Mls waded accross it and stopped the remainder of the day I had a severe attack of Rheumatism in my knees and ankles but this was no place to be sick so we jogged along over the Black hills having plenty of wood water and fresh Buffaloe meat every night until the 18th when we reached fort William.[127] When I entered this Fort I was met by two of my old messmates who invited me to their apartments. I now felt myself at home as Mr. Fontanell was one of the chief proprietors of the establishment and who had been partly and I may say wholly the cause of our misfortunes at night I lay down but the pains in my legs and feet drove sleep from me The next day I walked round the Fort as well as I could in order to get my joints limber. And on the 3d day after our arrival I felt quite recovered and at breakfast I

The interior of Fort Laramie (earlier known as Fort William), a rendezvous familiar to trappers, is depicted in this drawing by Alfred Jacob Miller.

asked my messmates where the man was who had charge of the Fort[128] they replied in his house pointing accross the square I inquired if he was sick for I had not seen him out [They] said he was unwell but not so as to confine him to his rooms I observed I must go and see him as I discover he was not coming to see me so saying myself and Allen started accross the square and met him on his way from the Storehouse to his dwelling room. we bid him "good morning" which he coldly returned and was on the point of turning carelessly away when we told him we would like to get some robes for bedding likewise a Shirt or two and some other nessary articles well said he as for Blankets shirts or coats I have none and Mr Fontanell has left no word when there will be any come up. If that is the case I replied you can let us have some Buffaloc robes and Epishemores yes said he I believe I can let you have an Epishemore or two. here John go up into yonder bastion and show these men those Epishemores that were put up there some time ago I dont think theres any there replied John but some old ones and them the rats have cut all to pieces —Oh I guess you can find some there that will do" he replied turning around and swinging a key on his thumb and forefinger as the insignia of his dignified station walked with a stiff stride to his apartments whilst we followed the Major Domo of this elevated quadruped to the bastion where I took the best Epishemore I could find which was composed of 9 pieces of Buffaloe skin sewed together but necessity compelled me to take it knowing at the same time there was more than 500 new robes in the warehouse which did not cost a pint of whisky each. But they were for people in the U S and not for trappers. This was the 21st day of Novr 1837 I never shall forget the time place nor circumstance but shall always pity the being who held the Imperial sway over a few sticks of wood with 5 or 6 men to guard them it was not his fault for how should he depart from the way in which he had been brought up? and what is more trappers have no right to meet with bad luck for it is nothing

more or less than the result of bad management. This is the lit-
teral reasoning of band box and counter hopping Philosophers —
consoling the unfortunate by enumerating and multiplying their
faults which are always the occasions of their misfortunes and
so clearly to be seen after the event has occurred. I would rather
at any time take an emetic than to be compelled to listen to the
advice of such predicting and [?] Counsellors. If I must be told
of something I already know let it be that I have learned another
lesson by experience and then give me advice for the future. I
have often derived a good deal of information from a person who
kept silent in the crowd — and it is well known that a certain class
of individuals display the most wisdom when they say the least!

On the 4th day after our arrival a large Sioux Indian arrayed
in the costume of the whites with a Sword suspended by his side
entered the lodging where I staid and looked around on the
whites for some time without Speaking a word at length he gave
me a signal to follow him and conducted me outside of the Fort
to his lodge which I found had been prepared for the reception
of a stranger. The Epishemores and robes had been arranged in
the back part of the lodge I was invited to sit by my mute con-
ductor who being the proprietor seated himself on my right The
big pipe went round with the usual ceremonies and the necessary
forms of Indian etiquette being complied with mine host commenced asking questions by signs without moving his lips and
having acquired the knowledge of conversation by signs without
uttering a word. It is impossible for a person not acquainted with
the Customs of Indians to form a correct idea in which [way] a
continuous conversation is held by hours between two individuals who cannot understand each others language but frequent
practice renders it faultless and I have often seen two Americans
conversing by signs by way of practice, but to return to my story
my inquisitive host gathered in the course of an hour the minute
details of my defeat by the Crows with my tedious journey to the
Fort and in return gave me a brief history of his life and inter-

course with the Whites since he had first seen them minutely describing the battles he had been in with the Crows the places where they were fought and their results particularly the rank of the Killed and wounded on both sides. After an hours dumb conversation a dish of roasted Buffaloe tongues was set before me accompanied by a large cake made of dried meat and fruit pounded together mixed up with Buffaloe marrow. It is considered an insult by an Indian for a Stranger whether White man or Indian to return any part of the food which is set before him to eat: If there is more than he wishes to eat at one time he must to avoid giving offense take the remainder with him when he leaves the lodge It is their general custom to set the Vituals their lodge affords before a stranger to eat. On the 22d Novr. a small trapping party arrived under the direction of Mr Thomas Biggs who intended to remain in the vicinity of the Fort until he receives further orders from Mr. Fontanell. On alighting from his horse he directed his course to our lodging Well boys said he on entering the door "The Crows found you did they?" and could not let you go without bestowing some of their National favors upon you?" Yes I observed and we have not mended the matter much by coming to this place and related what had passed between me and the Superintendent Well said he after I had done That is too ridiculous I thought before that Mr. - - - - - - had a soul but I am glad I have found you here I will see that you get such articles as you want if they can be had at this place and you must go with me. I shall go up about 15 Mls on the Plate and encamp—I have 200 lbs of lead and powder to shoot it and about 30 of the Company's horses which you well know were left after more than 200 were chosen out of the band to go into the Blackfoot country and I have not one which has not from one to three of his legs standing awry but such as they are you are welcome to them or anything there is in the Camp even to the half chew of tobacco. Nearly all of my Men are French and but little company for me and I want to see you slay the fat Cows and eat." So saying he turned and walked to the appartments of his wisdom, the overseer. Presently one of the Interpreters came and told us that Mr. - - - - - - wished us to come and get our things Oh said Allen he has got "things" has he? and has found out the Company is owing of us money? he is afraid of getting turned out of employment by his superior. Well let us go and get some of his things and yet inform Mr. Fontanell of his conduct" After getting our things we went to Mr. Bigg's camp as soon as possible. Then I felt a little more independent The rheumatism had left me and I felt as tho. I had rather walk than ride a poor horse. This section of Country which is called the "black hills" has always been celebrated for the game with which it abounds I passed most of my time hunting Black Tailed deer among the hills on foot, which has always been my favorite sport One day as myself and one of my fellow hunters were travelling thro. the hills coming toward us at full speed. [?] We stopped and they passed within 80 yds of us without making a halt we Shot the charges that were in our rifles loaded and Shot 2 more each before they had all passed by. As the hindmost were passing I could see the foremost passing over a ridge covered with snow more than 3 miles distant apparently at the same rate they had passed by us. They made a trail about 30 paces wide and went in as compact a body as they could consistently They consisted mostly of females. 20th Decr Mr Fontanell arrived at the Camp with 15 Men bringing the furs he had collected during the hunt for the purpose of depositing them at the Fort. he informed us he had left the main party on Powder river[129] and expressed his sorrow that he had been the cause of our Misfortunes he had mistaken the day agreed on to meet at Clarks fork and sent two men to the place on the 18th of Novr. who found the Note I had left. But said he I have met with that Village of Crows and recovered all your property that could be identified. I told them when I heard the circumstance that if they did not produce your property forthwith their heads would pay for it within 24 hours.

On hearing this they immediately gave up as they repeatedly affirmed all except the Beaver skins which they had traded to a Portugese by the name of Antonio Montaro[130] who had built some log cabins on Powder River for the purpose of trading with the Crows. I immediatcly continued he went to the Cabins and asked Mr. Montaro what right he had to trade Beaver skins from Indians with white mens names marked upon them knowing them to be stolen or taken by force from the Whites?" and asked him to deliver them to me which he refused to do. I then ordered him to give me the key of his warehouse which he reluctantly did I then ordered my clerk to go in and take all the Beaver skins he could find with your names marked upon them and have them carried to my camp which was done without further ceremony. Here then was the sum and substance of the sorrows expressed by the Crow Chief whose feelings were so much hurt to think that we were robbed by men or dogs belonging to his village yet I have no doubt if we had gone to the Village with him we would have received our things and fared better than we did by the course we persued but we were like all Mortals of the present day destitute of foreknowledge On the 28th of Jany the party started for Powder river with supplies for the Main Camp leaving Mr. Fontanell[131] at the Fort. The weather being cold we were compelled to travel on foot most of the time to keep ourselves from freezing. The snow was about 10 inches deep generally but driftet very much in many places. On the 7th of Feby we reached the encampment all in good health fine spirits and with full stomachs Here we found the Camp living on the fat of the land The bottoms along Powder river were crowded with Buffaloe insomuch that it was difficult keeping them from among the horses who were fed upon Sweet Cottonwood bark as the buffaloe had consumed everything in the shape of grass along the river

We passed the remainder of the winter very agreeably until 25th of March when the winter began to break the Buffaloe to leave the stream and scatter among the hills and the Trappers to prepare for the Spring hunt. After making the usual arrangements we started on the 29th down Powder river making short marches as our animals were very poor On the 3d of April we left the river and travelled accross the country which was generally comprised of rolling hills in a North Direction until the 18th when we reached the Little horn river[132] and travelled down it to the forks This river empties into the Big horn about 40 Mls below the lower Mountain. April 21st we left the forks and travelled nearly west over a broken and uneven country about 18 Mls and encamped on a small spring branch After we had encamped the Trappers made preparations for starting the next day to hunt Beaver as we had set but few traps since we left winter quarters for the Crows had destroyed nearly all the Beaver in the part of country thro. which we had been travelling. Early next morning about 30 of us were armed equipped and mounted as circumstances required. A Trappers equipments in such cases is generally one Animal upon which is placed one or two Epishemores a riding Saddle and bridle a sack containing six Beaver traps a blanket with an extra pair of Mocasins his powder horn and bullet pouch with a belt to which is attached a butcher Knife a small wooden box containing bait for Beaver a Tobacco sack with a pipe and implements for making fire with sometimes a hatchet fastened to the Pommel of his saddle his personal dress is a flannel or cotton shirt (if he is fortunate enough to obtain one, if not Antelope skin answers the purpose of over and under shirt) a pair of leather breeches with Blanket or smoked Buffaloe skin, leggings, a coat made of Blanket or Buffaloe robe a hat or Cap of wool, Buffaloe or Otter skin his hose are pieces of Blanket lapped round his feet which are covered with a pair of Moccassins made of Dressed Deer Elk or Buffaloe skins with his long hair falling loosely over his shoulders complets his uniform. He then mounts and places his rifle before him on his Saddle. Such was the dress equipage of the party my-

This Charles M. Russell painting, titled "Free Trappers" por-
trays a group of Mountain Men emerging from the high country.
(Reproduced by courtesy of the Historical Society of Montana)

self included now ready to start. After getting the necessary information from Mr. Bridger concerning the route he intended to take with the Camp we all started in gallop in a West direction and travelled to the Big horn[133] and there commenced separating by two's and three's in different directions I crossed the river with the largest party still keeping a west course most of the time in a gallop until sun about an hour high at night when we Killed a Bull and each taking some of the meat for supper proceeded on our journey till Sunset when I found myself with only one Companion All had turned to the right or left without once hinting their intentions for it was not good policy for a Trapper to let too many know where he intends to set his traps particularly if his horse is not so fast as those of his companions. I am sure my remaining companion who was a Canadian Frenchman knew not where I intended to set until I stopped my horse at a Beaver dam between sunset and dark We set three traps each and went down the Stream ½ a Mile and encamped Sometime after dark. This day I travelled about 40 Mls with a poor horse over a rough and broken country intersected with deep ravines The next morning we set the remainder of our traps and started down the stream about a Mile where we found two more trappers we encamped with them hobbled our horses and turned them out to feed and before night our number had increased to 12 Men. The Camp came to us on the 26th of April and found us nearly all together we raised our traps and moved on with them to the west Fork of Priors River where we arrived on the 29th The next morning we made another start as formerly. My intentions were to set my traps on Rocky fork which we reached about 3 oclk P.M. our party having diminished to three men beside myself. In the meanwhile it began to rain and we Stopped to approach a band of Buffaloe and as myself and one of My comrades (a Canadian) were walking along half bent near some bushes secreting ourselves from the Buffaloe a large Grizzly Bear who probably had been awakened from his slumbers by our approach sprang upon the Canadian who was 5 or 6 feet before me and placing one forepaw upon his head and the other on his left shoulder pushed him one side about 12 ft. with as little ceremony as if he had been a cat still keeping a direct course as tho. nothing had happened. I called to the Cannadian and soon found the fright exceeded the wound as he had received no injury except what this impudent stranger had done by tearing his coat but it was hard telling which was the most frightened the man or the Bear. We reached Rocky fork about Sunset and going along the edge of the timber saw another Bear lying with a Buffaloe Calf lying between his forepaws which he had already killed while the Mother was standing about 20 paces distant Moaning very pitifully for the loss of her young The bear on seeing us dropped the calf & took to his heels into the brush. The next day we travelled up Rocky fork till about 11 ock when I discovered there were trappers ahead of me I then altered my course leaving the stream at right Angles in a Westerly direction and travelled accross the Country paralell with the Mountain in company with a Cannadian for about 10 Mls set my traps on a stream called Bodairs fork (named after a Cannadian who was killed by the Blackfeet in 1836) [134] after setting our traps travelled down the stream, encamped and before night our party consisted of 15 men who had set their traps and come to this place to spend the night without any previous arrangement whatever. But an old trapper can form some idea where his companions will encamp tho. they seldom tell before their traps are set. I stopped at this place until the 6th of May when learning that the Camp had arrived on Rocky fork below I left my traps setting and went to it to get a fresh horse On the 7th the Camp moved near to where my traps were set and the next day moved on to the right hand fork of "Rosebud" 9th I raised my traps and overtook them at the junction of the three forks of Rosebud. The next day I started with two more to trap the head streams of this river we travelled up the middle fork to the mountain where we found signs of 4 or 5 trappers being there before us and to follow a fresh horse track in trapping time is neither wise nor profitable with such a number of trappers as our Camp contained on the 14th we started to the Camp which we found on the YellowStone at the mouth of the Cross Creeks The next day the Camp crossed the Yellow Stone and moved up the Nth side to the Mouth of "25 yard river" There I stopped with the Camp till the 19th when I started again with 3 others Travelled up 25 yard river about 25 Mls in a North direction then left it and took over a low point of Mountain in a West direction and fell on to a branch of the Same river which forms a half circle from the north point of the mountain from where we first struck the river We found this part of the country had been recently trapped by the Blackfeet

The next morning May 20th 2 of my comrades returned to the Camp as it rained very hard. The other asked me which way I was going I replied to hunt Beaver and started off as I spoke he mounted his horse and followed me without further ceremony We left the stream and took up the mountain in a SW direction after travelling about 6 Mls. we fell into a defile running thro. the Mountains on to Cherry river[135] a branch of the Gallatin. We travelled down this branch until near night and encamped The next day continued down the stream and reached the plains about 3 oclk PM within about 25 Mls. of the junction of the 3 forks of Missouri. We here left the stream we had descended and took up a small right hand fork of it in an East direction where we remained until the Camp arrived on the 25th. 27th We moved with the Camp to the Gallatin Fork the next day we crossed it with some difficulty but without accident except the loss of 3 Rifles the current ran so swift that several horses lost their footing and were washed down the stream which compelled their riders to abandon both horses and guns and swim ashore May 29th Travelled up this stream to the mountain about 15 Mls. and encamped. This Valley[136] is the largest in the Rocky Mountains except the valley of the Snake River but far smoother than the latter and more fertile. May 30th Travelled up the Gallatin fork about 10 Mls into the mountain and encamped 31st We travelled up a small branch in a west direction about 25 Mls. June 1st We crossed the mountain in the same direction and camped in the Valley[137] on the Madison fork which after leaving the valley runs thro. deep rocky kanyon into the plains below June 2 We crossed this fork and travelled up on the West side about 15 Mls on a trail made by a village of Blackfeet which had passed up 3 or 4 days previous. They were to all appearances occasionally dying of the Small Pox which has made terrible havoc among the Blackfeet during the last winter. To day we passed an Indian lodge standing in the prarie near the river which contained 9 dead bodies 3d Continued up the stream on their trail until 10 oclk a.m. when Mr. Bridger having Charge of the Camp tried to avoid them by taking into the mountain but the Majority of the men remonstrated so hard against trying to avoid a Village of Blackfeet which did not contain more than 3 times our numbers that he altered his course and turned back towards the Madison and encamped about two Ms from the river on a small spring branch This branch runs thro a ridge in a narrow passage in the rocks a hundred feet perpendicular on both sides about a quarter of a Ml. from the Madison. The next morning as we were passing over the ridge around this place we discovered the Village about 3 Mls above us on the river We immediately drove into this Kanyon with the Camp and prepared for battle Our leader was no military commander therefore no orders were given after the company property was secured about 15 men mounted horses and started for the Village in order to commence a skirmish. The Village was situated on the West bank of the river about 30 rods behind it arose a bench of land 100 ft high running parralell with the river and gradually ascending to the westward until it terminated in a high range of mountains about 2 Mls distant. While our men were approaching the Village I took a telescope and ascended the highest point of rock which over hung the camp to view the manoeuver. They rode within a short distance of the edge of the bench, then dismounted and crept to the edge and opened a fire on the Village which was the first the Indians knew of our being in the country. They fired 3 or 4 rounds each before the Indians had time to mount their horses and ascend the bluff one hundred and fifty yards above them The whites then mounted their horses and retreated towards the Camp before about 5 times their numbers a running fire was kept up on both sides untill our men reached the Camp when the Indians took possession of an elevated point formed of broken rocks about 300 paces distant on the South side of the Camp from which they kept shooting at intervals for about 2 hours without doing any damage when one of them called to us in the flathead tongue and Said that we were not men but women and had better dress ourselves as such for we had bantered them to fight and then crept into the rocks like women. An Old Iroquois trapper[138] who had been an experienced warrior trained on the Shores of Lake Superior understanding this harangue turned to the Whites about him and made a speech in imperfect English nearly as follows My friend you see dat Ingun talk? He not talk good he talk berry bad He say you me all same like squaw, dat no good, spose you go wid me I make him no talk dat way" On saying this he stripped himself entirely naked throwing his powder horn and bullet pouch over his right shoulder and taking his rifle in his hand began to dance and utter the shrill war cry of his Nation. 20 of us who stood around and near him cheered the sound which had been the death warrant of so many whites during the old French war He started and we followed amid a shower of balls: the distance as I said before was about 300 yards up a smooth and gradual ascent to the rocks where the Blackfeet had secreted themselves to the number of 150. The object of our leader was to make an open charge and drive them from their position which we effected without loss under an incessant storm of fusee balls. When we reached the rocks we stoped to breath about half a minute not having as yet discharged a single gun. We then mounted over the piles of granite and attacked them muzzle to muzzle Altho 7 or 8 times our number they retreated from rock to rock like hunted rats among the ruins of an old building whilst we followed close at their heels loading and shooting until we drove them entirely into the plain where their horses were tied. They carried off their dead with the exception of two and threw them into the river They then placed their wounded on horses and started slowly towards their village with a mournful cry We then packed our animals and followed them with the Camp within a quarter of a Mile of their village where we stopped for the night. During the night they moved the Village up about 3 Mls further. Next morning we ascended the bench intending to pass with the camp by the Village we soon found however that they had formed a line of mounted warriors from the river to the thick pines which grew on the mountain about 30 of us concluded to try the bravery of those cavaliers on the field leaving the remainder of the camp to bring up the rear we rode into a thicket under cover of the Camp out of their sight and turned into a deep ravine which led us undiscovered within 20 or 30 paces of their line They in the meantime were watching the motions of the Camp intending to attack it while crossing this ravine we approached nearly to the top of the bank where we concluded to rest our horses a moment and then Charge their line in front near the left wing we were close enough to hear them talking as they pranced back and forward on the bench above us after tightening our girths and examining our arms we put each of us 4 or 5 bullets in our mouths and mounted without noise—Our leader (the same old Iroquois) Sallied forth with a horrid yell and we followed the Indians were so much surprised with such a sudden attack that they made no resistance whatever but wheeled and took toward the village as fast as their horses could carry them whilst we pursued close at their heels until within about 300 yards of their lodges where we made a halt and stopped until the Camp had passed then rode quietly away to our own party. After leaving them we travelled up the Madison about 8 Mls and encamped near the place where we had fought the Blackfeet in Septr. 1835. The Madison after leaving the mountains runs westerly to this place forms a curve and turning east of north in which direction it runs to the junction of the three forks. The next day (June 6th) we left the Madison and travelled in a South [direction over an] undulating plain[139] about 15 Mls and encamped at Henrys Lake. This lake is about 30 Mls in circumference surrounded by forests of pine except on the SE side where there is a small prarie about one Mile wide and two long terminating almost to a point to the two extremities. Here we discovered another village of Blackfeet of about 15 lodges who were encamped on our route at the SE side of the Lake. The next morning we concluded to move camp to the village and smite it without leaving one to tell their fate—but when within about 2 miles of the village we met six of them coming to us unarmed who invited us in the most humble and submissive manner to their village to smoke and trade. This proceeding conquered the bravest in our camp. For we were ashamed to think of fighting a few poor Indians nearly dwindled to skeletons by the small Pox and approaching us without arms. We stopped however and traded with them for sometime and then started on our journey encamping at night in the edge of the pine woods June 8th We commenced our March thro. the pine woods by the lower track which runs South nearly parralell with the cours of Henry's fork and on the 11th we emerged from the pine woods into the plains of Snake river where we stopped and trapped until the 14th From thence we went to Pierre's hole where we found a party of 10 Trappers who had left the Camp at the mouth of 25 yard river they had been defeated by the Blackfeet lost most of their horses and one man was wounded in the thigh by a fusee ball.

June 18th we left Pierr's hole and crossed the mountain to Jacksons big hole. The next day myself and another trapper left the Camp crossed Lewis fork and travelled down the valley to the south end The next day we travelled in a SW direction over high and rugged spurs of Mountain and encamped on a small stream running into Gray's river which empties into Lewis fork above the mouth of Salt river 21st Travelled down the stream to Gray's river and set Traps We remained hunting the small streams which run into this river until the 28 of June then crossed the mountains in a SE direction and fell on to a stream running into Green River about 35 miles below the mouth of horse creek Called Lebarges fork[140] July 1st we travelled down this stream to the plains and steered our course NE towards "horse creek"[141] where we expected to find the Rendezvous. The next day we arrived at the place but instead of finding the Camp we found a large band of buffaloe near the appointed place of *of* meeting. We rode up to an old log building which was formerly used as a store house[142] during the Rendezvous where I discovered a piece of paper fastened upon the wall which informed me that we should find the Whites at the forks of Wind river. This was unwelcome news to us as our animals were very much jaded. We then went down Green river crossed and encamped for the night The next day we travelled to Little Sandy 3d day—we camped on the point of the mountain on a branch of Sweetwater 4th We encamped at the Oil Spring on Po po azia and the next day we arrived at Camp. There we found Mr Dripps from St Louis with 20 horse carts loaded with Supplies and again met Capt. Stewart likewise several Missionaries with their families on their way to the Columbia river On the 8th Mr. F. Ermatinger arrived with a small party from the Columbia accompanied by the Rev. Jason Lee who was on his way to the U S On the 20th of July the meeting broke up and the parties again dispersed for the fall hunt. I started with about 30 trappers up Wind river expecting the Camp to follow in a few days During our Stay at the Rendezvous it was rumored among the men that the Company intended to bring no more supplies to the Rocky Mountains and discontinue all further operations.[143] This caused a great deal of discontent among the Trappers and numbers left the party 21st We travelled up Wind river about 30 Mls and encamped 22d Continued up the river till noon then left it to our right travelled over a high ridge covered with pines in a west direction about 15 Mls and fell on to the Gros vent fork Next day we travelled about 20 Mls down the Gros vent fork. 24th Myself and another crossed the Mountain in a NW direction fell on to a stream[144] running into Lewis fork about 10 Mls below Jacksons lake, here we staid and trapped until the 29th Then we started back to the Gros vent fork where we found the Camp consisting of about 60 men under the direction of Mr. Dripps James Bridger Pilot.

The next day the Camp followed down the Grosvent fork to Jacksons hole In the meantime myself and Comrade returned to our traps which we raised and took over the Mountain in a SW direction and overtook the Camp on Lewis fork. The whole company were starving fortunately I had killed a Deer in crossing the Mountain which made supper for the whole camp Aug 1st We crossed Lewis fork and encamped and staid the next day 4th Camp crossed the Mountain to Pierres hole and the day following I started with my former comrade to hunt beaver on the streams which run from the Tetons. about the middle of the afternoon as we were winding down a steep declivity which overhung a precipice of rocks nearly 200 ft perpendicular my horse slipped fell headlong down and was dashed to pieces 6th I returned to camp in Pierre's valley. On the next day made another start with the same Comrade. After leaving Camp we travelled in a SW direction[145] across the valley then took over low hills covered with pines until sun about an hour high when we stopped and set our traps. On the 8th we travelled down the stream about 3 Mls and then ascended a left hand branch in a

NE direction After travelling about 10 Mls we fell into a Valley surrounded by high mountains except on the S.W. Side This Valley is about 4 Mls long and one wide whilst the huge piles of rocks reaching above the clouds seemed almost to overhang the place on the North and East sides. We stopped here on the 9th and on the 10th returned to hunt the Camp when leaving the Valley we took up the valley in a west direction and from thence travelled a NW course thro. dense forests of pine about 15 Mls. when we struck the trail of the Camp going North we followed the track which still led us thro. the forest about 12 Mls when we came to a prarie about 5 Mls in circumference in which the Camp had stopped the night previous We stopped here a few minutes then resumed our journey on the trail and after winding about among the fallen trees and rocks about 6 Mls we fell on to the middle branch of Henrys fork which is called by hunters "The falling fork"[146] from the numerous Cascades it forms whilst meandering thro. the forest previous to its junction with the main river. At the place where we struck the fork is one of the most beautiful cascades I ever saw[147] The stream is about 60 yds wide and falls over the rock in a straight line about 30 ft perpendicular It is very deep and still above where it breaks and gradually shallows to the depth of 3 ft on the brink it is also very deep below and almost dead except the motion caused by the waters falling into the deep pond like stream and boiling from the bottom rolls off into small ripples and dies away into a calm smooth surface. We ascended this stream passing several beautiful cascades for about 12 Mls when the trail led us into a prarie seven or 8 miles in circumference[148] in which we found the Camp just as the Sun was sitting.

The next morning Aug. 11th we bid adieu to the camp and started on the back track to trap the stream we had left the day previous We however took a nearer route and reached the little valley where we staid until the 25th This day we had a tremendous thunder storm which broke in peals against the towering

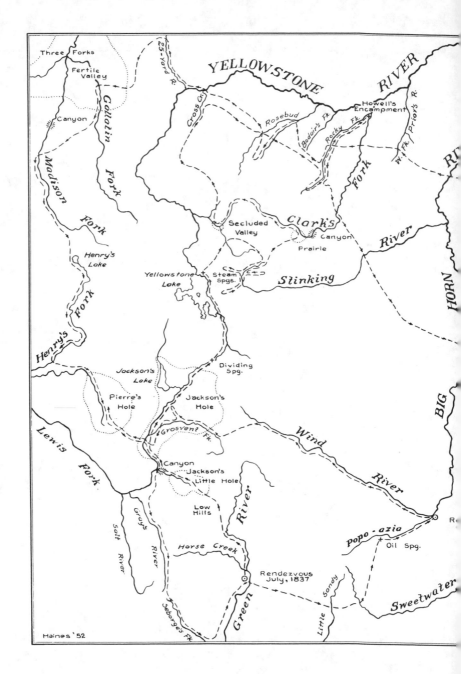

Haines '52

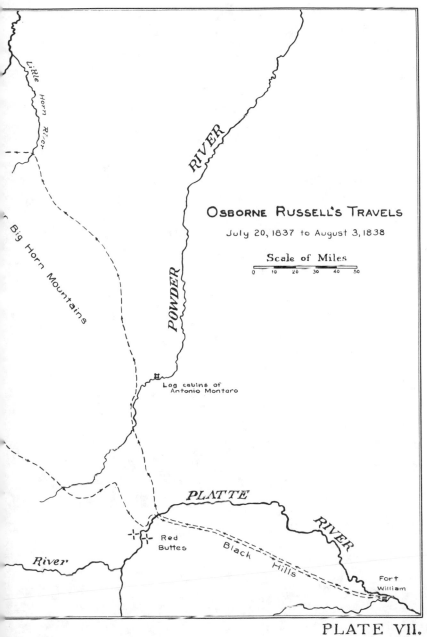

Little Horn River

Big Horn Mountains

RIVER

POWDER

OSBORNE RUSSELL'S TRAVELS

July 20, 1837 to August 3, 1838

Scale of Miles

0   10   20   30   40   50

Log cabins of
Antonio Montaro

PLATTE

RIVER

River

Red
Buttes

Black Hills

Fort
William

PLATE VII.

rocks above us with such dreadful clashing that it seemed as if they would have been torn from their foundations and hurled into the Valley upon our heads Such storms are very frequent about these Mountains and often pass over without rain 27th We left the Valley and ascended the mountain S.W. and travelled about 15 Mls to a branch of Henry's fork. Here we staid until the 7th of Septr. and then started down Henry's fork SW. After travelling about 12 Mls we left the pines and travelled parralelle with the stream over rolling ridges among scattered groves of quaking asps when we arrived at the edge of the plains in travelling about 8 Mls. Here we discovered a trail made by a war party of Blackfeet evidently the night previous. We then took a South course and travelled our horses in a trot all day and encamped an hour after dark on Lewis fork about 15 miles above the junction. The next day we Travelled to Blackfoot creek and the day following to Fort Hall we remained at the Fort until the 20th and then started down Snake River trapping with a party of 10 men besides ourselves 22d We arrived at a stream called Cozzu (or Raft River) [149] This we ascended and hunted until the 5th of Octr. when finding the country had been recently hunted we returned to Fort Hall. From thence we started on the 18th with the Fort hunter and six men to kill and dry Buffaloe meat for winter We cruised about on Snake river and its waters until the 23d of Novr. when the weather becoming very cold and the snow about 15 inches deep we returned with our horses loaded with meat to Fort Hall where we stopped until the 1st of Jany 1839 when we began to be tired of dried meat and concluded to move up the river to where Lewis fork leaves the Mountain and there spend the remainder of the winter killing and eating Mountain Sheep We were Six in company and started on the 2d travelling slowly as the snow was deep and the weather cold and arrived at the destined place on the 20th Jany. We were followed by 7 lodges of Snake Indians. We found the snow shallow about the foot of the Mountain with a plenty of

Sheep Elk and some few Bulls among the rocks and low Spurs 26th I started with two white men and several Indians thro the kanyon to hunt Elk after travelling about 4 Mls I left the party and took up the river on the north side whilst the remainder crossed the river on the Ice to follow the trail of some Bulls. I ascended the river travelling on the ice and land alternately about 4 Ms further and encamped for the night. This was a severe cold night but I was comfortably situated with one Blanket and two Epishemores and plenty of dry wood to make a fire, when I arose in the morning I discovered a band of Elk about half a mile up the mountain. I took my rifle and went to approach them thro the snow 3 ft deep and when within about 250 paces of them they took the wind of me and ran off leaving me to return to my encampment with the consolation that this was not the first time the wind had blown away my breakfast. When I arrived at my camp I found plenty of fresh Buffaloe meat hanging on the bushes near where I had slept. I immediately began to roast and eat as 24 hour's fasting would naturally dictate. Presently a Snake Indian arrived to whom the meat belonged. Near where I was encamped was a small stream which ran from a spring about a 100 paces distant and emptied into the river the water was a little more than blood warm. The Beaver had taken the advantage of the situation Damed it up at the Mouth and built a large lodge on the bank at sunrise I discovered three of them swimming and playing in the water.

The next day I killed a Bull and returned thro. the kanyon to our Camp On the 30th I started with my old comrade (Elbridge) back with our traps to try the Beaver the snow was about 2 ft deep on the level plain and it took us till near night to reach the place we encamped in a cave at the foot of the Mountain nearby and I set 4 traps The weather was extremely cold but I felt very comfortable whilst walking about in the warm water but on coming out and running as fast as I could to the Camp 40 rods distant my feet were both frozen. I soon drew out the frost however by stripping them and holding them in the cold snow— next morning I found 4 large fat Beaver in my traps and on the 2d of Feby. we returned to Camp with 12 Beaver. Feby 10th Moved with the camp up the river to where we had caught the Beaver and encamped, Lewis fork comes thro. this kanyon for about 12 Mls. where the rock rises 2 or 300 feet forms a bench and ascends gradually to the Mountain which approaches very close on the Nth side and on the South is about 3 or 4 Mls distant and an occasional ravine running from the mountain to the river thro the rocks on the Nth side forms convenient places for en- camping as the bench and low Spurs are well clothed with bunch grass. Here we found imense numbers of Mountain Sheep which the deep snows drive down to the low points of rocks facing the South near the river We could see them nearly every morn- ing from our lodges standing on the points of rock jutting out so high in the air that they appeared no larger than Weasels. It is in this position that hunter delights to approach them from behind and shoot whilst their eyes are fixed on some object below. It is an exercise which gives vigor health and appetite to a hunter to shoulder his rifle at day break on a clear cold morn- ing and wind his way up a rugged mountain over rocks and crags at length killing a fat old Ewe and taking the meat to Camp on his back: this kind of exercise gives him an appetite for his breakfast. But hunting sheep is attended with great danger in many places especially when the rocks are covered with sleet and ice. I have often passed over places where I have had to cut steps in the ice with my butcher Knife to place my feet in directly over the most frightful precipices, but being excited in the pursuit of game I would think but little of danger until I had laid down to sleep at night, then it would make my blood run cold to meditate upon the scenes I had passed thro. during the day and often have I resolved never to risk myself again in such places and as often broken the resolution. The sight of danger is less hidious than the thought of it. On the 18th of March the winter commenced breaking up with a heavy rain and 4 of us started up the river to commence the spring hunt whilst the remainder of the party returned to the Fort. After travelling thro. the kanyon we found the ground bare in many places whilst it still continued to rain. On the 30th of Mch we travelled to the mouth of 'Muddy' this we ascended and crossed the mountain with some difficulty as the snow was very deep on to the head waters of "Gray's Creek." There two of our party (who were Canadians) left us and struck off for themselves. Our Camp then consisted of myself and my old comrade Elbridge,[150] I say old comrade because we had been sometime together but he was a young man, from Beverly Mass and being bred a sailor he was not much of a landsman, woodsman or hunter but a great easy good natured fellow standing 5 feet 10—and weighing 200 lbs On the 2d of april we crossed a high ridge in a Nth direction and encamped on a stream that sinks in the plain soon after leaving the Mountain here we set our traps for Beaver but their dams were nearly all covered with ice excepting some few holes which they had made for the purpose of obtaining fresh provisions we stopped on this stream until the 25th of April and then travelled out by the same way which we came 26th we travelled in a South direction about 25 Mls Crossing several of the head branches of 'Grays Creek' On the 1st of May we travelled about 10 Mls East course and the next day went to the head of Grays Marsh about 20 Mls South course There we deposited the Furs we had taken and the next day [started] for Salt river to get a supply of salt we took an east direction about 6 Mls and fell on to Gardners fork which we descended to the Valley and on the 6th arrived at the Salt Springs[135] on Scotts fork of Salt River Here we found 12 of our old Comrades who had come like our selves to gather salt We staid two nights together at this place when myself and Elbridge took leave of them and returned to Grays Marsh from there we started towards fort Hall travelling one day and laying by 5 or 6 to fatten our horses and arrived

at the Fort on the 5th of June. This Post now belongs to the
British Hudsons Bay Company who obtained it by purchase
from Mr Wyeth in the year 1837 We stopped at the Fort until
the 26th of June then made up a party of 4 for the purpose
of trapping in the YellowStone and Wind river mountains
and arrived at Salt river valley on the 28th 29 we crossed the
Valley NE then left it ascending Grays river in an E. direction
about 4 Mls into a narrow rugged pass encamped and killed a
Sheep 30th We travelled up this srteam 30 Mls East and encamped in a small Valley and Killed a bull and the next day we
encamped in the South end of Jacksons big hole July 3d we
travelled thro. the valley Nth. until night and the next day
arrived at Jacksons Lake where we concluded to spend the 4th
of July, at the outlet. July 4th I caught about 20 very fine
salmon trout which together with fat mutton buffaloe beef and
coffee and the manner in which it was served up constituted
a dinner that ought to be considered independent even by
Britons.[151] July 5 we travelled north paralell with the Lake on
the East side and the next day arrived at the inlet or northern
extremity 7th We left the lake and followed up Lewis fork about
8 Mls in a NE direction and encamped. On the day following
we travelled about 5 Mls when we came to the junction of two
equal forks[152] we took up the left hand, on the west sid thro the
thick pines and in many places so much fallen timber that we
frequently had to make circles of a quarter of a mile to gain a
few rods ahead, but our general course was north and I suppose
we travelled about 16 Mls in that direction at night we encamped at a lake [153] about 15 Mls in circumference formed by the
stream we had ascended July 9th we travelled round this lake
to the inlet on the west Side and came to another lake[154] about
the same size This has a small prarie on the west side whilst the
other is completely surrounded by thick pines. The next day we
travelled along the border of the lake till we came to the NW.
extremity and where we found about 50 springs of boiling hot

water[155] We stopped here some hours as one of my comrades had
visited this spot the year previous he wished to show us some
curiosities The first Spring we visited was about 10 feet in
diameter which threw up mud with a noise similar to boiling
soap close about this were numerous [others] similar to it throwing up the hot mud and water 5 or 6 feet high about 30 or 40
paces from these along the side of a small ridge the hot steam
rushed forth from holes in the ground with a hissing noise which
could be heard a mile distant. On a near approach we could hear
the water bubbling under ground some distance from the surface. The sound of our footsteps over this place was like thump-
ing over a hollow vessel of imense size in many places were peaks
from 2 to 6 feet high formed of lime Stone, deposited by the
boiling water, which appeared of snowy whiteness. The water
when cold is perfectly sweet except having a fresh limestone
taste. After surveying these natural wonders for sometime my
comrade conducted me to what he called the "hour Spring"[156]
at that this spring the first thing that attracts the attention is a
hole about 15 inches in diameter in which the water is boiling
slowly about 4 inches below the surface at length it begins to
boil and bubble violently and the water commences raising and
shooting upwards until the column arises to the hight of sixty
feet from whence it falls to the ground in drops on a circle of
about 30 feet in diameter being perfetly cold when it strikes the
ground It continues shooting up in this manner five or 6 minutes
and then sinks back to its former state of Slowly boiling for an
hour and then shoots forth as before My Comrade Said he
had watched the motions of this Spring for one whole day and
part of the night the year previous and found no irregularity
whatever in its movements After Surveying these wonders for a
few hours we left the place and travelled north about 3 Mls over
ascending ground then desended a steep and rugged mountain
4 mile in the same direction and fell on to the head branch of
the Jefferson branch of the Missouri[157] The whole country still

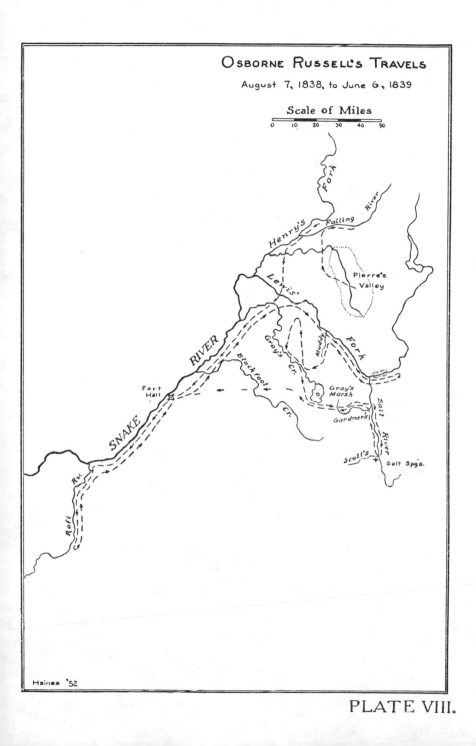

OSBORNE RUSSELL'S TRAVELS

August 7, 1838, to June 6, 1839

Scale of Miles

0   10   20   30   40   50

Fork

Henry's

Falling

River

Pierre's
Valley

Lewis'

Fork

Grays Cr.

Muddy

RIVER

Blackfoot

Gray's
Marsh

Salt

Fort
Hall

Cr.

Gardner's

River

SNAKE

Scott's

Salt Spgs.

Rv.

Roft

Haines '52

PLATE VIII.

thickly covered with pines except here and there a small prarie. We encamped and set some traps for Beaver and staid 4 dys. At this place there is also large numbers of hot Springs some of which have formed cones of limestone 20 feet high of a Snowy whiteness which make a splendid appearance standing among the ever green pines Some of the lower peaks are very service-able to the hunter in preparing his dinner when hungry for here his kettle is always ready and boiling his meat being suspended in the water by a string is soon prepared for his meal without further trouble Some of these spiral cones are 20 ft in diameter at the base and not more than 12 inches at the top the whole being covered with small irregular semicircular ridges about the size of a mans finger having the appearance of carving in bass relieve formed I suppose by the waters running over it for ages unknown. I should think this place to be at least 3,000 ft lower than the Springs we left on the mountain[158] Vast numbers of Black Tailed Deer are found in the vicinity of these springs and seem to be very familiar with hot waters and steam. The noise of which seems not to disturb their slumbers for a Buck may be found carelessly sleeping where the noise will exceed that of 3 or 4 engines in operation. Standing upon an eminence and super-ficially viewing these natural monuments one is half inclined to believe himself in the neighborhood of the ruins of some ancients City whose temples had been constructed of the whitest marble. July 15 we travelled down the stream NW. about 12 Mls passing on our route large numbers of hot Springs with their snow white monuments scattered among the groves of pines. At length we came to a boiling Lake about 300 ft in diameter forming nearly a complete circle as we approached on the South side The tsream which arose from it was of three distinct Colors from the west side for one third of the diameter it was white, in the middle it was pale red, and the remaining third on the east light sky blue Whether it was something peculiar in the state of the atmos-phere the day being cloudy or whether it was some Chemical

properties contained in the water which produced this phenomenon I am unable to say and shall leave the explanation to some
scientific tourist who may have the Curiosity to visit this place
at some future period—The water was of deep indigo blue boiling
like an imense cauldron running over the white rock which had
formed [round] the edges to the height of 4 or 5 feet from the
surface of the earth sloping gradually for 60 or 70 feet.[159] What a
field of speculation this presents for chemist and geologist. The
next morning we crossed the stream travelled down the east side
about 5 Mls then ascended another fork in an east direction
about 10 mls. and encamped. From where we left the Main fork
it runs in a NW direction about 40 Mls before reaching the
Burnt hole[160] July 17 we travelled to the head of this branch
about 20 Mls East direction 18th After travelling in the same
direction about 7 mls. over a low spur of mountain we came into
a large plain[161] on the Yellow Stone river about 8 Mls below the
Lake we followed up the Yellow Stone to the outlet of the Lake
and encamped and set our traps for beaver. We stopped here
trapping until the 28th and from thence we travelled to the
"Secluded Valley" where we staid one day. From thence we
travelled East to the head of Clarks fork where we stopped and
hunted the small branches until the 4th of Aug. and then returned to the Valley On the 9th we left the Valley and travelled
two days ovr the mountain NW and fell on to a stream running
South into the YellowSone where we staid until the 16th[162] and
then crossed the mountain in a NW direction over the snow and
fell on to a stream running into the YellowStone plains and entering that river about 40 Mls above the mouth of 25 yard river.
18th We descended this stream within about a mile of the plains
and set our traps. The next day my comrades started for the
plains to Kill some Buffaloe Cows I remonstrated very hard
against their going into the plains and disturbing the buffaloe in
such a dangerous part of the country when we had a plenty of
fat deer and mutton but to no purpose off they Started and

returned at night with their animals loaded with cow meat. They told me they had seen where a village of 3 or 400 lodges of Blackfeet had left the Yellowstone in a NW direction but 3 or 4 days previous. Aug 22 we left this Stream and travelled along the foot of the mountain at the edge of the plain about 20 Mls west cours and encamped at a spring. The next day we crossed the Yellowstone river and travelled up it on the west side to the mouth of Gardnes fork where we staid the next day 25th We travelled to "Gardners hole" then altered our cousre SE crossing the eastern point of the valley and encamping on a small branch among the pines 26 We encamped on the YellowStone in the big plain below the lake The next day we went to the lake and set our traps on a branch running into it near the outlet on the NE side[163] 28th after visiting my traps I returned to the Camp where after stopping about an hour or two I took my rifle and sauntered down the shore of the Lake among the [scattered] groves of tall pines until tired of walking about (the day being very warm) I took a bath in the lake for probably half an hour and returned to camp about 4 ockk PM Two of my comrades observed let us take a walk among the pines and kill an Elk" and started off whilst the other was laying asleep—Sometime after they were gone I went to a bale of dried meat which had been spread in the Sun 30 or 40 feet from the place where we slept here I pulled off my powder horn and bullet pouch laid them on a log drew my butcher knife and began to cut We were encamped about a half a mile from the Lake on a stream running into it in a S.W. direction thro. a prarie bottom about a quarter of a mile wide On each side of this valley arose a bench of land about 20 ft high running paralell with the stheam and covered with pines On this bench we were encamped on the SE side of the stream The pines immediatcly behind us was thickly intermingled with logs and fallen trees—After eating a few [minutes] I arose and kindled a fire filled my tobacco pipe and sat down to smoke My comrade whose name was White was still sleeping. Presently I cast my eyes towards the horses which were feeding in the Valley and discovered the heads of some Indians who were gliding round under the bench within 30 steps of me I jumped to my rifle and aroused White and looking towards my powder horn and bullet pouch it was already in the hands of an Indian and we were completely surrounded We cocked our rifles and started thro. their ranks into the woods which seemed to be completely filled with Blackfeet who rent the air with their horrid yells. on presenting our rifles they opened a space about 20 ft. wide thro. which we plunged about the fourth jump an arrow struck White on the right hip joint I hastily told him to pull it out and I spoke another arrow struck me in the same place but they did not retard our progress At length another arrow striking thro. my right leg above the knee benumbed the flesh so that I fell with my breast accross a log. The Indian who shot me was within 8 ft and made a Spring towards me with his uplifted battle axe: I made a leap and avoided the blow and kept hopping from log to log thro. a shower of arrows which flew around us like hail, lodging in the pines and logs. After we had passed them about 10 paces we wheeled about and took [aim] at them They then began to dodge behind the trees and shoot their guns we then ran and hopped about 50 yards further in the logs and bushes and made a stand—I was very faint from the loss of blood and we set down among the logs determined to kill the two foremost when they came up and then die like men we rested our rifles accross a log White aiming at the foremost and Myself at the second I whispered to him that when they turned their eyes toward us to pull trigger. About 20 of them passed by us within 15 feet without casting a glance towards us another file came round on the [opposite] side within 20 or 30 paces closing with the first a few rods beyond us and all turning to the right the next minute were out of our sight among the bushes They were all well armed with fusees, bows & battle axes We sat still until the rustling among the bushes had died away

The campsite east of Pelican Creek in present Yellowstone National Park where a band of Blackfoot Indians despoiled Russell's party of trappers in 1838. (*Photo courtesy of Aubrey L. Haines*)

then arose and after looking carefully around us White asked in a whisper how far it was to the lake I replied pointing to the SE about a quarter of a mile. I was nearly fainting from the loss of blood and the want of water We hobbled along 40 or 50 rods and I was obliged to sit down a few minutes then go a little further and rest again. we managed in this way until we reached the bank of the lake Our next object was to obtain some of the water as the bank was very steep and high. White had been perfectly calm and deliberate until now his conversation became wild hurried and despairing he observed "I cannot go down to that water for I am wounded all over I shall die" I told him to sit down while I crawled down and brought some in my hat. This I effected with a great deal of difficulty. We then hobbled along the border of the Lake for a mile and a half when it grew dark and we stopped. We could still hear the shouting of the Savages over their booty. We stopped under a large pine near the lake and I told White I could go no further "Oh said he let us go up into the pines and find a spring" I replied there was no spring within a Mile of us which I knew to be a fact. Well said he if you stop here I shall make a fire" Make as much as you please I replied angrily This is a poor time now to undertake to frighten me into measurs. I then started to the water crawling on my hands and one knee and returned in about an hour with some in my hat. While I was at this he had kindled a small fire and taking a draught of water from the hat he exclaimed Oh dear we shall die here, we shall never get out of these mountains, Well said I if you presist in thinking so you will die but I can crawl from this place upon my hands and one knee and Kill 2 or 3 Elk and make a shelter of the skins dry the meat until we get able to travel. In this manner I persuaded him that we were not in half so bad a Situation as we might be altho. he was not in half so bad a situation as I expected for on examining I found only a slight wound from an arrow on his hip bone but he was not so much to blame as he was a young man who had been

brot up in Missouri the pet of the family and had never done
or learned much of anything but horseracing and gambling whilst
under the care of his parents (if care it can be called). I pulled
off an old piece of a coat made of Blanket (as he was entirely
without clothing except his hat and shirt) Set myself in a leaning position against a tree ever and anon gathering such leaves
and rubbish as I could reach without altering the position of My
body to keep up a little fire in this manner miserably spent the
night. The next morning Aug 29th I could not arise without
assistance When White procured me a couple of sticks for
crutches by the help of which I hobbled to a small grove of pines
about 60 yds distant. We had scarcely entered the grove when
we heard a dog barking and Indians singing and talking. The
sound seemed to be approaching us. They at length came near
to where we were to the number of 60 Then commenced shooting at a large bank of elk that was swimming in the lake killed
4 of them dragged them to shore and butchered them which
occupied about 3 hours. They then packed the meat in small
bundles on their backs and travelled up along the rocky shore
about a mile and encamped. We then left our hiding place crept
into the thick pines about 50 yds distant and started in the
direction of our encampment in the hope of finding our comrades My leg was very much swelled and painful but I managed
to get along slowly on my crutches by Whites carrying my rifle
when we were within about 60 rods of the encampment we discovered the Canadian hunting round among the trees as tho he
was looking for a trail we approached him within 30 ft before
he saw us and he was so much agitated by fear that he knew
not whether to run or stand still. On being asked where Elbridge
was he said they came to the Camp the night before at sunset
the Indians pursued them into the woods where they seperated
and he saw him no more. At the encampment I found a sack of
salt—everything else the Indians had carried away or cut to
pieces They had built 7 large Conical forts near the spot from

which we supposed their number to have been 70 or 80 part
of whom had returned to their Village with the horses and
plunder. We left the place heaping curses on the head of the
Blackfoot nation which neither injured them or alleviated our
distress We followed down the shores of the lake and stopped
for the night My companions threw some logs and rubbish to
gether forming a kind of shelter from the night breeze but in the
night it took fire (the logs being pitch pine) the blaze ran to the
tops of the trees we removed a short distance built another fire
and laid by it until Morning We then made a raft of dry poles
and crossed the outlet upon it. We then went to a small grove of
pines nearby and made a fire where we stopped the remainder of
the day in hopes that Elbridge would see our signals and come
to us for we left directions on a tree at the encampment which
route we would take. In the meantime the Cannadian went to
hunt something to eat but without success. I had bathed my
wounds in Salt water and made a salve of Beavers Oil and
Castoreum which I applied to them This had eased the pain
and drawn out the swelling in a great measure. The next morning
I felt very stiff and sore but we were obliged to travel or starve
as we had eaten nothing since our defeat and game was very
scarce on the West side of the Lake and morover the Cannadian
had got such a fright we could not prevail on him to go out of
our sight to hunt So on we truged slowly and after getting warm
I could bear half my weight on my lame leg but it was bent
considerably and swelled so much that my Knee joint was stiff.
About 10 oclk the Cannadian killed a couple of small Ducks
which served us for breakfast. after eating them we pursued our
journey. At 12 oclk it began to rain but we still kept on until
the Sun was 2 hours high in the evening when the weather
clearing away we encamped at some hot springs[164] and killed a
couple of geese. Whilst we were eating them a Deer came swimming along in the lake within about 100 yards of the shore
we fired several shots at him but the water glancing the balls he

remained unhurt and apparently unalarmed but still Kept swimming to and fro in the Lake in front of us for an hour and then started along up close to the shore. The hunter went to watch it in order to kill it when it should come ashore but as he was lying in wait for the Deer a Doe Elk came to the water to Drink and he killed her but the Deer was still out in the lake swimming to and fro till dark. Now we had a plenty of meat and drink but [were] almost destitute of clothing I had on a par of trowsers and a cotton shirt which were completely drenched with the rain. We made a sort of shelter from the wind of pine branches and built a large fire of pitch Knots in front of it, so that we were burning on one side and freezing on the other alternately all night. The next morning we cut some of the Elk meat in thin slices and cooked it slowly over a fire then packed it in bundles strung them on our backs and started by this time I could carry my own rifle and limp along half as fast as a man could walk but when my foot touched against the logs or brush the pain in my leg was very severe We left the lake at the hot springs and travelled thro. the thick pines over a low ridge of land thro. the snow and rain together but we travelled by the wind about 8 Mls in a SW direction when we came to a Lake about 12 Mls in circumference[165] which is the head spring of the right branch of Lewis fork. Here we found a dry spot near a number of hot springs under some thick pines our hunter had Killed a Deer on the way and I took the skin wrapped it around me and felt prouder of my Mantle than a Monarch with his imperial robes. This night I slept more than 4 hours which was more than I had slept at any one time since I was wounded and arose the next morning much refreshed These Springs are similar to those on the Madison and among these as well as those Sulphur is found in its purity in large quantities on the surface of the ground. We travelled along the Shore on the south side about 5 Mls in an East direction fell in with a large band of Elk killed two fat Does and took some of the meat. We then

left the lake and travelled due South over a rough broken country covered with thick pines for about 12 Mls when we came to
the fork again which ran thro. a narrow prarie bottom followed
drown it about six miles and encamped at the forks We had
passed up the left hand fork on the 9th of July on horse back
in good health and spirits and came down on the right[166] on the
31st of Aug. on foot with weary limbs and sorrowful countenances. We built a fire and laid down to rest, but I could not
sleep more than 15 or 20 minutes at a time the night was so very
cold. We had plenty of Meat however and made Mocasins of raw
Elk hide The next day we crossed the stream and travelled down
near to Jacksons Lake on the West side then took up a small
branch in a West direction to the head.[167] We then had the Teton
mountain to cross which looked like a laborious undertaking as
it was steep and the top covered with snow. We arrived at the
summit however with a great deal of difficulty before sunset and
after resting a few moments travelled down about a mile on the
other side and stopped for the night. After spending another
cold and tedious night we were descending the Mountain thro.
the pines at day light and the next night reached the forks of
Henrys fork of Snake river.[168] This day was very warm but the
wind blew cold at night we made a fire and gathered some dry
grass to sleep on and then sat down and eat the remainder of
our provisions. It was now 90 Mls to Fort Hall and we expected
to see little or no game on the route but we determined to travel
it in 3 days we lay down and shivered with the cold till daylight then arose and again pursued our journey towards the fork
of Snake river where we arrived sun about an hour high forded
the river which was nearly swimming and encamped The
weather being very cold and fording the river so late at night
caused me much suffering during the night Septr 4th we were
on our way at day break and travelled all day thro. the high
Sage and sand down Snake river We stopped at dark nearly
worn out with fatigue hunger and want of sleep as we had now

travelled 65 Mls in two days without eating. We sat and hovered
over a small fire until another day appeared then set out as usual
and travelled to within about 10 Ms of the Fort when I was
seized with a cramp in my wounded leg which compelled me to
stop and sit down ever 30 or 40 rods at length we discovered a
half breed encamped in the Valley who furnished us with horses
and went with us to the fort where we arrived about sun an hour
high being naked hungry wounded sleepy and fatigued. Here
again I entered a trading post after being defeated by the
Indians but the treatment was quite different from that which
I had received at Larameys fork in 1837[169] when I had been
defeated by the Crows

The Fort was in charge of Mr. Courtney M. Walker[170] who
had been lately employed by the Hudsons Bay Company for
that purpose He invited us into a room and ordered supper to
be prepared immediately. Likewise such articles of clothing and
Blankets as we called for. After dressin ourselves and giving a
brief history of our defeat and sufferings supper was brot. in
consisting of tea Cakes butter milk dried meat etc I eat very
sparingly as I had been three days fasting but drank so much
strong tea that it kept me awake till after midnight. I continued
to bathe my leg in warm salt water and applied a salve which
healed it in a very short time so that in 10 days I was again
setting traps for Beaver On the 13th of Sptr. Elbridge arrived
safe at the Fort he had wandered about among the Mountains
several days without having any correct knowledge, but at
length accidentally falling onto the trail which we had made in
the Summer it enabled him to reach the plains and from thence
he had travelled to the Fort by his own Knowledge 20th of
Octr. we started to hunt Buffaloe and make meat for the winter.
The party consisted of 15 men. We travelled to the head of the
Jefferson fork of the Missouri where we Killed and dried our
meat from there we proceeded over the mountain thro. "Cam-
mas prarie"[171] to the forks of Snake river where most of the party

concluded to spend the winter 4 of us however (who were the only Americans in the party) returned to Fort Hall on the 10th of Decr. We encamped near the Fort and turned our horses among the springs and timber to hunt their living during the winter whilst ourselves were snugly arranged in our Skin lodge which was pitched among the large Cotton wood trees and in it provisions to serve us till the Month of April. There were 4 of us in the mess One was from Missouri one from Mass. one from Vermont and myself from Maine We passed an agreeable winter We had nothing to do but to eat attend to the horses and procure fire wood We had some few Books to read[172] such as Byrons Shakespeares and Scotts works the Bible and Clarks Commentary on it and other small works on Geology Chemistry and Philosophy — The winter was very mild and the ground was bare in the Valley until the 15 of Jany. when the snow fell about 8 inches deep but disappeared again in a few days. This was the deepest snow and of the longest duration of any we had during the winter On the 10th of March I started again with my old companion Elbridge We travelled from the Fort on to the Black-foot near the foot of the Mountain where the ice being broke up we set some traps for Beaver On the 15th we tried to cross the mountain to Grays Valley but were compelled to turn back for the snow On the 20th made another trial and succeeded and encamped at the Forks of 'Gray's creek' here the ground was bare along the stream and some [on] the South sides of the hills but very deep on the high plains I killed two Bulls which came in good time after living upon Dried meat all winter Mch 19 we travelled up Grays creek about 10 Mls. There we found the snow very deep and hard enough to bear our horses in the morning. On the 22d we travelled on the snow up this stream about 5 Mls and encamped on a bare spot of ground where we staid three days Then started on the snow as usual and went about 8 Mls to the Valley about Grays Marsh where we found a bare spot about 40 rods square on the South side of a ridge and encamped

The snow in the Valley was about 3 feet deep on a level Mch 28th We started on foot in the morning on the snow to hunt Buffaloe after going about 2 Mls we found 11 Bulls aproached and killed 10 of them on the spot we then butchered some of them and took out the tongues of the others buried the meat about 3 ft. deep in a snow drift laid some stones on the snow over it and burned gun powder upon them to keep away the wolves. We then took meat enough for our suppers and started for the Camp by this time the snow was thawed so much that we broke thro. nearly every step. Early next morning the snow being frozen we took two horses and went for our meat but when we reached the place where we had buried it we found the wolves had dug it up and taken the best of its notwithstanding our precautions. The Carcasses of the Bulls yet remained untouched by them and from these we loaded our horses and returned to camp. About noon the rays of the sun shining up on the Snow and reflecting upwards began to affect our eyes in somuch that towards night we could scarcely look abroad We lay down to sleep but it was useless for our eyes felt as if they were filled with coarse Sand after suffering 4 days severely with what the trappers call snow blindness we began to recover our eye sight by degrees altho we had not been at any time totally blind yet we had been the whole time very near it. We staid here until the 10th of April when finding the snow did not abate we returned to the forks of Grays Creek where we remained until the 20th We then travelled to the fork which sinks in the plain on Lewis fork where we set our traps and staid until the 1st of May On the 2d we arrived again at the Marsh on Grays creek where we found the ground mostly bare but the streams overflowing their banks. On the 5 crossed the mountain in an East direction fell on to a stream running into Lewis fork 10 Ms below the mouth of Salt River we travelled down this stream which runs thro a narrow cut in the mountain for about 15 Mls and then forms a small valley where we stopped and set our traps and staid until

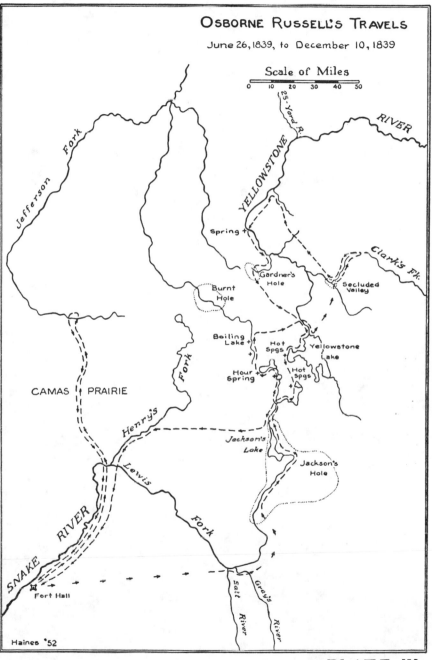

OSBORNE RUSSELL'S TRAVELS

June 26, 1839, to December 10, 1839

Scale of Miles

0   10   20   30   40   50

YELLOWSTONE

25-Yard R.

RIVER

Clark's Fk.

Jefferson Fork

Spring +

Gardner's Hole

Secluded Valley

Burnt Hole

Boiling Lake +

Hot Spgs

Yellowstone Lake

Hour Spring +

Hot Spgs

Fork

CAMAS   PRAIRIE

Henry's

Jackson's Lake

Jackson's Hole

Lewis

SNAKE   RIVER

Fork

Fort Hall

Salt River

Gray's River

Haines '52

PLATE IX.

the 20th when Elbridge observed he thought we had better leave our traps setting turn and go to Salt river Valley spend a few days killing bulls and then return I remonstrated against the proposal as our horses were very poor the streams high and the ground very muddy but I told him if he wished to go to take his traps with him and not be at the trouble of coming back after them. The next morning he packed his horses and left me My two horses were now my only companions with the exception of some books which I brot from the Fort. I staid here trapping until the 28th Then travelled up a branch about 15 Mls. crossed the Mountain in a NW direction fell on to the head of Muddy Creek where I killed a Bull and stopped for the night. The next day I stopped at this place and dried some meat 30th went on to the Right fork of Muddy and set some traps, here I staid 6 days and then went to Gray's marsh intending to kill and dry some meat and go to the Fort but finding no Buffaloe here I crossed on to Salt River and finding no Buffaloe there I ascended Gardners fork crossed the Mountain and fell on to Blackfoot creek where I killed a fat Bull dried the meat and started for fort Hall where I arrived on the 10th of June. June 14th Mr. Ermatinger arrived at the fort with 80 horse loads of goods to supply the post the ensuing year. On the 15 Elbridge arrived having fallen in with a party of hunters soon after leaving me in the Mountains after having lost his traps in crossing Grays river. A few days after he arrived he expressed a wish that I would go with him and two others to make a hunt in the Yellow Stone mountains I replied I had seen enough of the Yellow Stone Mountains and moreover I intended to trap in future with a party who would not leave me in a 'pinch.' On the 22d of June I started with two horses six traps and some few books intending to hunt on the waters of Snake river in the vicinity of Fort Hall. I went to Grays hole set my traps and staid 5 days. From there I went on to Milk fork[173] where I staid until the 15 of July From thence I took a north direction thro the Mountains and fell on to a stream running into Lewis Fork near the mouth of Salt River where I staid 12 days and then returned to Grays Marsh and staid until the 3d of August I then travelled thro. the mountains SE on to the head streams of Gardners fork where I spent the time hunting the small branches until the 15th —From there I started towards the Fort hunting the streams which were on the route and arrived on the 22d—After stopping here a few days I started in Company with 3 trappers one of whom was 'Major Meek' and travelled to the forks of Snake river From there we ascended Henry's fork about 15 Mls and then took up a stream in a SW direction into the Mountain but finding no Beaver we crossed the mountain and struck Lewis fork in the kanyon where after trapping some days we went on to Grays creek where after staying some days we killed a fat Grizzly Bear and some antelope loaded the meat on our horses and started to the Fort where we arrived on the 22 of Septr. On the first of Octr. I again left the Fort with a Frenchman who had an Indian wife and two children and was going on to Green river to pass the winter there. We travelled up Portneuf about 15 Mls where we stopped the next day and hunted antelope and the day following we travelled up the stream about 20 Mls when after staying 10 dys we went to the Soda Springs on Bear river here we concluded to spend a month on Bar river travelling slowly hunting Beaver and Antelope as the latter is the only game in this part of the country. Beaver also were getting very scarce. On the 15th of Novr. the snow began to fall and my comrade started with his family accross the mountain to Green river and I returned towards the fort On my way down bear river I met thousands of antelope travelling towards their winter quarters which is generally in Green river Valley I followed Bear River down to Cache Valley where I found 20 lodges of Snake Indians and staid with them several days They had a considerable number of Beaver Skins but I had nothing to trade for them. They told me if I would go to the Fort and get some goods return and spend the winter with them they would trade their Furs with me. I started for the Fort with one of them whom I engaged to assist me with my horses. I arrived at the Fort on the 23rd of Novr. when after getting such articles for trade as I wished and my personal supplies for the winter I returned to Cache Valley accompanied by a halfbreed On arriving at the Village I found several Frenchmen and half breed trappers encamped with the Snakes One Frenchman having an Indian wife and child invited me to pass the winter in his lodge and as he had a small family and large lodge I accepted the invitation. And had my baggage taken into his lodge and neatly arranged by his wife who was a flathead but the neat manner in which her lodge and furniture was kept would have done honor to a large portion of the "pale faced" fair sex in the civilized world. We staid in this valley until the 15th of Decr. when it was unanimously agreed on to go to the Salt lake and there spend the remainder of the winter The next day we travelled accross the Valley in a SW direction Then took into a narrow defile which led us thro. the mountain in to the valley on the East borders of the lake. The day following we moved along the Valley in a South direction and encamped on a small branch close by the foot of the mountain. The ground was still bare and the Autumnal growth of grass was the best I ever saw at this season of the year 18th I arose about an hour before daylight took my rifle and ascended the Mountain on foot to hunt sheep The weather was clear and cold but the Mountain being steep and rugged and my rifle heavy the exercise Soon put me in a perspiration. After Climbing about half a mile I sat down on a rock to wait for daylight and when it came I discovered a band of about 100 rams within about 80 yds of me I shot and killed one the others ran about 50 yds further and stopped. Whilst I was reloading my rifle one of them ascended a high pinnacle of rock which jutted over a precipice there were others nearer to me but I wished to fetch this proud animal from his elevated position.

I brought my rifle to my face the [ball] whistled thro. his heart
and he fell headlong over the precipice I followed the band at
some distance among the crags and killed two more butched
them then returned and butchered the two I had first killed and
returned to camp—and sent some men with horses to get the
Meat. 20th Decr. we moved along the borders of the Lake about
10 Mls. and encamped on a considerable stream running into it
called "Weaver's river"[174] At this place the Valley is about 10
Mls wide intersected with numerous Springs of salt and fresh
hot and cold water which rise at the foot of the Mountain and
run thro. the Valley into the river and Lake—Weavers river is
well timbered along its banks principally with Cottonwood and
box elder—there are also large groves of sugar maple pine and
some oak growing in the ravines about the Mountain—We also
found large numbers of Elk which had left the Mountain to
winter among the thickets of wood and brush along the river.
Decr. 25th It was agreed on by the party to prepare a Christmas
dinner but I shall first endeavor to describe the party and then
the dinner. I have already said the man who was the proprietor
of the lodge in which I staid was a French man with a flat head
wife and one child The inmates of the next lodge was a half
breed Iowa a Nez percey wife and two children his wifes brother
and another half breed next lodge was a half breed Cree his wife
a Nex percey 2 children and a Snake Indian The inmates of
the 3d lodge was a half breed Snake his wife (a Nez percey and
two children). The remainder was 15 lodges of Snake Indians
Three of the party spoke English but very broken therefore that
language was made but little use of as I was familiar with the
Canadian French and Indian tongue. About 1 oclk we sat down
to dinner in the lodge where I staid which was the most spacious
being about 36 ft. in circumference at the base with a fire built
in the center around this sat on clean Epishemores all who
claimed kin to the white man (or to use their own expression
all that were gens d'esprit) [175] with their legs crossed in true

Turkish style—and now for the dinner The first dish that came on was a large tin pan 18 inches in diameter rounding full of Stewed Elk meat The next dish was similar to the first heaped up with boiled Deer meat (or as the whites would call it Venison[176] a term not used in the Mountains) The 3d and 4th dishes were equal in size to the first containing a boiled flour pudding prepared with dried fruit accompanied by 4 quarts of sauce made of the juice of sour berries and sugar Then came the cakes followed by about six gallons of strong Coffee already sweetened with tin cups and pans to drink out of large chips or pieces of Bark Supplying the places of plates. on being ready the butcher knives were drawn and the eating commenced at the word given by the landlady as all dinners are accompanied with conversation this was not deficient in that respect The principal topic which was discussed was the political affairs of the Rocky Mountains The state of governments among the different tribes, the personal characters of the most distinguished warriors Chiefs etc One remarked that the Snake *Chief Pah da-hewak um da* was becoming very unpopular and it was the opinion of the Snakes in general that *Moh woom hah* his brother would be at the head of affairs before 12 mos as his village already amounted to more than 300 lodges and moreover he was supported by the bravest men in the Nation among whom were *Ink a tush e poh Fibe bo un to wat su* and *Who sha kik* who were the pillars of the Nation and at whose names the Blackfeet quaked with fear. In like manner were the characters of the principal Chiefs of the Bonnak Nez percey Flathead and Crow Nations and the policy of their respective governments commented upon by these descendants of Shem and Japhet with as much affected dignity as if they could have read their own names when written or distinguish the letter B from a Bulls foot.[177] Dinner being over the tobacco pipes were filled and lighted while the Squaws and children cleared away the remains of the feast to one side of the lodge where they held a Sociable tite a tite[178] over the fragments.

After the pipes were extinguished all agreed to have a frolic shooting at a mark which occupied the remainder of the day. Jany. 1st The ground was still bare but the weather cold and the fresh water streams shut up with ice On the 3d we moved Camp up the stream to the foot of the mountain where the stream forks The right is called Weavers fork and the left Ogden's both coming thro. the mountain in a deep narrow cut The mountain is very high steep and rugged which rises abruptly from the plain about the foot of it are small rolling hills abounding with springs of fresh water. The land bordering on the river and along the Stream is a rich black alluvial deposite but the high land is gravelly and covered with wild sage with here and there a grove of scubby oaks and red cedars On the 10th I started to hunt Elk by myself intending to stop out 2 or 3 nights I travelled up Weavers fork in a SE direction thro the mountains The route was very difficult and in many places difficult travelling over high points of rocks and around huge precipices on a trail just wide enough for a single horse to walk in, in about 10 Mls I came into a smooth plain 5 or 6 Mls in circumference just as the Sun was setting here I stopped for the night the snow being about 5 inches deep and the weather cold I made a large fire—As I had not Killed any game during the day I had no supper at night but I had a blanket horse to ride and a good rifle with a plenty of Amunition I was not in much danger of Suffering by hunger cold or fatigue So I wrapped myself in my blanket and laid down on some dry grass I had collected before the fire. About an hour after dark it clouded up and began to snow but as I was under some large trees it did not trouble me much and I soon fell asleep at daylight it was still snowing very fast and had [?] about 8 inches during the night—I saddled my horse and started in a North direction over high rolling hills covered with Scrubby oaks quaking asp and maples for about 10 Mls where I came into a smooth valley about 20 Mls in circumference called "Ogdens hole"[179] with the fork of the same

name running thro. it. Here the snow was about 15 inches deep
on a level. Towards night the weather cleared up and I discovered a band of about 100 Elk on the hill among the Shrubbery.
I approached and killed a very fat old doe which I butcherd and
packed the meat and skin on my horse to an open spring about
a quarter of a mile distant where I found plenty of dry wood
and stopped for the night. I had now a good appetite for supper
which after eating I scraped away the Snow on one side of the
fire spread down the raw Elk hide and laid down covering myself with my blanket. In the morning when I awoke it was still
snowing and after eating breakfast I packed the Meat on my
horse and started on foot leading him by the bridle Knowing it
was impossible to follow down this Stream with a horse to the
plains I kept along the foot of the Mountain in a Nth. direction
for about 2 Mls then turning to the left into a steep ravine began
to ascend winding my way up thro. the snow which grew deeper
as I ascended I reached the Summit in about 3 hours in many
places I was obliged to break a trail for my horse to walk in
I descended the mountain West to the plains with comparative
ease and reached the Camp about dark On arriving at the lodge
I entered and sat down before a large blazing fire My landlady soon unloaded my horse and turned him loose and then
prepared supper with a good dish of Coffee whilst I as a matter
of course related the particulars of the hunt. We staid at this
place during the remainder of January The weather was very
cold and the snow about 12 inches deep but I passed the time
very agreeably hunting Elk among the timber in fair weather
and amusing myself with books in foul The 3d day of Feby. I
took a trip up the mountain to hunt Sheep I ascended a spur
with my horse sometimes riding and then walking until near the
top where I found a level bench where the wind had blown the
snow off. I fastened my horse with a long cord and took along
the side of the mountain among the broken crags to see what the
chance was for supper just as the sun was sinking below the dark

green waters of the Salt Lake I had not rambled far before I
discovered 3 rams about 300 ft perpendicular below me I shot
and killed one of them but it being so late and the precipice
so bad I concluded to sleep without supper rather than to go
after it I returned to my horse and built a large fire with fragments of dry sugar maple which I found scattered about on the
Mountain having for a shelter from the wind a huge piece of
Coarse Sandstone of which the mountain was composed the air
was calm serene and cold and the stars shone with an uncommon
brightness after sleeping till about Midnight I arose and renewed the fire My horse was continually walking backwards
and forwards to keep from freezing I was upwards of 6,000 ft
above the level of the lake, below me was a dark abyss silent
as the night of Death I set and smoked my pipe for about an
hour and then laid down and slept until near daylight — My
Chief object in Sleeping at this place was to take a view of the
lake when the Sun arose in the Morning. This range of mountains lies nearly Nth & South and approaches the Lake irregularly within from 3 to 10 Mls. About 8 Mls from the SE shore
stands an Island about 25 Mls long and six wide having the
appearance of a low Mountain extending Nth & South and
rising 3 or 400 ft Above the water To the Nth [W] of this about
8 Mls. rises another Island apparently half the size of the first.
Nth of these about six Mls. and about half way between rises
another about 6 Mls. in circumference which appears to be a
mass of basaltic rock with a few scrubby Cedars Standing about
in the Cliffs the others appear to be clothed with grass and wild
Sage but no wood except a few bushes near to the western horizon arose a small white peak just appearing above the water.
which I supposed to be the mountain near the west Shore. On
the Nth. side a high Promontory about Six Mls wide and 10 long
projects into the lake covered with grass and scattering Cedars
On the South Shore rises a vast pile of huge rough mountains;
which I could faintly discern thro. the dense blue atmosphere[180]

The water of the lake is too much impregnated with Salt to freeze any even about the shores. About sun an hour high I commenced hunting among the rocks in search of Sheep but did not get a chance to shoot at any till middle of the afternoon when crawling cautiously over some shelving cliffs I discovered 10 or 12 Ewes feeding some distance below me I shot and wounded one reloaded my rifle and crept down to the place where I last saw her when I discovered two standing on the side of a precipice Shot one thro the head and she fell dead on the cliff where she stood. I then went above and fastened a cord (which I carried for the purpose) to some bushes which overhung the rocks by this means I descended and rolled her off the cliff where she had caught when she fell upwards of 100 ft. I then pulled myself up by the cord and went round the rook down to where she fell butcherd her hung the meat on a tree then pursued and killed the other After butchering the last I took some of the [meat] for my supper and started up the mountain and arrived at the place where I had slept about an hour after dark I soon had a fire blazing and a side of ribs roasting and procured water by heating Stones and melting snow in a piece of skin by the time supper was over it was late in the night And I lay down and slept till morning At sun rise I started on foot to get my meat and left my rifle about half way down the Mountain when I came to where the first sheep had been hung in a tree I discovered a large Wolverine sitting at the foot of it I then regretted leaving my rifle but it was too late he saw me and took to his heels as well he might for he had left nothing behind worth stopping for All the traces I could find of the sheep were some tufts of hair scattered about on the snow. I hunted around for sometime but to no purpose. In the meantime the cautious thief was sitting on the snow at some distance watching my movements as if he was confident I had no gun and could not find his meat. and wished to agravate me by his antic gestures he had made roads in every direction from the

root of the tree dug holes in a 100 places in the snow apparently
to decieve me but I soon got over my ill humour and gave it up
that a Wolverine had fooled a Yankee. I went to the other Sheep
and found all safe carried the meat to my horse mounted and
went to Camp. Feby 15 the weather began to moderate and rain
and on the 23d the ground was bare about the Mountain Feby
24th I left the Camp with a determination to go to the Eutaw
Village at the SE extremity of the Lake to trade furs I travelled
along the foot of the Mountain about 10 Mls when I stopped
and deposited in the ground such articles as I did not wish to
take with me The next day I travelled along the foot of the
Mountain South about 30 Mls and encamped on a small spring
branch which runs in a distance of 4 Mls from the mountain to
the lake. This is a beautiful and fertile Valley intersected by large
numbers of fine springs which flow from the mountain to the
Lake and could with little labour and expense [be] made to irri-
gate the whole Valley. The following day I travelled about 15
Mls along the lake when a valley opened to my view stretching
to the SE about 40 Mls and upwards of 15 Mls wide At the
farther extremity of this valley lies Trimpannah or Eutaw lake[181]
composed of fresh water about 60 Mls in circumference The
outlet of it is a stream about 30 Yds wide which, after cutting this
valley thro the middle empties into the Salt Lake. I left the Lake
and travelled up this Valley over smooth ground which the snow
had long since deserted and the green grass and herbage were
fast supplying its place After crossing several small streams
which intersected this vale I arrived at the Village rode up to a
lodge and asked of a young Indian who met me where Want a
Sheep's lodge was but before he could reply a tall Indian very
dark complected with a thin visage and a keen piercing eye
having his Buffaloe robe thrown carelessly over his left shoulder
gathered in folds around his waist and loosely held by his left
hand stepped forth and answered in the Snake tongue "I am
Want a Sheep", follow me' at the same time turning round and

directing his course to a large white lodge. I rode to the door dismounted and followed him in he immediately ordered my horses to be unsaddled and turned loose to feed whilst their loads were carefully arranged in the lodge After the big pipe had gone round several times in silence he then began the conversation — I was asked the news, where travelling for what whom and how I replied to these several inquiries in the Snake tongue which was understood by all in the lodge. He then gave me an extract of all he had seen heard and done for 10 years past He had two Sons and one daughter grown to man and womanhood and the same number of less size his oldest son was married to a Snake Squaw and his daughter to a man of the Same nation The others yet remained single. After supper was over the females retired from the lodge and the principal men assembled to smoke and hear the news which occupied the time till near midnight when the assembly broke up the men retiring to their respective lodges and the women returned. I passed the time as pleasantly at this place as ever I did among Indians in the daytime I rode about the Valley hunting water fowl who rend the air at this season of the year with their cries and at night the Old Chief would amuse me with traditionary tales mixed with the grossest superstition some of which were not unlike the manners of Ancient Israelites. There seems to be a happiness in ignorance which knowledge and Science destroys here is a nation of people contented and happy they have fine horses and lodges and are very partial to the rifles of the white man If a Eutaw has 8 or 10 good horses a rifle and ammunition he is contented if he fetches a deer at night from the hunt joy beams in the faces of his wife and children and if he returns empty a frown is not seen in the countenances of his companions. The Buffaloe have long since left the shores of these Lakes and the hostile blackfeet have not left a footprint here for many years. During my stay with these Indians I tried to gain some information respecting the southern limits of the Salt Lake but all that I could learn was that it was a sterile barren mountainous Country inhabited by a race of depraved and hostile savages who poisoned their arrows and hindered the exploring of the country. The Chiefs son informed me he had come from the largest Island in the lake a few days previous having passed the winter upon it with his family which he had conveyed backwards and forth on a raft of bulrushes about 12 ft square. He said there was large numbers of antelope on the Island and as there was no wood he had used wild Sage for fuel. The Old Chief told me he could recollect the time when the Buffaloe passed from the main land to the island without swimming and that the depth of the waters was yearly increasing. After obtaining all the furs I could from the Eutaws I started towards Fort Hall on the 27th of March and travelled along the borders of the Lake about 25 Mls. The fire had run over this part of the country the previous autumn and consumed the dry grass The new had srpung up to the height of 6 inches intermingled with various kinds of flowers in full Bloom. The shore of the Lake was swarming with waterfowls of every species that inhabits inland lakes. The next day I went on to Weavers river April 1st I left Wavers river and travelled along the [shore] to the NE extremity of the lake about 25 Mls. The next day I went on to Bear river and struck it about 15 Mls below Cache Valley and twelve Mls from the mouth There I found my winter Comrades and staid one night and then pursued my journey towards Fort Hall where I arrived on the 7th of April I hunted Beaver round the country near the Fort until the 15 of June when the party arrived from the Columbia river accompanied by a Presbyterian Missionary with his wife and one child on their way to the States. I left the Fort with them and conducted them to Green river where we arrived on the 5th of July when learning that no party was going to the States they concluded to return to the Columbia River and we retraced our steps to Fort Hall where we arrived on the 8th dy of August.[182] I remained at the Fort until the 15 Septr. and then

started with Elbridge and my old Comrade from Vermont to
hunt a few more Beaver we went to the head waters of Blackfoot where we staid 10 dys. and then crossed the mountain in a
SW direction on to Bear river which we struck about 25 Mls
below the Snake Lake. We continued huntin Beaver and Antelope between this place and the Soda Springs until the 10th of
Octr. We then travelled down Bear river to Cache valley where
we stopped until the 21st thence we followed down the river
near where it empties into the Salt Lake. Along the bank of this
stream for about 10 Mls from the Lake extends a barren clay
flat destitute of Vegetation excepting a few willows along the
banks of the river and scattering spots of Salt grass and Sage
in one place there was about 4 or 5 acres covered about 4 inches
deep with the most beautiful salt I ever saw. two crusts had
formed one at the bottom and the other on the top which had
protected it from being the least soiled—between those crusts
the salt was Completely dry loose and composed of very small
grains of a snowy whiteness. We stopped about this place until
the 5 of Novr. and then returned to Fort Hall where after remaining a few days we concluded to go on to the head streams
of Port Neuf and stop until the waters froze up. We travelled up
about 40 Mls and arranged an encampment in a beautiful valley
as the weather began to grow cold—In the year 1836 large bands
of Buffaloe could be seen in almost every little Valley on the
small branches of this Stream at this time the only traces which
could be seen of them were the scattered bones of those that had
been killed. Their trails which had been made in former years
deeply indented in the earth were over grown with grass and
weeds The trappers often remarked to each other as they rode
over these lonely plains that it was time for the White man to
leave the mountains as Beaver and game had nearly disappeared On the 15th of Novr I started up a high mountain in
search of sheep after hunting and scrambling over the rocks for
half the day without seeing any traces of them I sat down upon

a rock which overlooked the country below me at length casting a glance along the South side of the Mountain I discovered a large Grizzly bear sitting at the mouth of its den I approached within about 180 paces shot and missed it. he looked round and crept slowly into his den I reloaded my rifle went up to the hole and threw down a stone weighing 5 or 6 lbs which soon rattled to the bottom and I heard no more I then rolled a stone weighing 3 or 400 lbs into the den stepped back two or three steps and prepared myself for the out come. The Stone had scarcely reached the bottom when the Bear came rushing out with his mouth wide open and was on the point of making a spring at me when I pulled trigger and Shot him thro. the left shoulder which sent him rolling down the Mountain It being near night I butchered him and left the Meat lying and returned to Camp. The next day I took the meat to camp where we salted and smoked it ready for winters use. We stopped about on these streams utill the 15th Decr. then returned to Fort Hall where we staid until the 24th Mrch. The winter was unusually Severe. The snow was 15 inches deep over the valley after settling and becoming hard, we had no thawing weather until the 18th of Mrch. when it began to rain and continued 4 dys and nights which drove the snow nearly all from the plains. Mch. 25 I started in company with Alfred Shutes my old Comrade from Vermont to go to the Salt Lake and pass the Spring hunting water fowls eggs and Beaver. We left the Fort and travelled in a South direction to the mountain about 30 Mls. The next day we travelled South about 15 Mls thro. a low defile and the day following we crossed the divide and fell onto a stream called "Malade" or Sick river[183] which empties into Bear river about 10 Mls from the mouth. This stream takes its name from the Beaver which inhabit it living on poison roots. Those who eat their meat in a few hours become sick at the stomach and the whole system is filled with cramps and severe pains but I have never known or heard of a persons dying with this disease We arrived at the mouth of Bear river on the 2d of April. Here we found the ground dry the grass green and myriads of Swans, Geese Brants and Ducks which kept up a continual hum day and night assisted by the uncouth notes of the Sand hill Cranes. The geese Ducks and Swans are very fat at this season of the year We caught some few Beaver and feasted on Fowls and Eggs, until the 20th May and returned to the Fort where we stopped until the 20th June when a small party arrived from the Mouth of the Columbia river on their way to the United States and my comrade[184] made up his mind once more to visit his native Green Mountains after an absence of 16 years whilst I determined on going to the Mouth of the Columbia and settle myself in the Willamette or Multnoma Valley I accompanied my comrade up Ross's fork about 25 Mls on his journey and the next morning after taking an affectionate leave of each other. I started to the mountain for the purpose of killing Elk and drying meat for my journey to the Willamette Valley. I ascended to the top of Rosses mountain[185] (on which the snows remain till the latter part of Aug.) Sat down under a pine and took a last farewell view of a country over which I had travelled so often under such a variety of circumstances The recollections of the past connected with the scenery now spread out before me put me somewhat in a Poetical humour and for the first time I attempted to frame my thoughts into rhyme but if Poets will forgive me for this intrusion I shall be cautious about trespassing on their grounds in future. In the evening I killed an Elk and on the following day cured the meat for packing from thence I returned to the fort where I staid till the 22d Aug In the meantime there arrived at the Fort a party of Emigrants from the States on their way to Oregon Territory among whom was Dr. E White[186] U S sub agent for the Oregon Indians. 23d I started with them and arrived at the Falls of the Willamette river on the 26 day of Septr. 1842. It would be natural for me to suppose that after escaping all the danger attendant for upon nearly nine years residence in a wild inhospitable region like the Rocky Mountains where I was daily and a great part of the time hourly anticipating danger from hostile Savages and other sources, I should on arriving in a civilized and enlightened community live in comparative security free from the harassing intrigues of Dames Fortunes Eldest daughter but I found it was all a delusion for danger is not always the greatest when most apparent as will appear in the sequel. On arriving at the Falls of the Willamette I found a number of Methodist Missionaries and American Farmers had formed themselves into a Company for the purpose of Erecting Mills and a Sawmill was then building on an Island standing on the brink of the Falls which went into operation in about 2 months after I arrived In the meantime Dr John McLoughlin a chief Factor of the Hudson Bay Co. who contemplated leaving the service of the Company and permanently settling with his family and Fortune in the Willamette Valley laid off a town (the present Oregon City) on the east side of the falls and began erecting a sawmill on a site he had prepared some years previous by cutting a race thro. the rock to let the water on to his works when they should be constructed. The following Spring the American Co commenced building a flour Mill and I was employed to assist in its construction. On the 6th day of June I was engaged with the contractor in blasting off some points of rock in order to sink the water sill to its proper place—when a blast exploded accidentally by the concussion of small particles of rock near the Powder a piece of rock weighing about 60 lbs. struck me on the right side of the face and knocked me senseless 6 feet backwards

I recovered my senses in a few minutes and was assisted to walk to my lodgings. Nine particles of rock of the size of wild goose shot Each, had penetrated my right eye and destroyed it forever. the Contractor escaped with the loss of two fingers of his left hand

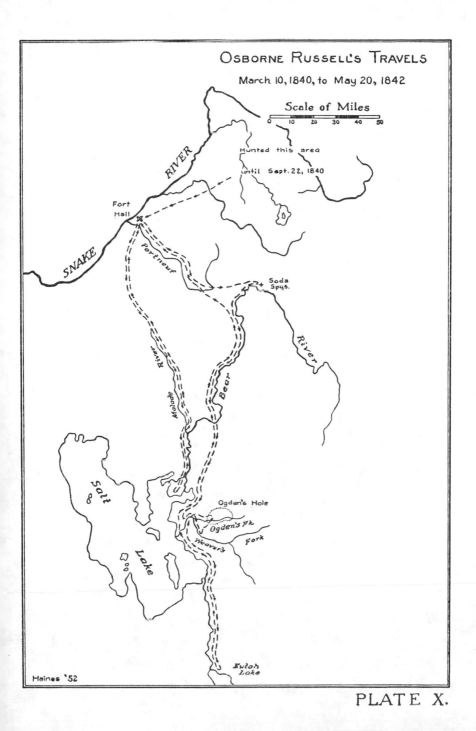

OSBORNE RUSSELL'S TRAVELS

March 10, 1840, to May 20, 1842

Scale of Miles

0   10   20   30   40   50

Hunted this area

until Sept. 22, 1840

Fort
Hall

SNAKE RIVER

Portneuf

Soda
Spgs.

River

Malade River

Bear River

Salt Lake

Ogden's Hole

Ogden's Fk.

Weavery   Fork

Eutah
Lake

Haines '52

PLATE X.

APPENDIX

It has been my design whilst Keeping a journal to note down the principal circumstances which came under my immediate observation as I passed along and I have mostly deferred giving a general description of Indians and animals that inhabit the Rocky Mountains until the latter end in order that I might be able to put the information I have collected in a more compact form. I have been very careful in gathering information from the most intelligent Indians and experienced White hunters but have excluded from this journal such parts (with few exceptions) as I have not proved true by experience. I am fully aware of the numerous statements which have been given to travellers in a jocular manner by the hunters and traders among the Rocky Mountains merely to hear themselves talk or according to the Mountaineers expression give them a long yarn or 'Fish Story" to put in their journals. and I have frequently seen those 'Fish Stories" published with the original very much enlarged which had not at first the slightest ground for truth to rest upon It is utterly impossible for a person who is merely travelling thro. or even residing one or two years in the Rock Mountains to give an accurate description of the Country or its Inhabitants

I have never known but one Rocky Mountain[eer] to keep a regular journal, and he could not have visited the Northern part of them as I am confident his Compiler (Mr. Flint) would not knowingly be led into such errors as occur in James O'Pattie's Journal, both in regard to the location of the country and Indians inhabiting the northern section of it. He says the 'Flathead nation of Indians flattened their heads[187] and lived between the Platte and Yellow Stone rivers" which is not nor ever was the case in either instance, he also says that Lewi's river and the Arkansas head near each other in Long's Peak. I never was at

Longs Peak or the head of the Arkansas river but am fully confident can [not] be within 300 Mls. of the source of Lewi's river. These are among the numerous errors which I discovered in reading James O Pattie's Journal Embellished by Mr. Flint of Cincinnati—These are among the reasons for which I offer this to public view hoping that it not only may be of interest to myself but the means of correcting some erroneous statements which have gone forth to the world unintentionally perhaps by their authors.

THE WOLVERINE, CARCAJOU OR GLUTTON

This Species of animals is very numerous in the Rocky Mountains and very mischievous and annoying to the Hunters They often get into the traps setting for Beaver or searching out the deposits of meat which the weary hunter has made during a toilsome days hunt among mountains too rugged and remote for him to bear the reward of his labors to the place of Encampment, and when finding these deposits the Carcajou carries off all or as much of the contents as he is able secreting it in different places among the snow rocks or bushes in such a manner that it is very difficult for man or beast to find it. The avaricious disposition of this animal has given rise to the name of Glutton by Naturalists who suppose that it devours so much at a time as to render it stupid and incapable of moving or running about but I have never seen an instance of this Kind on the contrary I have seen them quite expert and nimble immediately after having carreyd away 4 or 5 times their weight in meat. I have good reason to believe that the Carcajou's appetite is easily satisfied upon meat freshly killed but after it becomes putrid it may become more Voracious but I never saw one myself or a person who had seen one in a stupid dormant state caused by Gluttony altho I have often wished it were the case —

The body is thick and long the legs short, the feet and Claws are longer in proportion than those of the Black bear which it very much resembles. with the exception of its tail which is 12 inches long and bushy. Its body is about 3 ft long and stands fifteen inches high its colour is black except along the sides which are of a dirty white or light brown —

Its movements are somewhat quicker than those of the Bear and it climbs trees with ease. I have never known either by experience or information the Carcajou to prey upon animals of its own killing larger than very young fawns or lambs altho. it has been described by Naturalists and generally believed that it climbs trees and leaps down upon Elk Deer and other large animals and clings to their back till it kills them in spite of their efforts to get rid of it by speed or resistance but we need go no further than the formation of the animal to prove those statements erroneous. Its body legs feet and mouth are shaped similarly to the Black Bear as has been already stated but its claws are somewhat longer and straighter in proportion and like the Bear its claws are somewhat blunted at the points which would render it impossible for them to cling to the back of an Elk or Deer while running. I do not pretend to say however what may be its habits in other countries I only write from Experience. They do not den up like the Bear in winter but ramble about the streams among the high mountains where they find springs open—its hair is 3 inches long and in the Summer is coarse like the Bear but in winter it is near as fine as that of the Red Fox The female brings forth its young in April and generally brings two at a birth

THE WOLF

Of this Species of animals there are several kinds as the Buffaloe Wolf the Big Prarie Wolf and the small prarie or Medicine Wolf.[188] The Buffaloe wolf is from 2 to 3 ft high and from 4 to 5 ft long from the tip of the nose to the insertion of the tail its hair is long coarse and shaggy Its color varies from a dark gray to a snowy whiteness. They are not ferocious towards man and will run at sight of him. The big Prarie wolf is 2 ft high and 3½ ft long;

its hair is long and shaggy: its color is a dirty grey often inclining to a brown or brindle. The least kind is little Prarie or Medicine Wolf: its size is somewhat larger than the red fox: its color is brownish grey and its species something between the Big Wolf and the Fox. The Indians are very superstitious about this animal when it comes near a Village and barks they say there is people near Some pretend to distinguish between its warning the approach of friends and enemies and in the latter case I have often seen them secure their horses and prepare themselves to fight. I have often seen this prophecy tolerably accurately fulfilled and again I have as often seen it fail but a supperstitious Indian will always account for the failure The habits of these three kinds of wolves are similar Their rutting season is in March, the female brings forth from 2 to 6 at a birth

The Panther

This animal is rarely seen in the plains but confines itself to the more woody and mountainous districts its color is light brown on the back and the belly is a sort of ash color: its length is 5 ft from the tip of the nose to the insertion of the tail which is about ½ the length of the body it is very destructive on Sheep and other animals that live on high mountains but will run at the sight of a man and has a great antipathy to fire —

The Marmot[189]

This animal inhabits the rocks and precipices of the highest mountains its color is a dark brown its size less than the smallest rabbit: its ears *are ears* are shaped like those of the rat and its cry resembles that of the bleating of the young lamb during the summer it collects large quantities of hay and moss with which it secures its habitation from the cold during the winter. On my first acquaintance with this animal I was led to suppose that the hay which they accumulated in Summer was calculated to supply them with food during the winter but this I found to be erroneous by visiting their habitation in the early part of Spring and finding their stock in nowise diminished. I have good reason to suppose that they lie dormant during the winter.

THE PORCUPINE

This species of animals are too well known to need a minute description in this place they are however very numerous and their flesh is much esteemed by some of the Indian tribes for food and their quills are held in the highest estimation by all for embroidering their dresses and other [furniture] which is done with peculiar elegance and uncommon skill it subsists chiefly on the bark of trees and other Vegetables.

THE BADGER

This species of animals are numerous in the Rocky Mountains their skins are much used by the Snake and Bonnak Indians for clothing as well as their flesh for food. They make their habitation in the ground in the most extensive plains and are found 10 Mls from water—

THE GROUND HOG[190]

These animals are also very numerous and their skins much used by the Indians for clothing in sections of country where Deer and Buffaloe are not to be found they are not so large as the ground hog of the N States but are in all respects the same species. They live among the rocks near streams and feed upon grass and other vegetables. The shrill cry with which their sentinels give warning danger resembles that of the U States

THE GRIZZLY BEAR

Much has been said by travellers in regard to this animal yet while giving a description of animals that inhabit the Rocky Mountains I do not feel justified in silently passing over in silence the most ferocious species without endeavoring to contribute some little information respecting it which altho it may not be important I hope some of it at least will be new It lives chiefly upon roots and berries being of too slow a nature to live much upon game of its own killing and from May to Septr. it never tastes flesh. The rutting season is in Novr. and the Female brings forth from 1 to 3 at a birth I have not been able to ascertain the precise time that the female goes with young but I suppose from experience and enquiry it is about 14 weeks. The young are untameable and manifest a savage ferocity when scarcely old enough to crawl Several experiments have been tried in the Rocky Mountains for taming them but to no effect. They are possessed with great muscular strength I have seen a female which was wounded by a rifle ball in the loins so as to disable her kill her young with one stroke of the fore paw as fast as they approached her. If a young Cub is wounded an commences making a noise the mother immediately springs upon it and kills it when grown they never make a noise except a fearful growl they get to be fatter than any other animals in the Rocky Mts. during the season when wild fruit is abundant. The flesh of the Grizzly Bear is preferable to Pork — It lives in winter in caves in the Rocks or holes dug in the ground on high Ridges It loses no flesh while confined to its den in the winter but is equally as fat in the Spring when it leaves the den as when it enters it at the beginning of the winter. There is seldom to be found more than one in a den excepting the female and her young. I have seen them measure seven feet from the tip of the nose to the insertion of the tail. It will generally run from the scent of a man but when it does not get the scent it will often let him approach close enough to spring upon him and when wounded it is a dangerous animal to trifle with. Its speed is comparatively slow down hill but much greater in ascending it never climbs trees as its claws are too straight for that purpose.

THE BLACK BEAR

The Black Bear of the Mountains are much the same species of those in the States. In comparison with the Grizzly it is entirely harmless. It is seldom found in the plains but inhabits the Timbered and mountanous districts They are not very numerous and their habits are too well known to need a detailed description here

THE MOUNTAIN SHEEP OR BIG HORN

These animals answer somewhat to the description given by Naturalists of the Musmon or wild sheep which are natives of Greece Corsica and Tartary. The male and female very much resemble the domestic ram and Ewe but are much larger The horns of the males are much larger in proportion to the body than the domestic rams but those of the females are about in the same proportion to the domestic Ewe. In the Month of May after they have shed their old coat and the new one appears their color is dark blue or mouse color except the extremity of the rump and hinder parts of the thighs which are white. As the season advances and the hair grows long it gradually turns or fades to a dirty brown In the Mo. of Decr its hair is about 3 inches long thickly matted together rendering it impenetrable to the cold. Its hair is similar in texture to that of the Deer and like the latter it is short and smooth upon its forehead and legs. They inhabit the highest and most craggy mountains and never descend to the plains unless compelled by necessity. In the winter season the snow drives them down to the low craggy mountains facing the South but in the spring as the snow begins to recede they follow it, keeping close to where the grass is short and tender—Its speed on the smooth ground is slower than the Deer—but in climbing steep rocks or precipices it is almost incredible insomuch that the wolf lynx and panther give up the Chase when ever the sheep reach the rugged crags

The fearful height from which it jumps and the small points

on which it alights without slipping or missing its footing is astonishing to its pursuers whether man or beast its hooves are very hard and pointed and it reposes upon the most bleak points of rocks both in summer & winter. The male is a noble looking animal as he stands upon an elevated point with his large horns curling around his ears like the coils of a serpent and his head held proudly erect disdaining the lower region and its inhabitants its flesh has a similar taste to Mutton but its flavor is more agreeable and the meat more juicy Their rutting season is in Novr. when the rams have furious battles with each other in the same manner as the domestic rams—The victor often Knocks his opponent over a high precipice when he is dashed to pieces in the fall. The sound of their heads coming in contact is often heared a mile distant—The Female produces from one to 3 at a birth the lambs are of a whitish color very innocent and playful. Hunting Sheep is often attended with great danger especially in the winter season when the rocks and precipices are covered with snow and ice but the excitement created by hunting them often enables the hunter to surmount obstacles which at other times would seem impossible The skins when dressed are finer softer and far superior to those of the Deer for clothing It is of them that the Squaws make their dresses which they embroider with beads and Porcupine quills dyed with various colors which are wrought into figures displaying a tolerable degree of taste and ingenuity

The Gazelle or Mountain Antelope

This animal for beauty and fleetness surpasses all the ruminating animals of the Rocky Mountains: its body is rather smaller than the common Deer: its color on the back and upper part of the sides is light brown the hinder part of the thighs and belly are white the latter having a yellowish cast. The under part of the neck is white with several black stripes running across the throat down to the breast: its legs are very slim neat and small;

its ears are black on the inside and around the edges with the remainder brown its horns are also black and flattened. the horns of the males are much longer than those of the females but formed in the same manner they project up about 8 inches on the males and then divide into 2 branches the one inclining backwards and the other forward with sometimes an additional branch coming out near the head inclining inward the two upper branches are 6 inches long the hindermost forming a kind of hook the nose is black and a strip of the same color runs round under the eyes and terminates under the ears: it runs remarkably smooth and in the summer season the fleetest horses but rarely overtake it. Its natural walk is stately and elegant but it is very timid and fearful and can see to a great distance but with all its timidity and swiftness of foot its curiosity often leads it to destruction if it discovers anything of a strange appearance (particularly anything red) it goes directly to it and will often approach within 30 paces they are very numerous in the plains but seldom found among timber, their flesh is similar to venison the female produces two at a birth and the young are suckled until a month old—They are easily domesticated

THE BLACK TAILED DEER

This animal is somewhat larger than the common Deer of the U S: its ears are very long from which it has derived the appellation of Mule Deer: its color in summer is red but in the latter part of Aug. its hair turns to a deep blue ground with about half an inch of white on each hair one fourth of an inch from the outer ends which presents a beautiful grey color: it lives among the mountains and seldom descends among the plains: its flesh is similar in every respect to the common Deer. the tail is about 6 inches long and the hair's upon it smooth excep upon the end where there is a small tuft of black. The female goes six months with young and generally produces two at a birth the young is brot forth in April and remains in an almost helpless state for one month during its state of inability the mother secrets it in some secure place in the long grass and weeds where it remains contented while she often wanders half a mile from it in search of food. The color of the fawn is red intermingled with white spots, and it is generally believed by Indians that so long as those spots remain (which is about 2½ months) that no beast of prey can scent them—This I am inclined to believe as I have often seen wolves pass very near the place where fawns were laying without stopping or altering their course and were it not for some secret provision of nature the total anihilation of this species of animal would be inevitable in those countries invested by wolves and other beasts of prey as in the Rocky Mts—This safeguard is given by the Great Founder of nature not only to the Black Tailed Deer but all of the species including Elk and Antelope whose young are spotted at their birth I do not consider that the mere white spots are a remedy against the Scent of wild beasts. but they mark the period of inability for when those disappear the little animals are capable of eluding their pursuers by flight; the male like the common Deer drops its horns in Feby. it then cannot be distinguished from the female except by its larger size

THE RABBIT

This species of animals is very numerous and various in their sizes and colors. The large Hares of the plains are very numerous, the common sized rabbit are equally or more numerous than the others and there is also the small brown rabbit which does not change its color during the winter as do the others, but the most singular kind is the black rabbit it is a native of mountaneous forests its color is Coal black excepting two small white spots which are on the throat and lower part of the belly In winter its color is milk white: its body is about the size of the common rabbit with the exception of its ears which are much longer Another kind is the Black tailed Rabbit of the plains it is rather larger than the common rabbit and derives its name from the color of its tail which never changes its color

THE ELK

This animal is Eight feet long from the tip of the nose to the insertion of the tail and stands 4½ ft. high its proportions are similar to those of the Deer except the tail which is 4 inches long and composed of a black gummy substance intermingled with fibres around the bone, the whole being clothed with skin and covered with hair like the body. Its color in summer is red but in winter is a browish grey except the throat and belly the former being dark brown and the latter white inclining to yellow extending to the hind part of the thighs as far as the insertion of the tail—They are very timid and harmless even when so disabled as to render escape impossible its speed is very swift when running single but when running in large bands they soon become wearied by continual collision with each other and if they are closely pursued by the hunter on horse back they soon commence dropping down flat on the ground to elude their pursuers and will suffer themselves to be killed with a knife in this position: when the band is first located the hunters keep at some distance behind to avoid dispersing them and to frighten them the more a continual noise is kept up by hallooing and shooting over them which causes immediate confusion and collision of the band and the weakest Elk soon begin to drop on the ground exhausted: their rutting time is in Scpr. when they collect in imense bands among the timber along the streams and among the Mts. It has been stated by Naturalists that the male is a very formidable and dangerous animal when pursued but I never saw it act on the offensive neither have I ever known one to offer resistance in defense of itself against man otherwise than by involuntary motions of its head or feet when too much disabled to raise from the ground. I have often seen the female come about the hunter who has found where her young is secreted uttering the most pitiful and persuasive moans and pleading in the most earnest manner that a dumb brute is capable of for the life of her young— This mode of persuasion would I think excite sympathy in the breast of any human that was not entirely destitute of the passion—The fawn has a peculiar cry after it is able to run which resembles the faint scream of a child by which it answers the Dam who calls it by a note similar to the scream of a woman in distress

In the month of Septr. the males have a peculiar shrill call which commences in a piercing whistle and ends in a coarse gurggling in the throat by this they call the females to assemble and each other to the combat in which by their long antlers they are rendered formidable to each other the hair stands erect and the head is lowered to give or receive the attack but the Victor seldom pursues the vanquished

THE BUFFALOE OR BISON

This animal has been so minutely described by travellers that I have considered it of little importance to enter into the details of its shape and size, and shall therefore omit those descriptions with which I suppose the public to be already acquainted, and try to convey some idea of its peculiarities which probably are not so well known. The vast numbers of these animals which once traversed such an extensive region in Nth. America are fast diminishing. The continual increasing demand for robes in the civilised world has already and is still contributing in no small degree to their destruction, whilst on the other hand the continual increase of wolves and other 4 footed enemies far exceeds that of the Buffaloe when these combined efforts for its destruction is taken into consideration, it will not be doubted for a moment that this noble race of animals, so useful in supplying the wants of man, will at no far distant period become extinct in North America. The Buffaloe is already a stranger, altho so numerous 10 years ago, in that part of the country which is drained by the sources of the Colerado, Bear and Snake Rivers and occupied by the Snake and Bonnack Indians. The flesh of the Buffaloe Cow is considered far superior to that of the domestic Beef and it is so much impregnated with salt that it requires but little seasoning when cooked. All the time, trouble and care bestowed by man upon improving the breed and food of meat cattle seems to be entirely thrown away when we compare those animals in their original state which are reared upon the food supplied them by Nature with the same species when domesticated and fed on cultivated grasses and grains and the fact seems to justify the opinion that Nature will not allow herself to be outdone by art for it is fairly proved to this enlightened age that the rude and untaught savage feasts on better beef and Mutton than the most learned and experienced Agriculturists now if every effect is produced by a cause perhaps I may sumble upon the cause which produces the effect in this instance at any rate I shall attempt it—In the first place, the rutting season of the Buffaloe is regular commencing about the 15th of July when the males and females are fat, and ends about the 15 of Aug. Consequently the females bring forth their young in the latter part of April and the first of May when the grass is most luxuriant and thereby enables the cow to afford the most nourishment for her calf and enables the young to quit the natural nourishment of its dam and feed upon the tender herbage sooner than it would at any other season of the year. Another proof is that when the rutting season commences the strongest healthiest and most vigorous Bulls drive the weaker ones from the cows hence the calves are from the best breed which is thereby kept upon a regular basis. In summer season they generally go to water and drink once in 24 hours but in the winter they seldom get water at all. The cows are fattest in Octr and the Bulls in July The cows retain their flesh in a great measure throughout the winter until the Spring opens and they get at water from whence they become poor in a short time So much for the regularity of their

habits and the next point is the food on which they subsist
The grass on which the Buffaloe generally feeds is short, firm
and of the most nutritious kind. The salts with which the mountain regions is much impregnated are imbibed in a great degree
by the vegetation and as there is very little rain in Summer
Autumn or winter the grass arrives at maturity and dries in the
sun without being wet it is made like hay; in this state it remains
throughout the winter and while the spring rains are divesting
the old growth of its nutricious qualities they are in the meantime pushing forward the new—The Buffaloe are very particular
in their choice of grass always preferring the short of the uplands
to that of the luxuriant growth of the fertile alluvial bottoms.
Thus they are taught by nature to choose such food as is most
palatable and she has also provided that such as is most palatable is the best suited to their condition and that condition the
best calculated to supply the wants and necessities of her rude
untutored children for whom they were prepared. Thus nature
looks with a smile of derision upon the magnified efforts of art to
excel her works by a continual breach of her laws—The most
general mode practiced by the Indians for killing Buffaloe is
running upon horseback and shooting them with arrows but it
requires a degree of experience for both man and horse to kill
them in this manner with any degree of safety particularly in
places where the ground is rocky and uneven. The horse that is
well trained for this purpose not only watches the ground over
which he is running and avoids the holes ditchs and rocks by
shortening or extending his leaps but also the animal which he
is pursuing in order to prevent being 'horned' when tis brot
suddenly to bay which is done instantaneously and if the Buffaloe wheel to the right the horse passes as quick as thought to the
left behind it and thereby avoids its horns but if the horse in
close pursuit wheels on the same side with the Buffaloe he comes
directly in contact with its horns and with one stroke the horses
entrails are often torn out and his rider thrown healong to the

ground After the Buffaloe is brought to bay the trained horse will immediately commence describing a circle about 10 paces from the animal in which he moves continually in a slow gallop or trot which prevents the raging animal from making a direct bound at him by keeping it continually turning round until it is killed by the rider with arrows or bullets. If a hunter discovers a band of Buffaloe in a place too rough and broken for his horse to run with safety and there is smooth ground nearby he secretly rides on the leward side as near as he can without being discovered he then starts up suddenly without apparently noticing the Buffaloe and gallops in the direction he wishes the band to run the Buffaloe on seeing him run to the plain start in the same direction in order to prevent themselves from being headed and kept from the smooth ground The same course would be pursued if he wished to take them to any particular place in the mountains—One of the hunters first instructions to an inexperienced hand is "run towards the place where you wish the Buffaloe to run but do not close on them behind until they get to that place" for instance if the hunter is to the right the leading Buffaloe keep inclining to the right and if he should fall in behind and crowd upon the rear they would separate in different directions and it would be a mere chance if any took the direction he wished them—When he gets to the plain he gives his horse the rein and darts thro the band selects his victim reins his horse up along side and shoots and if he considers the wound mortal he pulls up the rein the horse knowing his business keeps along galloping with the band until the rider has reloaded when he darts forward upon another Buffaloe as at first A Cow seldom stops at bay before she is wounded and therefore is not so dangerous as a Bull who wheels soon after he is pushed from the band and becomes fatigued whether he is wounded or not. When running over ground where there is rocks holes or gullies the horse must be reined up gradually if he is reined at all there is more accidents happens in running Buffaloes by the riders getting frightened and suddenly checking their horses than any other way. If they come upon a Gully over which the horse can leap by an extra exertion the best plan is to give him the rein and the whip or spur at the same time and fear not for any ditch that a Buffaloe can leap can be cleared with safety by a horse and one too wide for a Buffaloe to clear an experienced rider will generally see in time to check his horse gradually before he gets to it—And now as I have finished my description of the Buffaloe and the manner of killing them I will put a simple question for the reader's solution—

If Kings Princes Nobles and Gentlemen can derive so much sport and Pleasure as they boast of in chasing a fox or simple hare all day? which when they have caught is of little or no benefit to them what pleasure can the Rocky Mountain hunter be expected to derive in running with a well trained horse such a noble and stately animal as the Bison? which when killed is of some service to him. There are men of noble birth noble Estate and noble minds who have attained to a tolerable degree of perfection in fox hunting in Europe and Buffaloe hunting in the Rocky Mountains, and I have heard some of them decide that the points would not bear a comparison if the word Fashion could be stricken from the English language It also requires a considerable degree of practice to approach on foot and kill Buffaloe with a Rifle A person must be well acquainted with the shape and make of the animal and the manner which it is standing in order to direct his aim with certainty—And it also requires experience to enable him choose a fat animal the best looking Buffaloe is not always the fattest and a hunter by constant practice may lay down rules for selecting the fattest when on foot which would be no guide to him when running upon horseback for he is then placed in a different position and one which requires different rules for choosing.

The Snake Indians

The appellation by which this nation is distinguished is derived from the Crows but from what reason I have never been able to determine—They call themselves Sho-sho-nies but during an acquaintance of nine years during which time I made further progress in their language than any white man had done before me I never saw one of the nation who could give me either the derivation or definition of the word Sho sho nie[191]—Their country comprises all the regions drained by the head branches of Green and Bear rivers and the East and Southern head branches of Snake River—They are kind and hospitable to whites thankful for favors indignant at injuries and but little addicted to theft in their large villages I have seldom heard them accused of inhospitality on the contrary I have found it to be a general feature of their character to divide the last morsel of food with the hungry stranger let their means be what it might for obtaining the next meal The Snakes and in fact most of the Rocky Mountain Indians believe in a supreme Deity who resides in the Sun and in infernal Deities residing in the Moon and Stars but all subject to the Supreme control of the one residing in the Sun—They believe that the Spirits of the departed are permitted to watch over the actions of the living and every warrior is protected by a pecular guardian Angel in all his actions so long as he obeys his rules a violation of which subjects the offender to misfortunes and disasters during the displeasure of the offended Deity. Their Prophets Jugglers or Medicine Men are supposed to be guided by Dieties diffring from the others insomuch as he is continually attended upon the devotee from birth gradually instilling into his mind the mysteries of his profession which cannot be transmitted from one mortal to another. The prophet or juggler converses freely with his supernatural director who guides him up from childhood in his manner of eating drinking and smoking particularly the latter for every Prophet has a different mode of handling filling lighting and smoking the big Pipe—Such as profound silence in the circle whilst the pipe is lighting the pipe turned round three times in the direction of the sun by the next person on the right previous to giving it to him or smoking with the feet uncovered Some cannot smoke in the presence of a female or a dog and a hundred other movements equally vague and superstitious which would be too tedious to mention here. A plurality of wives is very common among the Snakes and the marriage contract is dissolved only by the consent of the husband after which the wife is at liberty to marry again Prostitution among the women is very rare and fornication whilst living with the husband is punished with the utmost severity The women perform all the labor about the lodge except the care of the horses. They are cheerful and affectionate to their husbands remarkably fond and careful of their children

The Government is a Democracy deeds of valor promotes the Chief to the highest points attainable from which he is at any time liable to fall for misdemeanor in office: their population amts. to between 5 and 6,000 about half of which live in large Villages and range among the Buffaloe: the remainder live in small detached companies comprising of from 2 to 10 families who subsist upon roots fish seeds and berries They have but few horses and are much addicted to thieving from their manner of living they have received the appellation of "Root Diggers —they rove about in the mountains in order to seclude themselves from their warlike enemies the Blackfeet—their arrows are pointed with quartz or obsideon which they dip in poison extracted from the fangs of the rattle snake and prepared with antelopes liver these they use in hunting and war and however slight the wound may be that is inflicted by one of them—death is almost inevitable but the flesh of animals killed by these arrows is not injured for eating—The Snakes who live upon Buffaloe and live in large villages seldom use poison upon their arrows either in hunting or war—They are well armed with fusees and well supplied with horses they seldom stop more than 8 or 10 dys in one place which prevents the accumulation of filth which is so common among Indians that are Stationary. their lodges are spacious neatly made of dressed Buffaloe skins, sewed to gether and set upon 11 or 13 long smooth poles to each lodge which are dragged along for that purpose. In the winter of 1842 the principal Chief of the Snakes died in an appoplectic fit and on the following year his brother died but from what disease I could not learn. These being the two principal pillars that upheld the nation the loss of them was and is to this day deeply deplored —immediately after the death of the latter the tribe scattered in smaller villages over the country in consequence of having no chief who could control and keep them together—their ancient warlike spirit seemed to be buried with their leaders and they are fast falling into degradation, without a head the body is of little use

The Crow Indians

This once formidable tribe once lived on the North side of the Missouri East of the mouth of the Yellow Stone about the year 1790 they crossed the Missouri and took the region of country which they now inhabit, by conquest from the Snakes It is bounded on the East and South by a low range of Mountains called the "Black Hills" on the West by the Wind river Mountains and on the North by the Yellow Stone river The face of the country presents a diversity of rolling hills and Valleys and includes several plains admirably adapted for grazing. the whole country abounds with Coal and Iron in great abundance and signs of Lead and Copper are not infrequently seend and gypsum exists in imense quarries. timber is scare except along the streams and on the mountains wild fruit such as cherries service berries currants gooseberries and plums resembling the pomgranate are abundant—The latter grow on small trees generally 6 or 8 feet high varying in color and flavor from the most acute acid to the mildest sweetness—Hops grow spontaneously and in great abundance along the streams. When the Crows first conquered this country their numbers amtd to about 8,000 persons but the ravages of war and small pox combined has reduced their numbers to about 2,000. of which upwards of 1200 are females They are proud treacherous thievish insolent and brave when they are possessed with a superior advantage but when placed in the opposite situation they are equally humble submissive and cowardly Like the other tribes of Indians residing in the Rocky Mts. they believe in a Supreme Deity who resides in the Sun and lesser deitys residing in the Moon and Stars. Their government is a kind of Democracy The Chief who can enumerate the greatest number of valiant exploits is unanimously considered the Supreme ruler All the greatest warriors below him and above a certain grade are Counsillors and take their seats in the council according to their respective ranks. the voice of the lowest rank having but little weight in discussing matters of importance. When a measure is adopted by the council and approved by the head Chief it is immediately put in force by the order of the military commander who is appointed by the Council to serve for an indefinite period A standing Company of soldiers is kept up continually for the purpose of maintaining order in the Village. The Captain can order any young man in the Village to serve as a soldier in turn and the council only can increase or diminish the number of soldiers at pleasure. The greatest Chiefs cannot violate the orders which the Capt. receives from the Council—No office or station is hereditary neither does wealth constitute dignity. The greatest Chief may fall below the meanest citizen for misdemeanor in office and the lowest citizen may rise to the most exalted station by the performance of valiant deeds—The Crows both male and female are tall well proportioned handsomly featured with very light copper coloured skins. Prostitution of their wives is very common but sexual intercours between near relatives is [strictly] prohibited—when a young man is married he never after speaks

Indians, often a harassment of the trapper, are depicted here in Charles M. Russell's painting "On the Warpath" which depicts five braves moving down a mountain trail. (*Reproduced by courtesy of the Historical Society of Montana*)

to his mother in law nor the wife to the father in law altho they
may all live in the same lodge If the husband wishes to say
anything to the mother in law he speaks to the wife who con-
veys it to the mother and in the same way communication is
conveyed between the wife and father in law—This custom is
peculiar to the Crows They never intermarry with other nations
but a stranger if he wishes can always be accommodated with a
wife while he stops with the Village but cannot take her from it
when he leaves—Their laws for killing Buffaloe are most rigidly
enforced. No person is allowed to hunt Buffalo in the vicinity
where the village is stationed without first obtaining leave of
the council—for the first offense the offenders hunting apparatus
are broken and destroyed for second his horses are killed his
property destroyed and he beaten with rods the third is punished by death by shooting—When a decree is given by the
council it is published by the head Chief who rides to and fro
thro. the village like a herald and proclaims it aloud to all—
They generally kill their meat by surrounding a band of Buffaloe
and when once enclosed but few escape—The first persons who
arrive at a dead Buffaloe is entitled to one third of the meat and
if the person who killed it is the fourth one on the spot he only
gets the hide and tongue but in no wise can he get more than
one third of the meat if a second and third person appears before
it is placed on the horses designed for packing. A person whether
male or female poor or rich gets the 2d or 3d division according
to the time of arrival each one knowing what parts they are
allowed—This is also a custom peculiar to the Crows which has
been handed down from time immemorial—Their language is
clear distinct and not intermingled with guttural sounds which
renders it remarkably easy for a stranger to learn It is a high
crime for a father or mother to inflict corporeal punishment on
their male children and if a Warrior is struck by a stranger he is
irretriveably disgraced unless he can kill the offender immediately

Taking prisoners of war is never practiced with the exception of subjecting them to servile employments—Adult males are never retained as prisoners but generally killed on the spot but young Males are taken to the Village and trained up in their mode of warfare until they imbibe the Crow Customs and language when they are eligible to the highest station their deeds of valor will permit. The Crows are remarkably fond of gaudy and glittering ornaments. The Eye teeth of the Elk are used in connexion with [?] are used as a circulating medium and are valued according to their size—There exists among them many customs similar to those of the ancient Israelites A woman after being delivered of a male child cannot approach the lodge of her husband under 40 dys and for a female 50 is required—and 7 dys seperation for every natural menses. The distinction between clean and unclean beasts bears a great degree of similarity to the Jewish law. They are remarkable for their cleanliness and variety of cookery which exceeds that of any other tribe in the Rocky Mts. They seldom use salt but often season their cookery with herbs of various kinds and flavors.

Sickness is seldom found amongst them and they naturally live to a great age. There is no possibility of ascertaining the precise age of any Mountain Indians but an inference may be drawn with tolerable correctness from their outward appearance and such indefinite information from their own faint recollections of dates as may be collected by an intimate acquaintance with their habits customs traditions and manner of living I have never known a Mountain [Indian] to be troubled with the tooth ache or decayed teeth nither have I ever known a case of insanity except from known and direct causes. I was upon one particular occasion invited to smoke in a circle comprising thirteen aged Crow warriors the youngest of whom appeared to have seen upwards of 100 winters and yet they were all in good health and fine spirits—they had long since left the battle ground and council room to young aspirants of 60 and under it is really diverting to hear those hoary headed veterans when they are collected together conversing upon the good old times of their forefathers and condemning the fashions of the present age—They have a tradition among them that their most powerful Chief (who died sometime since) commanded the Sun and Moon to stand still two days and nights in the valley of Wind River whilst they conquered the Snakes and that they obeyed him. They point out the place where the same chief changed the wild sage of the prarie into a band of Antelope when the Village was in starving condition I have also been shown a spring on the west side of the Big horn river below the upper Mountain which they say was once bitter but thro. the medicine of this great Chief the waters were made sweet.

They have a great aversion to distilled spirits of any kind terming it the 'White mans fool water' and say if a Crow drink it he ceases to be a Crow and becomes a foolish animal so long as he senses are absorbed by its influence

THE BEAVER

The Beaver as almost every one knows is an amphibeous animal but the instinct with which it is possessed surpasses the reason of a no small portion of the human race. Its average size is about $2\frac{1}{2}$ feet long from the point of the nose to the insertion of the tail, which is from 10 to 15 inches long and from 5 to 9 broad flat in the shape of a spade rounded at the corners covered with a thick rough skin resembling scales. the tail serves the double purpose of steering and assisting it thro. the water by a quick up and down motion The hind feet are webbed and the toe next the outside on each has a double nail which serves the purpose of a toothpick to extract the splinters of wood from their teeth as they are the only animals that cut large trees for subsistence they are also the only animals known to be furnished with nails so peculiarly adapted to the purpose for which they are used. Its color is of a light brown generally but I have seen them of a jet black frequently and in one instance I saw one of a light cream color having the feet and tail white The hair is of two sorts the one longer and coarser the other fine short and silky Their teeth are like those of the rat but are longer and stronger in proportion to the size of the animals. To a superficial observer they have but one vent for their excrements and urine but upon a closer examination without dissection seperate openings will be seen likewise 4 glands opening forward of the arms two containing oil with which they oil their coats the others containing the castorum a collection of gummy substance of a yellow color which is extracted from the food of the animal and conveyed thro. small vessels into the glands. it is this deposit which causes the destruction of the Beaver by the hunters—When a Beaver Male or female leaves the lodge to swim about their pond they go to the bottom and fetch up some mud between their forepaws and breast carry it on to the bank and emit upon it a small quantity of castorum—another Beaver passing the place does the same and should a hundred Beaver pass within the scent of the place they would each throw up mud covering up the old castorum and emit new upon that which they had thrown up. The Trapper extracts this substance from the gland and carries it in a wooden box he sets his trap in the water near the bank about 6 inches below the Surface throws a handful of mud on the bank about one foot from it and puts a small portion of the castorum thereon after night the Beaver comes out of his lodge smells the fatal bait 2 or 300 yds. distant and steers his course directly for it he hastens to ascend the bank but the traps grasps his foot and soon drowns him in the struggle to escape for the Beaver though termed an amphibeous animal cannot respire beneath the water. The female brings forth her young in April and produces from 2 to 6 at a birth but what is most singular she seldom raises but 2 a male and a female. This peculiarity of the Beaver has often been a matter of discussion among the most experienced hunters whether the dam or father kills the young but I have come to the conclusion that it is the mother for the following reasons 1st The Male is

Trappers carefully set their traps for the wily beaver.

seldom found about the lodge for 10 or 15 days after the female brings forth. 2dly there is always a male and female saved alive 3dly I have seen the dead kittens floating in the ponds freshly killed and at the same times have caught the male where he was living more than ½ a mile from the Lodge. I have found where beaver are confined to a limited space they kill nearly all the kittens which is supposed to be done to keep them from becoming too numerous and destroying the timber and undergrowth too fast—I have caught 50 full grown Beaver in a valley surrounded by mountains and cascades where they had not been disturbed for 4 yrs and with this number there were but 5 or 6 kittens and yearlings. The young ones pair off generally at 3 yrs. of age to set up for themselves and proceed up or down a stream as instinct may suggest until they find the best place for wood and undergrowth connected with the most convenient place for building a dam which is constructed by cutting small trees and brush dragging them into the water on both sides of the stream and attaching one end to each bank while the other extends into the stream inclining upwards against the current then mud small stones and rubbish are dragged or pushed on to it to sink it to the bottom they proceed in this manner until the two ends meet in the middle of the stream the whole forming a sort of curved line accross but the water raising often forces the dam down the stream until it becomes nearly strait—In the meantime they have selected a spot for the lodge either upon the bank or upon a small Island formed by the rising water— but it is generally constructed on an island in the middle of the pond with sticks and mud in such a manner that when the water is raised sufficiently high which is generally from 4 to 7 ft. it has the appearance of a potash kettle turned on the surface bottom upwards standing from 4 to 6 ft above the water there is no opening above the water but generally two below. The floor on which they sleep and have their beds of straw or grass is about 12 inches above the water level the room is arched over and kept neat and clean When the leaves begin to fall the Beavers commence laying in their winter store. They often cut down trees from 12 to 18 inches in diameter and cut off the branches covered with smooth bark into pieces from two to six feet long these they drag into the water float them to the lodge sink them to the bottom of the pond and there fasten them in this manner they proceed till they have procured about ½ a cord of wood solid measure for each Beavers winters supply— by this time the dam freezes over and all is shut up with ice. The Beaver has nothing to do but leap into the water thro. the subterranean passage and bring up a stick of wood which is to furnish him his meal this he drags by one end into the lodge eats off the bark to a certain distance then cuts off the part he has stripped and throws it into the water thro. another passage and so proceeds until he has finished his meal. When the Ice and snow disappears in the spring they clear their pond of the stripped wood and stop the leaks which the frosts have occasioned in their dam. Their manner of enlarging their lodge is by cutting out the inside and adding more to the out—the covering of the lodge is generally about 18 inches thick formed by sticks and mud intermingled in such a manner that it is very difficult for Man beast or cold to penetrate through it

The Hunter's Farewell

Adieu ye hoary icy mantled towers
That ofttimes pierce the onward fleeting mists
Whose feet are washed by gentle summer showers
While Phoebus' rays play on your sparkling crests
The smooth green vales you seem prepared to guard
Beset with groves of ever verdant pine
Would furnish themes for Albions noble bards
Far 'bove a hunters rude unvarnish'd rhymes

Adieu ye flocks that skirt the mountains brow
And sport on banks of everliving snow
Ye timid lambs and simple harmless Ewes
Who fearless view the dread abyss below—
Oft have I watched your seeming mad career
While lightly tripping o'er those dismal heights
Or cliffs o'erhanging yawning caverns drear
Where none else treads save fowls of airy flight

Oft have I climbed those rough stupendous rocks
In search of food 'mong Nature's well fed herds
Untill I've gained the rugged mountain's top
Where Boreas reigned or feathered Monarchs soar'd
On some rude cragg projecting from the ground
I've sat a while my wearied limbs to rest
And scann'd the unsuspecting flock around
With anxious care selecting out the best

The prize obtained with slow and heavy step
Pac'd down the steep and narrow winding path
To some smooth vale where chrystal streamlets met
And skillful hands prepared a rich repast
Then hunters jokes and merry humor'd sport
Beguiled the time enlivened every face
The hours flew fast and seemed like moments short
'Til twinkling planets told of midnights pace

But now those scenes of cheerful mirth are done
The horned [herds] are dwindling very fast
The numerous trails so deep by Bisons worn
Now teem with weeds or over grown with grass
A few gaunt Wolves now scattered or the place
Where herds since time unknown to man have fed
With lonely howls and sluggish onward pace
Tell their sad fate and where their bones are laid

Ye rugged mounts ye vales ye streams and trees
To you a hunter bids his last farewell
I'm bound for shores of distant western seas
To view far famed Multnomahs fertile vale
I'll leave these regions once famed hunting grounds
Which I perhaps again shall see no more
And follow down led by the setting sun
Or distant sound of proud Columbia's roar

NOTES

1. Thomas Nuttall and John Kirk Townsend.

2. This Boston sea captain, who was a Kentuckian by birth, remained with Wyeth's enterprise to its end as second-in-command. He led several trapping expeditions, and, after 1835, was in charge of Fort Hall, where he became noted for his generous Southern hospitality. His astronomical observations were quite inaccurate when compared with those made eight years later by the "Pathfinder," Captain John P. Fremont.

3. Marston G. Clark, whom Jason Lee (p. 118) speaks of as a "... cousin to Gen. Clark who went to the Columbia with Lewis." However, Washington Irving (Bonneville, p. 274) says the relationship was that of a brother.

4. The date of arrival at the Platte appears to be in error. Jason Lee (p. 123), the most consistent journalist of this expedition, gives the date as May 17, while John Townsend (p. 157) notes it as May 18.

5. The Laramie River, which heads in the Laramie and Medicine Bow Ranges of Wyoming and joins the Platte River near the eastern boundary of the state. It was named for Jacques Laramie, a free trader killed by Indians on its headwaters in about the year 1821. Little is known of either the man or the event.

6. The Laramie Range. In that day the term "Black Hills" was used to indicate all the outlying foothills of the Rocky Mountains, but now it is applied only to the prominent mountains of western South Dakota.

7. The Red Buttes, in Natrona County, Wyoming, were first seen in 1811 by the returning Astorians under Robert Stuart. He gave the name of "Fiery Narrows" to this cleft through which the Platte River rushes in a furious cataract, but later travellers knew the place as the Red Buttes, from the prominent hills which cap the flanking rocks and form a landmark visible for many miles. The date of the crossing was June 7, according to Jason Lee (p. 131).

8. Three different stories concerning the origin of this name are current. C. J. Coutant (Vol. I, p. 122) says: "The trappers found the water superior for drinking purposes and claimed that it left a pleasant taste in the mouth. General Ashley consequently named it Sweetwater ..." The other two accounts both indicate the river was sweetened to that taste. According to W. A. Ferris (p. 37), "This river owes its name to the accidental drowning in it of a mule loaded with sugar, some years since." And similarly, A. J. Allen (p. 160) states: "A company were once passing the stream, and during a drunken carousel, emptied into it a large bag of sugar, thereby, as they said, christening it, and declaring that it should hereafter be called Sweetwater Valley as long as the waters ran."

9. This divide is South Pass. The discoverer of this important route over the Rocky Mountains is not certainly known, but it is probable that the returning Astorians used it in 1811.

10. This date should be June 19; Wyeth, Lee and Townsend agree on it.

11. The rendezvous of 1834 was held on Ham's Fork. The site of the encampment was changed on the twenty-seventh by ascending the stream a short distance, probably to obtain better pasturage.

12. Andrew Dripps and Lucien Fontanelle.

13. Bear Lake, Utah. On subsequent visits Russell calls it "Snake Lake," a name often used by the trappers. However, it was also known as "Black Bear Lake," and as "Little Lake" or "Sweet Lake," to distinguish it from the Great Salt Lake.

14. Soda Point, Idaho. This prominent landmark forms the craggy northern end of the Bear River Range.

15. Soda Springs, Idaho. The trappers knew them as the "Beer Springs."

16. Captain Benjamin Louis Eulalie De Bonneville, on leave from the United States Army.

17. The place where Wyeth built his fort is not the point marked "Fort Hall" on present maps, but a site farther west on the sandy plain between Portneuf and Snake Rivers. All that remains of the old fort are some low ridges and patches of adobe amidst the deep grass on a small point between Snake River and a shallow slough. They probably mark the location of the walls and out-buildings of the Hudson's Bay Company fort with which the original structure was replaced prior to 1839. The south wall line is a prominent ridge two or three feet high and 78 feet in length, while only portions of the east and west wall lines still remain. It is likely that the stockaded walls were merely replaced with adobe since the dimensions of the fort as given by Russell agree with those of Wislizenus (pp. 106-7). The impounding of the waters of Snake River in the American Falls Reservoir has raised the water level and may have changed the appearance of the site considerably, both in its vegetative cover and in its relationship to the river. A monument has been erected by the Oregon Trail Society.

18. Both Wyeth and Townsend describe this dedication. In his journal (p. 227) Wyeth writes, "6th [August] Having done as much as was requisite for safety to the Fort and drank a bale of liquor and named it Fort Hall in honor of the oldest partner of our concern we left it and with it Mr. Evans in charge of 11 men and 14 horses and mules and three cows—Fort Hall is in Latt. 43°14′ Long. 111°35′." Townsend (p. 230) says of it, "August 5th—At sunrise this morning, the 'star-spangled banner' was raised on the flag-staff at the fort, and a salute fired by the men . . ."

19. The eleven men left with Russell to garrison Fort Hall were Robert Evans, who was in charge; William Richmonds, Robert Cairnes, John Hynds, John Maxwell, Charles Schriver, John Timmer, Samuel Nott, John Ward, Thomas Callahan, and Peter Rost. The spelling of the names varies considerably in the account books of Fort Hall, and Russell is always referred to as "John Russell."

20. Probably named for Alexander Ross, who led a Hudson's Bay Company brigade into the Snake River country in 1824.

21. The Portneuf River was named for one of Peter Skene Ogden's men, a French-Canadian trapper, killed there by the Indians.

22. A cold fit, accompanied by shivering, which precedes a fever. In Russell's time the term "ague" was used to designate several intermittent fevers, particularly malaria.

23. The Snake or Shoshone Indians are an important tribe of the linguistic group which, in Russell's day, roamed the great basin and the mountains east and north of it. They were mainly nomadic hunters, subsisting on big game and dwelling in tepees. At an earlier date the Shoshones probably lived on the great plains from which they were driven by Indians who had obtained firearms. Their name is said to be an uncomplimentary Siouian expression.

24. The Bannock Indians were closely related to the Shoshones. In earlier times they dwelt in the great valleys of Montana, but the pressure of the Blackfeet forced them southward so that, in Russell's day, they roamed through what is now southern Idaho and western Wyoming.

25. A term applied to smooth-bored, flintlock guns traded to the Indians, particularly by the Hudson's Bay Company, and usually shortened for ease of handling from horseback. The word is a corruption of the French *fusil*, which itself probably comes from the Italian *fucile*, a flint. Originally, the French word was applied to flintlock muskets to distinguish them from the wheel-lock arms previously used. These trade guns were so inferior to the rifled guns of the trappers in range and accuracy that the Indian's ability to wage open war was seriously limited.

26. The American Fur Company and the remnant of the Rocky Mountain Fur Company doing business under the name of Fitzpatrick, Sublette and Bridger.

27. Joseph Gale was born near Washington, D. C., in 1800, and he came to Oregon in October of 1834 with a party under the leadership of Ewing Young and Hall Kelley. He entered Wyeth's service, remained about five years in the Rocky Mountains and then returned to the Willamette Valley, where he settled on the Tualatin Plains.

28. The direction from Fort Hall to the Portneuf River is southeast.

29. Cache Valley, lying along Bear River where it crosses the Idaho-Utah state line, received its name in the early days of the fur trade. According to Chittenden, the name may stem from a shadowy event wherein General Ashley is purported to have "lifted" beaver furs cached there by Peter Skene Ogden. Ferris (pp. 47-48) gives it a starker origin as follows:

"A man in the employ of Smith, Sublette and Jackson, was engaged ... in constructing one of those subterranean vaults for the reception of furs ... [and when] nearly completed ... a large quantity of earth fell in upon the poor fellow ... His companions *believed* him to have been instantly killed, *knew* him to be well buried, and the cache destroyed, and therefore left him and accomplished their object elsewhere."

30. It is not clear which stream the name Rush Creek was applied to. Ferris (p. 142) says it is 35 miles from the head of Cache valley, and describes it as "... a small stream (that flows into Bear River on the south side) bordered by dense thickets, ..."

31. Bear Lake. See note 13.

32. Thomas Fork. W. A. Ferris (p. 52) states that it was named in honor of the French tragedian Francis Joseph Talma (1763-1826).

33. Scott's Fork appears to be the stream now known as "Stump Creek," which joins Salt River near Auburn, Wyoming. Nothing is known of the origin of the earlier name.

34. Gardner's Fork is the stream shown as Tincup Creek on current maps. It was probably named for one of General Ashley's men. N. J. Wyeth (p. 74) says, "Mr. Gardner, one of his agents, met a Mr. Ogden, clerk of the H. B. Co., in the Snake country at the head of a trapping party. Gardner induced the men of Ogden's party to desert by promises of supplies and good prices for furs." It is also likely that this man is the Johnson Gardner who appears at a later date as a free trapper on the Missouri and the headwaters of the Yellowstone River.

35. This canyon, in Caribou County, Idaho, is now known as "The Narrows."

36. The gorge is now occupied by the Blackfoot River Reservoir, Caribou County, Idaho.

37. Francis Ermatinger.

38. Captain William George Drummond Stewart, seventh Baronet of Grandtully; trapper, traveler, big-game hunter and author. This retired British Army officer toured the west for several years and was well liked by the traders and trappers. His home was in Perthshire, Scotland.

39. This stream is now known as Willow Creek, though a fork of it bears the name John Grey's Lake Outlet. It was named for John Gray, a half-breed Iroquois employed by Peter Skene Ogden. Gray is credited with the discovery of several prominent features in this region.

40. A craft of this type was called a "bull-boat" and was in common use among both trappers and Indians.

41. Abraham R. Patterson came to Fort Hall on June 10, 1835, with the small Hudson's Bay Company party under Francis Ermatinger, and he died June 22, 1835. So his service with the Columbia River Fishing and Trading Company amounted to only twelve days.

42. This is Swan Valley, Idaho; the mountains are the Pallisades and Big Hole Mountains.

43. The Teton Valley of Idaho. The first white men to describe it were the Astorians, though some of Henry's men undoubtedly were in it as they trapped from Fort Henry. The early name was given for Pierre, an Iroquois employee of the Hudson's Bay Company, who was killed there by the Blackfeet.

44. The Tetons are the "Pilot Knobs" which served as a landmark to the outward bound Astorians under Wilson Price Hunt. The first attempt to climb the principal peak was made by Michaud, a French explorer, in 1843. It was finally conquered by Captain James Stevenson, a member of the United States Geological Survey, and N. P. Langford, in 1872.

45. Now called the Teton River.

46. The crossing was made by what is now known as Teton Pass.

47. Named by William Sublette in 1829 for David E. Jackson who was fond of that beautiful basin at the foot of the Tetons. The name remains the most important relic of the day when such level, grassy valleys were called "holes."

48. The Gros Ventre River. Captain Raynolds notes in his Report (p. 88):
"Friday, June 1 [1860] ... We are now on waters flowing to the westward and into a branch of Lewis fork, which Bridger says is known to the trappers as Gros Ventre fork, the Gros Ventre Indians having been commonly in the habit of passing by this valley in their annual trips across the mountains."

49. They had reached the Du Noir River, a branch of the Wind River of Wyoming.

50. They were looking at the Absaroka Range, named for the Crow or Absaroka Indians—the "Bird People."

51. Probably *Washaki* Indians.

52. Lake Yellowstone.

53. The South Fork of the Shoshone River of Wyoming.

54. The Stinking River is now known as the North Fork of the Shoshone. The following excerpt from the *Report of the Chief of Engineers, U. S. Army* (p. 3781), explains the change in name:
"This stream has heretofore been known as the Stinkingwater River. It was so named in 1807 by its discoverer, John Colter, who came upon it where there

is a large tar spring near the junction of the two forks and gave it the name on account of the impression received at this particular point. The name was wholly inappropriate as the stream is one of the finest in the mountains, ... Local usage has succeeded in changing it to 'Shoshone', but this change has never received official recognition ... acting upon a recommendation from this office to the Governor of Wyoming, the legislature of that state passed an act (February 14, 1901) changing the name to Shoshone."

55. The Lamar River. It was at first called the East Fork of the Yellowstone, but was later renamed in honor of L. Q. C. Lamar, Secretary of the Department of Interior from March 6, 1885, to January 16, 1888.

56. This is the Lamar Valley in Yellowstone National Park. Russell calls it the "Secluded Valley" on subsequent visits.

57. Probably nomadic Sheepeater Indians, the only aborigines inhabiting the Yellowstone Plateau. They were a branch of the Shoshonean people, small, timid and impoverished. Unable to defend themselves against their better armed and aggressive neighbors, these Indians lived a hermit-like existence in constant fear of the hunting parties which frequented the area in summer. The last of the Sheepeaters were removed to reservations soon after the Yellowstone National Park was set aside in 1872, yet traces of them can still be found in isolated glens where their crude, conical shelters, made of small poles stood on end, resist decay very well.

58. This ford is directly east of Tower Falls and is the one where the Bannock or Great Trail of the Indians crossed the Yellowstone River.

59. Gardner's Hole is the valley at the head of the Gardiner River in Yellowstone National Park. Chittenden (Fur Trade, p. 746) says, "In an open valley of most attractive surroundings on one of the upper tributaries of the Yellowstone, a free-trapper, Johnson Gardner, plied his trade as far back as 1830, and gave the river and valley his name. 'Gardner's Hole' was the uncouth name of this beautiful spot ..." The present spelling of Gardiner for the name of the river probably originated with the Washburn expedition of 1870, through misunderstanding of information obtained by N. P. Langford from Jim Bridger.

Johnson Gardner may be the same Gardner for whom Gardner's fork on Salt River was named.

60. The Burnt Hole is the valley now occupied by the Hebgen Reservoir near West Yellowstone, Montana. W. A. Ferris (pp. 85-86), gives the following origin for the name: "The Burnt Hole is a district on the north side of the Piney Woods, which was observed to be wrapped in flames a few years since. The conflagration that occasioned this name must have been of great extent, and large forests of half-consumed pines still evidence the ravages ..."

Captain Raynolds in his Report (p. 98), clearly locates this valley: "Monday, June 25 ... After crossing the Lake fork [Henry's River], Mr. Hutton, Dr.

Hayden, and ... turned to the east and visited the pass over the mountains [Targhee Pass], leading into the Burnt Hole valley. They found the summit distant only about 5 miles ... From it they could see a second pass upon the other side of the valley, which Bridger states to lead to the Gallatin." The "second pass" is the one Russell's party crossed on the 29th.

At a later time the name Burnt Hole was mistakenly attached to the geyser basins on the Firehole River in Yellowstone National Park. N. P. Langford in his preface to the book *The Folsom-Cook Exploration of the Upper Yellowstone in the Year 1869* (Folsom, p. 20) says, "... came to a small irregularly shaped valley, some six miles across in the widest place, from every part of which great clouds of steam arose. From descriptions which we had had of this valley from persons who had previously visited it, we recognized it as the place known as 'Burnt Hole,' or 'Death Valley'." Chittenden (*Yellowstone*, pp. 316-17) also attaches the name to the geyser basins of the Firehole River, apparently under the assumption that the name arose naturally from the superficial resemblance of a steaming geyser basin to a smoking burned-over area. The translocation of this name occurred easily enough as the two areas are close together.

On a later expedition into the Yellowstone country Russell locates the Burnt Hole with relation to the geyser basins of the Firehole River (cf. note 160).

61. Near the site of Hebgen Dam.

62. The Blackfeet and two other tribes of Algonquin Indians, Bloods and Piegans, were joined in a loose confederacy which held the plains between the upper Missouri and Saskatchewan Rivers. They were nomadic hunters without arts or agriculture; warlike, aggressive and consistently hostile to the whites. They were also at war with most of their Indian neighbors, particularly the Flatheads, Snakes and Crows, whose country they roamed as freely as their own. The Blackfeet preferred to travel afoot and to fight from ambush, and, when on the defensive, used conical log and brush forts. They were repeatedly decimated by the smallpox.

63. For an account of this battle by Joe Meek, see *River of the West* (Victor, pp. 166-69). He mentions Russell as one of a group which showed "game spirit" during the fight. A comparison of the Meek account with that given in *Four Years in the Rockies* (Marsh, pp. 55-61), leaves no doubt that Mr. Marsh borrowed freely from the earlier work, often without bothering to re-phrase. Other events common to the two books are strikingly similar in text and in chronological arrangement.

64. Piegans.

65. Probably Fort Union on the Missouri River six miles above the mouth of the Yellowstone.

66. See pp. 16-17.

67. See note 62.

68. The Ruby River in Madison County, Montana. This stream-of-many-names was called the "Philanthropy" by Lewis and Clark, while the trappers referred to it sometimes by that name and sometimes as the "Stinkingwater." Both names disappeared with the fur trade era, and the maps accompanying the Pacific Railroad Surveys use the name of "Hooked Man Cr." for the stream. However, the early settlers preferred to call it the "Passamari River" and it is so shown on the topographic map prepared by the Geological Survey in 1893 (Dillon Quadrangle).

69. Named for a prominent cliff which Lewis and Clark described as ". . . a clift of rocks 150 feet high St^d[right] side called by the Snake Indians the *Beavers head, . . ." (Original Journals,* Vol. VI, p. 19).

70. A tribe of the Salishan linguistic group of which the Flatheads were the principal tribe.

71. Probably the Lower Red Rock Lake. Russell appears unaware of the other lake nearby. His "head stream of the Jefferson Fork" is Red Rock Creek, known to the trappers as Pierre's Fork.

72. Ferris (p. 86), calls it ". . . Kammas Creek, (so called from a small root, very nutritious, and much prized as food by Indians and others, which abounds here) a small stream that rises with the sources of the Madison [Jefferson], flows southeast forty or fifty miles, and discharges itself into a pond . . ."

73. Probably Ray's Lake which is ten miles north of Mud Lake. In Russell's day Mud Lake did not exist; it was formed in a prairie basin, known to the trappers as "The Market," by flood waters from Snake River in 1853 (Mullan, *Pacific Railway Reports,* p. 330).

74. In attempting to retrace his route from the lake to the lava beds, Russell veered to the west and reached one of the streams which issues from the Salmon River Mountains to sink in the plain west of Mud Lake.

75. The junction of Snake River and Henry's Fork.

76. Probably between Lava Hot Springs and Chesterfield, Idaho.

77. Philoctetes, one of the heroes of Greek mythology. When Hercules wished to end his torment on the funeral pyre he had erected, none would set it alight; but finally Philoctetes did from his desire for the bow and poisoned arrows he was offered.

78. Joe Meek, George Ebberts, Cotton Mansfield and Jim Bridger were commonly known as "Major," "Squire," "Cotton," and "Gabe" by their fellow trappers, and it is likely they are the characters in this scene. The "Judge" may be Russell himself.

79. Smiths Fork ". . . receives its name from the late Jerediah [Jedediah]

Smith, of the firm of Smith, Sublette and Jackson." (Ferris, p. 140). He was one of the great leaders of the Rocky Mountain fur trade in its early days, combining untiring energy, great courage and an impetuous but deeply religious nature. His far-flung explorations opened vast reaches of the transmontane west to the trappers. Smith withdrew from the fur trade in 1830 and the following year he and his partners entered the Santa Fe trade, but on the first expedition, he was killed by Comanche Indians at a water-hole on the Cimarron River.

80. The rendezvous for 1836 was held at Horse Creek on Green River.

81. Probably Gannett Peak, elevation 13,785 feet, the highest point in Wyoming.

82. Pacific Creek.

83. This is Two Ocean Pass, the source of Atlantic and Pacific Creeks.

84. This is the valley of the Upper Yellowstone River — an area which has become known as the "Thorofare."

85. In the vicinity of the present Fishing Bridge settlement in Yellowstone National Park. Russell's distances for the 18th and 19th are in error; for the distance from the inlet to the outlet around the east shore of the lake is less than 25 miles.

86. Probably siliceous sinter or "geyserite." Limestone deposition is known only at the Mammoth Hot Springs, at a small group of hot springs on Snake River, and at the extinct springs at Soda Butte. (Allen and Day, pp. 94 and 145.)

87. See note 56.

88. This direction appears to be in error; a course west or north of west would be required.

89. Lt. Maynadier notes in his Report (pp. 140-42):

"June 29, [1860] ... we came to a stream called Twenty-five Yard river, the same I think that Captain Clark calls Shield's river; it is a narrow, shallow stream flowing from the Belt mountains into the Yellowstone."

"July 8 ...This is the river which Captain Clark calls Shield's river; and it would be well if the name were revived but as it now goes by the name of Twenty-five Yard river I have retained it."

Shields was the gunsmith of the Lewis and Clark Expedition of 1804-6.

90. This is the Stillwater River. The name "Rosebud" was given by Lewis and Clark and survives only in the name of a prominent fork, Little Rosebud Creek. Lt. Maynadier says "June 20, [1860] ... This stream is known as Big Rosebud by the trappers; Bonlon de Rose, by the Canadian voyageurs, and Bilskopay-agee, by the Crow Indians."

91. Rock Creek. The town of Red Lodge, Montana, is situated where it issues from the mountains. The Lewis and Clark map of 1814 shows it as the "Ap-sah sro ka R."

92. Joe Meek and Davis Crow. The latter is listed in the "Account books of Fort Hall" as an employee of the Columbia River Fishing and Trading Company from July 6, 1835 to January 1, 1836 (Ledger No. 1, pp. 269-70 and 377-88). There are references to him in *Four Years in the Rockies* (Marsh, pp. 107 and 215), including an account of his death following a Christmas celebration at which he fired an overloaded cannon and was gravely injured.

93. Named for Nathaniel Pryor, a sergeant who accompanied Lewis and Clark to the Pacific, 1804-6. Its aboriginal name was the Mampoa or Shot Stone river (Larocque, p. 20).

94. The reason for using this expression when referring to the Blackfeet is not clear; perhaps it stems from some frontier incident which was common knowledge at that time.

95. The "unfortunate Howell," as Isaac Rose calls him, became a trapper in an attempt to recoup his fortunes. He needed two hundred dollars to set himself up in the freighting business and win the hand of a St. Louis seamstress, but twice lost his "stake" through accidents and finally joined Wyeth's Columbia River Fishing and Trading Company. At the time of his death Howell was accompanied by Green, another unlucky lover who broke up his engagement by going on a drunken spree (Marsh, pp. 27, 122 and 123).

96. This is Beauvais Creek in Big Horn County, Montana.

97. The name of this trapper was Isaac P. Rose. His biographer, James Marsh, says that the ball struck the "... right elbow, entering at the back, below the joint, and passing out at the forepart of the arm." The wound left him crippled and he soon returned to his home in Pennsylvania where he became a school teacher after first teaching himself to read and write.

98. According to Rose, the name of the Delaware was "Manhead." His account of this fight adds some interesting details (Marsh, pp. 137 and 138).

99. From *traineaux*, more often referred to as "travois." These primitive vehicles were made of two poles crossed near the small ends over the back of a horse with the butt ends allowed to drag on the ground. Burdens were lashed across the drag poles behind the horse.

100. This encampment was near the present town of Park City, Montana. It is a very good description of that part of the Yellowstone Valley.

101. The name of the Spaniard was Maselino. Rose relates several events in which he had a part, and also credits him with bringing gold dust to Fort William during the winter of 1837-8 (Marsh, pp. 89, 143-4 and 216).

102. The trappers were in the country of the Crow or Absoruque Indians, a branch of the Siouan stock inhabiting central and northern Wyoming. They were accomplished thieves, and quick to press any advantage. The reports of early Indian agents call them "rascals."

103. Named by Lewis and Clark.

104. The name is now spelled "Greybull," but the reason for the change from the older, and more correct form, is not evident.

105. This name has disappeared from present maps, but probably referred to Gooseberry Creek. Irving mentions that Bonneville had a rendezvous with his trappers "at the Medicine Lodge," and Abbé Domenech shows a "Medicine R." between Wind and Grey Bull Rivers on the map opposite page 1 in *Seven Years Residence In The Great Deserts Of North America.* The Middle Fork and South Fork of Russell's account appears to be Grass and Cottonwood or Owl Creeks.

106. Crowheart Butte in Fremont County, Wyoming.

107. The Popo Agie River. "*Popo* in the Crow language signifying head; and *Agie,* river" (Irving, *Bonneville,* p. 315). It is a source of the Big Horn River of Wyoming.

108. Irving *(Bonneville,* p. 315) says ". . . the Captain made search for 'the great Tar spring,' one of the wonders of the mountains; . . . he found it at the foot of a sandbluff, a little to the east of the Wind River Mountains . . ."

109. The origin of the name is obscure.

110. Both Joe Meek and Isaac Rose give accounts of this fight.

111. This date should be July 18th, according to the journal of William H. Gray.

112. The valley at the source of the Hoback River near Bondurant, Wyoming.

113. The canyon of the Hoback River, named for one of Wilson Price Hunt's men who had trapped on its waters when in the service of Andrew Henry. He was later killed by the Indians while trapping with John Reed in the country of the Nez Perce Indians on Snake River.

114. The direction appears to be wrong; a course of east northeast from the outlet of Yellowstone Lake places the encampment south of the "Secluded Valley" and on the Lamar River.

115. Hoodoo Basin.

116. The meadows at the head of Eagle Creek.

117. Mountain Creek.

118. Middle Creek.

119. Sylvan Pass in Yellowstone National Park.

120. The Sunlight Basin.

121. Soda Butte Creek.

122. Slough Creek in Yellowstone National Park.

123. Hellroaring Creek.

124. This appears to be the Boulder River, one of the "Rivers a Cross" of

Lewis and Clark. It joins the Yellowstone about 25 miles below the mouth of Shields River. On May 14, 1838, Russell uses the plural, Cross Creeks, indicating that the trappers employed a corrupt form of the original name.

125. Ferris, p. 126, calls them "... square pieces of robes, used under our saddles in traveling or under our beds in camp ..." The word appears in various forms.

126. John Greenberry came West with Russell in the service of the Columbia River Fishing and Trading Company. The account books of Fort Hall show that he enlisted April 20, 1834, for the monthly wage of $13.88-8/9.

127. Fort William was built by William Sublette and Robert Campbell in order to control the trade with the Indians frequenting the upper Platte. Wyeth noted in his Journal on June 1, 1834, "At the crossing [Laramie's Fork] we found 13 of Sublette's men camped for the purpose of building a fort he having gone ahead ... ," and Jason Lee mentions that they were planting corn. William Anderson, who was present when the construction of Fort William was begun, says it was given the name in a humorous compromise to an argument as to whether it should be Fort Anderson or Fort Sublette. Thus, "... the foam flew, in honor of Fort William, which contained the triad prenames of clerk, leader and friend." (Partoll, pp. 4 and 5.)

The original fort was built on a slight eminence on the north bank of the Laramie River about one mile above its junction with the Platte, and probably stood on or very near the site now occupied by the building known as the Commanding Officer's Quarters. Wislizenus, page 67, has left the best description of the early fort:

"It is on a slight elevation, and is built in a rectangle of about eighty by a hundred feet. The outside is made of cottonwood logs, about fifteen feet high, hewed off, and wedged closely together. On three sides there are little towers on the walls that seem designed for watch and defense. In the middle a strong gate, built of blocks, constitutes the entrance. Within, little buildings with flat roofs are plastered all around against the wall, like swallows nests. One is a storehouse; another the smithy; the others are dwellings not unlike monks cells. A special portion of the court yard is occupied by the so-called horsepen, in which the horses are confined at night. The middle space is free, with a tall tree in it, on which the flag is raised on occasions of state."

In 1836 Fort William was sold to the American Fur Company, and in 1841 its decaying pickets were replaced with adobe walls encompassing a larger area. The rebuilt fort was called "Fort John on the Laramie," but convenience soon shortened the name to Fort Laramie. It was sold to the United States Government in 1849 and became a part of the military post established there. The remains were razed in 1862 to make room for the residence which now occupies the site.

128. Probably a Mr. Woods whom the missionary, W. H. Gray, noted was

in charge of the fort on August 2, 1836. The "Journal" of Mrs. Myra F. Eells indicates he was still at the post May 31, 1838.

129. The name is explained by Larocque (p. 13), who was probably the first white man to see the river: "... the water so muddy that it is scarcely drinkable. The savages say that it is always thus and that it is for this reason that they called the river Powder, for the wind rises and carries from the slope a fine sand which obscures and dirties the water."

130. This is the "Montero" who was the leader of one of Bonneville's brigades, and also the "Antonio Mateo" mentioned by Captain Raynolds as the builder of the trading post known as the Portugese houses. He is probably the partisan whom Bonneville sent into the Crow country to make a fall hunt in 1832. While there, he was robbed by the Crows, lost his men through desertion to the American Fur Company which tempted them with liquor at Tullock's Fort, and then, while trapping on the headwaters of Powder River with a party of free trappers, lost his horses to the Aricaras. The vengeance he took was as barbaric as his despoilers. Returning empty-handed to his captain, he was outfitted and sent out again in 1833 to trap the Crow country and the Arkansas. Apparently successful in this campaign, he wintered among the Crows on Powder River and rejoined Bonneville at the forks of Wind River late in June, 1834. Irving *(Bonneville,* pp. 235-6) says that Bonneville returned to the East "leaving Montero with a brigade of trappers to open another campaign ..."

Irving says no more about the venture, which is understandable, since it was yet a going enterprise at the time he wrote; an enterprise surrounded by enemies among whom the Indians were the least feared. In short, Bonneville remained in the fur trade with his business afield in the hands of Montero who established himself among the Crows on Powder River, hoping there to escape the ruinous competition of the other companies. However, Montero's trading post did not go long undiscovered.

In *River of the West* (Victor, pp. 223-4), Joe Meek says:

"About Christmas [1836] all the company went into winter quarters on Powder River, in the neighborhood of a company of Bonneville's men, left under the command of Antoine Montero, who had established a trading post and fort at this place, hoping, no doubt, that here they should be comparatively safe from the injurious competition of the older companies. The appearance of three-hundred men, who had the winter before them in which to do mischief, was therefore as unpleasant as it was unexpected; and the result proved that even Montero, who was Bonneville's experienced trader, could not hold his own against so numerous and expert a band of marauders as Bridger's men, assisted by the Crows, proved themselves to be; for by the return of spring Montero had very little remaining of the property belonging to the fort, nor anything to show for it."

It is not known if that disaster put an end to Montero's activities on Powder River, but it is significant that no other mention of the post has been found except that by Captain Raynolds in his Report on the Exploration of the Yellowstone, page 65:

"Monday, September 26 [1859]—... Bridger and myself turned our faces down stream to try and obtain some information in regard to Lieutenant Maynadier. After a ride of about 15 miles we came to the ruins of some old trading posts, known as the 'Portugese houses,' from the fact that many years ago they were erected by a Portugese trader named Antonio Mateo.

"They are now badly dilapidated, and only one side of the pickets remains standing. These, however, are of hewn logs, and from their character it is evident that the structures were originally very strongly built. Bridger recounted a tradition that at one time this post was beseiged by the Sioux for forty days, resisting successfully to the last alike the strength and the ingenuity of their assaults and the story is not only credible but probable."

The location of the Portugese houses is also given in Captain Raynolds' report. On p. 173, J. W. Hutton places them as three miles due West of the "upper ford," which is on Powder River about 200 yards above the mouth of Salt Creek. The site is now marked by a monument placed in 1928, which is on the north bank of Powder River at a point 11.1 miles east of Kaycee and one-quarter mile south of the highway on the SE¼ of Section 14, T43N, R80W, Sixth Principal Meridian. A faint, rectangular outline, 85 feet by 110 feet, which probably resulted from the subsidence of earth after the pickets rotted, can still be seen.

131. Lucien Fontanelle was a colorful figure about whose life legends have accumulated in lieu of facts. Among them is a story that he committed suicide at Fort Laramie at about this time while in a state of drunkenness (Victor, p. 224), but it is entirely false. A letter in the Collection of the Missouri Historical Society, written by Fontanelle to P. A. Sarpy, indicates he was still alive August 5, 1838. In fact, Bernard DeVoto, who made a study of the subject, believes Fontanelle died sober in bed at Bellevue in 1840.

132. This river was known to Larocque (pp. 15-17) as the "Little Horn," and appears on Captain Raynolds' map of 1860 in that form. However, the Indian name of "Ets-pot-Agie-caia" would support the present usage of Little Big Horn River.

133. Beginning as Wind River, this stream was known to the trappers as the "Horn River" after passing through the upper chain of the Big Horn Mountains, and as the "Bighorn River" after passing the lower chain (Irving, *Bonneville*, p. 315). The practise of attaching different names to distinct portions of a stream was sometimes followed by the trappers, probably in conformity with Indian usage.

134. Bodair, or Bodah, was killed September 7, 1836, on what is now known

as Red Lodge Creek (cf. p. 66). Captain Raynolds' map shows the stream as "Baudins Fork," probably from information given him by Jim Bridger, his scout.

135. Probably headwaters of the East Gallatin River.

136. The Gallatin Valley is one of the rich agricultural areas of the northern Rocky Mountains. The river which flows through it was named by Lewis and Clark for the American statesman Albert Gallatin.

137. This valley has since been dammed to create Ennis Lake. It was probably reached by way of Spanish Creek.

138. One of the group of Iroquois boatmen and trappers brought to the Oregon country by the old Northwest Company.

139. The "undulating plain" which they crossed is Raynolds Pass. Only a rude wagon road yet crosses the Continental Divide by this easy route which probably was known to the trappers from Major Henry's time.

140. LaBarge Creek, named for the father of Captain Joseph LaBarge of Missouri River steamboat fame.

141. Coutant (p. 124), gives two possible origins for the name of this stream: he says,

"As they proceeded up the river [a party of Ashley's men under Clements, and including Jim Beckworth, LeBrache and Baptiste — 1823] they came to a branch on the west side of the main stream, up which they saw a number of wild horses pasturing in the beautiful green meadows, and they promptly called it Horse Creek ..."

"... another origin ... is to the effect that Edward Rose, in 1824, while acting as interpreter and guide for a large party of trappers under Jedediah Smith and Thomas Fitzpatrick, instigated the Crows to steal the horses of the party, and that this branch ... took its name from that incident."

Irving supports the second version in *Bonneville* (p. 244),

"... Smith and Fitzpatrick were robbed of their horses in Green River Valley; the place where the robbery took place still bears the name of Horse Creek."

142. Captain Stewart also mentions the building. In his romantic novel, *Altowan* (Vol. I, p. 35) it is described as "... a trading house, still used when they rendezvoused in these parts." Apparently it was not a part of Bonneville's Fort Nonsense which Stewart also notes as lying in ruin.

H. E. Tobie, writing on "Joseph L. Meek, a Conspicuous Personality," says that Moses "Black" Harris left the note on the log store building, and that it read, "Come to Popoazua and you will find plenty trade, whiskey and white women."

143. Actually, one more rendezvous was held before the Rocky Mountain fur trade came to its end as an organized business.

144. Probably the stream now known as "Ditch Creek."

145. The direction is probably in error; it would need to be easterly.

146. This stream, which is now known as Falls River, originates in the southwest corner of Yellowstone National Park.

147. Sheep Falls.

148. The Bechler Meadows in Falls River Basin.

149. Raft River was called the "Cassia" by Ferris, and "Casu" by Wyeth. Jason Lee says it ". . . received its name from the circumstances that some of the traders were obliged to make a raft to cross it in high water." Certainly the name must have been given early for Peter Skene Ogden notes in his Journal (p. 356):

"Monday, March 20th [1825]. I sent two men with traps to examine Raft River."

150. The account books of Fort Hall show that Trask entered the service of the Columbia River Fishing and Trading Company September 30, 1835, as a crewman on the supply ship *May Dacre*. His monthly wage was sixteen dollars.

151. Compare this Fourth of July with the dismal one recorded on pp. 18-19.

152. The junction of Lewis River with Snake River in Yellowstone National Park.

153. This is Lewis Lake in Yellowstone National Park.

154. Shoshone Lake. This beautiful lake, which is the second largest in Yellowstone National Park, was first mapped by Captain W. W. DeLacy, who visited it with a party of prospectors in 1863. Many early maps gave the lake his name, but the United States Geological Survey supplanted it with the name of the linguistic group of Indians which includes the Snake tribe.

155. The Shoshone Geyser Basin. This thermal area contained thirteen active geysers in 1930, three of them erupting to heights of 50 feet or more, and Russell's estimate of 50 hot springs is certainly no exaggeration. A very good description of the area and its features is given by Allen and Day, pp. 307-19.

156. None of the geysers presently active in the Shoshone Basin resemble the "Hour Spring" in the interval between eruptions. However, the variability of geyser activity is so well established that a difference is to be expected after such a long span of time.

157. This is the Firehole River, a tributary of the Madison, not the Jefferson. Here Russell was among the great geysers of the Upper Geyser basin — the area dominated by Old Faithful.

158. The geyser basins of Shoshone Lake and the Firehole River lie at nearly the same elevation.

159. This is an excellent description of the Grand Prismatic Spring, the largest hot spring in the Midway Geyser Basin. The guidebook to Yellowstone National Park gives a remarkably similar description.

160. The route followed was down the Firehole River to the point where it joins the Gibbon to form the Madison River; then up the Gibbon River. Here the location of "Burnt Hole" is shown in relation to the Firehole geyser basins (cf. note 60).

161. Hayden Valley, named for Dr. Ferdinand V. Hayden of the United States Geological Survey.

162. Probably on Hell Roaring Creek; from there a northwest course would take them to Mill Creek.

163. The encampment was on the bank of Pelican Creek just north of the point where the highway now crosses it east of Fishing Bridge settlement. Where the stream enters Lake Yellowstone its course is only a few degrees west of south, however, the general course is southwest.

164. The hot springs at West Thumb.

165. This is Heart Lake. Following the wind for a guide led Russell southeast instead of southwest, bringing him out in the Heart Lake Geyser Basin.

166. Russell's references to "right" or "left" hand of a stream are always made as though looking upstream; just the opposite of the accepted practice today. The date here does not agree with that carried forward from previous entries; it should be September 2.

167. Probably Owl Creek in what is now Grand Teton National Park. Allyn Hanks, formerly Chief Ranger there, pointed the route out to me in 1945 as one commonly used by the "mountain men" in crossing the Teton Range. However, the route could have been the one later followed by the Marysville freight road which roughly paralleled the south boundary of Yellowstone National Park. While the distances the party covered — twenty miles the first day and thirty the second — seem long marches for wounded men, desperation undoubtedly spurred their exertions.

168. The junction of Henry's Fork and Falls River, or the "Falling Fork," as it was called by the trappers.

169. See pp. 101-106. Correcting the error in dating would make this September 6, 1839.

170. He was one of the "lay assistants" who accompanied the Rev. Jason Lee to Oregon. Walker stayed in the Oregon country, and Wyeth put him in charge of the properties on Sauvies Island at the time Fort Hall was sold. Apparently he took service with the Hudson's Bay Company when they leased the Island from Wyeth.

171. This area is still called the "Camas Meadow."

172. Dr. John McLoughlin circulated good books among his traders in isolated posts and it appears that Russell had access to the "library" at Fort Hall.

173. This stream cannot be identified.

174. The Weber River on which Ogden, Utah, is situated. It is joined by the Ogden River in the western suburbs of that town (cf. p. 116).

175. People of the same thought or kindred souls. The expression does not imply a blood relationship.

176. The word stems from the French word *venaison* and originally meant the flesh of any wild game, as its root, the Latin *venor*, to hunt, would suggest.

177. This figure of speech is still common in the southern part of the United States.

178. *Tête-a-tête*.

179. Named for Peter Skene Ogden, a trader for the Hudson's Bay Company, who led his brigade into it, probably as early as 1825. The city of Ogden, Utah, now occupies the valley.

180. In Russell's description the outstanding topographic features of the Great Salt Lake are readily recognized; Antelope, Stansbury and Fremont Islands, Terrace Mountain, and Promontory Mountain.

181. Utah Lake, which drains into Great Salt Lake.

182. The name of this missionary is unknown.

183. The name was originally applied to another stream, the Big Woody. The Alexander Ross map, an undated sheet in manuscript hand, shows the "River Malade or Poisonous Beaver" entering the Snake River from the north at a point just below "Snake Falls." Peter Skene Ogden says that it "... derives its name from the beaver living on a poisonous root. Formerly, in 1819, all who ate of the beaver taken here were seriously ill." Ferris (p. 65) has more to say about the effects: "The river ... is called 'La Riviere Maladi,' (Sick River), and owes its name to the fact that the beaver found upon it, if eaten by the unwary hunter, causes him to have a singular fit, the symptoms of which are, stiffness of the neck, pains in the bones, and nervous contortions of the face." On the following page Ferris says, "There is a small stream flowing into the Big Lake, the beaver taken from which, produce the same effect." It is of this stream that Russell speaks, and it is the one which has retained the name of "Malad."

184. Alfred Shutes.

185. This peak cannot be identified; probably it was a summit in the Portneuf Range.

186. Dr. Elijah White was earlier associated with the Methodist Mission of Jason Lee in the Willamette Valley. In 1842 he returned as a Federal Indian sub-agent, bringing with him a wagon train which marked the beginning of the "covered wagon" migration to Oregon. It was, however, a stormy undertaking with much quarreling and several divisions.

187. The myth that the Flathead Indians of Western Montana deformed

skulls of infants is most tenacious. In spite of the great weight of evidence to the contrary, it is still given credence in some places (see *The American Indian* by A. Hyatt Verrill, p. 334). Actually, the "Flatheads" were so called because their heads were normal rather than peaked by compression, as was the custom among some tribes on the Northwest coast. For a very thorough treatise on this often misunderstood name see "The Flathead-Salish Indian Name in Montana Nomenclature," by Albert J. Partoll.

188. The coyote, *Canis latrans.*

189. The Rocky Mountain Pika, *Ochotona princeps,* and related species, commonly known as the cony or rock rabbit.

190. The Golden-mantled Marmot, *Marmota flaviventris nosophora,* is the most common of the several Western woodchucks found in the Northern Rocky Mountains.

191. See note 23.

SOURCES

"Account-books of Fort Hall, 1834-1837," 3 ledgers, mss. collection of the Oregon Historical Society, Portland, 1,110 pp.

Allen, (Miss) A. J., *Ten years in Oregon; Travels . . . and adventures of Doctor E. White and lady west of the Rocky Mountains.* Ithaca, New York, 1848. 430 pp.

Allen, E. T. and Arthur L. Day, *Hot springs of the Yellowstone National Park,* Publication number 466, Carnegie Institution of Washington, 1935. 525 pp.

Atkinson, Rev. George H., "Diary of the Rev. George H. Atkinson, 1847-1858," Part IV, edited by E. Ruth Rockwood, *Oregon Historical Society Quarterly,* 40:345-61 (December, 1939).

Bancroft, Hubert Howe, *History of Oregon,* Vol. I, 1834-1848, *(Bancroft's works,* Vol. XXIX), San Francisco: The History Company, 1886.

Brown, J. Henry, *Brown's political history of Oregon,* Vol. I, Portland, Oregon: Wiley B. Allen, publisher (Press of the Lewis and Dryden Printing Company), 1892. 462 pp.

Burnett, Peter H., "Recollections and opinions of an old pioneer," Chaps. IV, V, *Oregon Historical Society Quarterly,* 5: (2) 151-98, (3) 272-305 (June, September, 1904).

Chittenden, Hiram Martin, *The American fur trade of the Far West,* 3 vols., New York: Francis P. Harper, 1902. 1,029 pp. (paged continuously).

Chittenden, Hiram Martin, *Yellowstone National Park,* Cincinnati, Ohio: Robert Clark Company, 1895. 397 pp.

Coutan, Charles Griffin, *History of Wyoming,* Vol. I, Laramie, Wyoming: Chaplin, Spafford and Mathison, printers, 1899. 712 pp. (Only Vol. I published).

DeVoto, Bernard, *Across the wide Missouri,* Cambridge, Massachusetts: Houghton Mifflin Company, The Riverside Press, 1947. 483 pp.

Dobbs, Caroline C., *Men of Champoeg,* Portland, Oregon: Metropolitan Press, 1932. 218 pp.

Domenech, Abbe Em., *Seven years residence in the great deserts of North America,* Vol. I, London: Longman, Green, Longman and Roberts, 1860. 445 pp.

Fenton, W. D., "The winning of the Oregon country," *Oregon Historical Society Quarterly,* 6: (4) 343-78 (December, 1905).

 176   SOURCES

Ferris, Warren Angus, *Life in the Rocky Mountains*, Paul C. Phillips editor, Denver, Colorado: Fred A. Rosenstock, The Old West Publishing Company, 1940. 365 pp.

Folsom, David E., *The Folsom-Cook exploration of the Upper Yellowstone in the year 1869*, preface by N. P. Langford, St. Paul, Minnesota: H. L. Collins Company, printers, 1894. 22 pp.

Griffin, J. S., "Subscribers to the *American and Unionist* in account with J. S. Griffin, June 1848," (account book in the Griffin records), Pacific University, Forest Grove, Oregon. 20 pp.

Grover, LaFayette, *The Oregon archives, including the journals, Governor's messages and public papers of Oregon*, Salem, Oregon; Asahel Bush, public printer, 1853. 333 pp.

"Hallowell, Maine, Vital Records," Vol. I (Births), p. 255.

Holman, Frederick V., "A brief history of the Oregon Provisional Government and what caused its formation," *Oregon Historical Society Quarterly*, 13: (2) 89-139 (June, 1912).

Hutton, J. D., "Reconnaissance from Platte to Powder River," Report of the Secretary of War—*Captain Raynolds' report on the exploration of the Yellowstone*, U. S., 40th Cong., 2nd Sess., Senate, Ex. doc. 77, Washington: Government Printing Office, 1868. pp. 170-74.

Irving, Washington, "Astoria, or anecdotes of an enterprise beyond the Rocky Mountains," *The works of Washington Irving*, Vol. II, New York: Pollard and Moss, publishers, 1882. pp. 301-435.

Irving, Washington, "The adventures of Captain Bonneville," *The works of Washington Irving*, Vol. III, New York: Pollard and Moss, publishers, 1882. pp. 269-371.

Langford, Nathaniel Pitt, *Diary of the Washburn expedition to the Yellowstone and Firehole Rivers in the year 1870*, St. Paul (?), Minnesota, 1905. 122 pp.

Larocque, Francois Antoine, *The journal of Francois Antoine Larocque from the Assiniboine River to the Yellowstone—1805*. Ruth Hazlitt, translator and editor, (University of Montana historical reprint no. 20), Missoula, Montana: State University of Montana, 1934. 26 pp.

Lee, Rev. Jason, "Diary of Rev. Jason Lee," *Oregon Historical Society Quarterly*, 17: 116-46, 240-66, 397-430, (June, September, December, 1916).

Lewis, Meriwether and William Clark, *Original journals of the Lewis and Clark expedition 1804-1806*, Vol. VI, Reuben Gold Thwaites, editor, New York: Dodd, Mead and Company, 1904-5. 280 pp.

SOURCES

Marsh, James B., *Four Years in the Rockies or the adventures of Issac P. Rose*, Columbus, Ohio: reprinted by Long's College Book Company, 1950. 262 pp.

Maynadier, Lt. H. E., "Report of First Lieutenant H. E. Maynadier, 10th Infantry, on route between the Yellowstone and Platte rivers, 1859," *Report of the Secretary of War — Captain Raynolds' report on the exploration of the Yellowstone*, U. S., 40th Cong., 2nd Sess., Senate Ex. doc. 77, Washington: Government Printing Office, 1868. pp. 127-54.

Mullan, Lt. John, "Report of an exploration from Cantonment Stevens to Fort Hall and back, by Lieutenant John Mullan, United States Army, with his route to St. Mary's and up the Jefferson fork of the Missouri," *Report of exploration of a route for the Pacific railroad — Governor Steven's report to the Secretary of War,* Washington, 1854. pp. 312-51.

Mullan, Lt. John, "Report of First Lieutenant John Mullan, 2d dragoons, on route from Fort Benton to Fort Union, between the Missouri and the Yellowstone rivers, 1860," *Report of the Secretary of War — Captain Raynolds' report on the the exploration of the Yellowstone*, U. S. 40th Cong., 2nd Sess., Senate, Ex. doc. 77, Washington: Government Printing Office, 1868. pp. 161-70.

National Resources Board, *Certain aspects of the land problems and government land policies*, Section V, Washington, D. C.: Government Printing Office, 1935. pp. 60-85.

Nesmith, Hon. J. W., "List of settlers in Oregon country in fall of 1843," *Oregon Pioneer Transactions*, 1875: 54.

Ogden, Peter Skene, "The Peter Skene Ogden journals," editorial notes by T. C. Elliott, *Oregon Historical Society Quarterly*, 10: (4) 331-365 (December, 1909).

"Oregon City donation land certificate file in the National Archives," (File microcopy FM 145), State Library Archives, Salem, Oregon.

Oregon land claim record, 1845-6, book 4 (book 1), Office of the Secretary of State, Salem, Oregon, 166 pp.

Oregon Supreme Court records, Oregon Territory — 1844, (microcopy of Supreme Court record book no. 1), State Library Archives, Salem, Oregon.

Oregon Supreme Court records, "Judges of the Supreme Court of Oregon," (unpublished biographical data compiled by the Clerk of the Supreme Court), c. 1936.

Partoll, Albert J., editor, *Anderson's narrative of a ride to the Rocky Mountains in 1834*, (University of Montana historical reprint No. 27), Missoula, Montana: State University of Montana, 1938. 12 pp.

Partoll, Albert J., "The Flathead-Salish Indian name in Montana nomenclature," *Montana Magazine of History*, 1: (1) 37-47. (January, 1951).

Pattie, James Ohio, *The personal narrative of James O. Pattie, of Kentucky*, edited by Timothy Flint, (Cincinnati, Ohio, 1833).

Placerville (California) *Mountain Democrat*, September 4, 1892.

Provisional Government of Oregon, documents 837, 920, 1079, 1369, 1521, 12220, Archives, State Library, Salem, Oregon.

Provisional Government of Oregon, Fee Record Book (Resignations, etc., 1848), Archives, State Library, Salem, Oregon.

Raynolds, W. F., "Captain Raynolds' report and journal," *Report of the Secretary of War — Captain Raynolds' report on the exploration of the Yellowstone*, U. S., 40th Cong., 2nd Sess., Senate Ex. doc. 77, Washington: Government Printing Office, 1868. pp. 18-127.

Report of the Chief of Engineers, Annual reports of the War Department, Part 5, Appendix FFF, "Yellowstone National Park," Washington: Government Printing Office, 1901. pp. 3777-3798.

Robertson, James R., "Origin of Pacific University," prepared from University records and other sources, *Oregon Historical Quarterly*, 6: (2) 109-146 (June, 1905).

Russell, Osborne, Letters to Martha Russell and Mrs. Eleanor Read, William Robertson Coe Collection of Western Americana, Yale University Library, New Haven, Connecticut.

Russell, Osborne, "Journal of a trapper, or, Nine years residence among the Rocky Mountains between the years of 1834 and 1843," (original manuscript in the William Robertson Coe Collection of Western Americana, Yale University Library, New Haven, Connecticut), 190 pp.

Scott, Leslie N., "First taxes in Oregon, 1844," *Oregon Historical Society Quarterly*, 31: (1) 1-24 (March, 1930).

Stewart, Sir William George Drummond, 7th bart., *Altowan: or, Incidents of life and adventure in the Rocky Mountains*, Vol. I., edited by J. Watson Webb, New York: Harper and Brothers, 1846. 255 pp.

The (Oregon) *Spectator*, June 24, 1847; November 25, 1847; March 9, 1848; June 15, 1848; and July 27, 1848.

Thornton, Hon. J. Quinn, "History of the Provisional Government," *Oregon Pioneer Transactions*, 1875: 43-96.

Thorpe, John, Letters, to Gen. Joseph Lane, July 23, 1851; November 7, 1851; November 22, 1851; and January 7, 1854, manuscript collection of the Oregon Historical Society Library, Portland, Oregon.

SOURCES

Tobie, H. E., "Joseph L. Meek, a conspicuous personality, II, 1834-1839," *Oregon Historical Quarterly*, 29:86-306 (1938).

Townsend, John Kirk, "Narrative of a journey across the Rocky Mountains to the Columbia River," Reuben Gold Thwaites, editor, *Early Western travels*, Vol. XXI, Cleveland, Ohio: Arthur H. Clark Company, 1905. pp. 107-369.

Tozier, Albert, Letter to Harriet C. Long, April 1936, State Library Archives, Salem, Oregon. 4 pp.

Tualatin Academy secretary's record book, Minute Book No. 1, 1848, Pacific University, Forest Grove, Oregon, 148 pp.

Vestal, Stanley, *Jim Bridger, mountain man*, New York: William Morrow and Company, 1946. 333 pp.

Victor, Mrs. Francis Fuller, *River of the West*, Hartford, Connecticut: Columbian Book Company, 1871. 602 pp.

Wislizenus, F. A., *A journey to the Rocky Mountains in the year 1839*, translated from the German by Frederick A. Wislizenus, St. Louis, Missouri: Missouri Historical Society, 1912. 162 pp.

Wyeth, Nathaniel Jarvis, "Correspondence and journals of Captain Nathaniel J. Wyeth, 1831-6," edited by F. G. Young, *Sources of the history of Oregon*, Vol. I, Parts 3-6, Eugene, Oregon: University Press, 1899. 262 pp.

York, L. A., editor, *Journal of a trapper, or, Nine years in the Rocky Mountains, 1834-1843*, Boise, Idaho: Syms-York Company, Inc., 1914. 105 pp.

Young, F. G., "Ewing Young and his estate," *Oregon Historical Quarterly*, 21: (3) 171-316, (September, 1920).

INDEX TO THE MAPS OF OSBORNE RUSSELL'S TRAVELS

Osborne Russell's Letters

This edition of *Journal of a Trapper* has been expanded by inclusion of Osborne Russell's known letters to his sisters, Martha and Eleanor, in Maine. Though intended only for his family, the letters are of lasting interest—as a source of biographical information concerning Russell, and for what they say about two phases of our westward expansion.

The first and second letters, penned from Oregon's Willamette Valley, provide a rare glimpse into the petulant thoughts of those Americans who were then upon the far western horizon of "manifest destiny." In them Russell voices the feeling of resentment with which the settlers viewed the Federal Government's failure to ease some of those same burdens which had caused them to seek territorial status under the jurisdiction of the United States. The third letter, written from the California gold mines, is alight with the enthusiasm of the Forty-niners; gone is the embittered outlook of the Oregon pioneer, metamorphosed into the expansiveness of the Argonaut. The change in attitude so noticeable in Osborne Russell's letters occurred with many other Oregonians, and enough of them returned to the Willamette Valley that it was never quite the same thereafter.

A.L.H.

To Miss Martha Russell, Hallowell, Maine.

Oregon, Polk County, April 3, 1848.

Dear Sister:

I received your letter, dated January 31st, '47, on the 18th of September last, and the one dated 16th March on the 1st October; and if your last letter speaks the language of your heart (which I do not doubt) you can imagine in some degree my feelings upon receipt of letters from the dearest female relations I have on earth. And when your eyes rest upon the date of this letter, do not impute it to a want of regard or negligence, that an answer to your letters has so long been delayed. In Oregon we are all mere creatures of chance so far as regards communication with the civilized world; and indeed, I sometimes fear the "masterly inactivity" of the government of the United States towards affording protection to the people of Oregon will drive them to a desperate extreme.

Congress has treated us with a shameful neglect which we do not deserve.

Notwithstanding our feeble resources, we are now involved in an expensive Indian war, the cause of which I shall briefly relate.

On the 29th of November last, the Cayuse Indians, who live 300 miles up the Columbia, massacred fourteen white persons, most of whom were missionaries residing among them, among whom were Dr. Marcus Whitman and his estimable lady, who had founded the mission among the Cayuses in 1837 under the auspices of the American Board of Boston. The only cause they could assign for the commission of such an atrocious deed was a report secretly spread among them, that Dr. Whitman and the whites wished to kill them and take their lands, and for that purpose, the last immigration from the the States had introduced the measles among them. It is true the last immigration did fetch the measles into all the inhabited parts of Oregon, the effects of which have proven severe on the Indians from their mode of treating the disease. There were several families of whites amounting to upwards of seventy persons residing among the Cayuse at the mission. The men were nearly all killed and the women subjected to indignities too horrid to be described, for about twelve days, when their freedom was purchased by the Hudson's Bay Company.

The name of Peter S. Ogden will long be remembered with

gratitude, not only by those he so timely released from such a dreadful captivity, but by every American in Oregon who has a heart susceptible of feeling.

Our Legislature being in session at the time the distressing news arrived at Oregon City, measures were immediately adopted for raising and equipping 500 men for the purpose of punishing the Cayuses as their crime deserved.

Whilst seated at the table writing this letter I have received intelligence from the regiment, which started on the campaign in January last. They have had several skirmishes with the Indians and killed sixty of them. The whites have lost four killed and fifteen wounded. The colonel has been killed in camp by an accidental shot from a rifle. The lieutenant colonel has been wounded in the knee. A treaty has been concluded with the neighboring tribes, and the Cayuses have been informed that a treaty of peace will be made with them on no other consideration than delivering up the murderers and paying of war expenses. And worse than all, the regiment is much in want of ammunition. I said worse than all, but I recall the expression; our worst treatment comes from our mother country, who instead of affording us the protection we have so long prayed for, she sent a ship to us modestly requesting 500 men to assist in the war with Mexico!

Alas! has it come to this? A colony of American citizens living on American soil, continually imploring protection in the most humiliating manner for nine years, and then meet with such a response as this! It is but too true. Citizens and subjects of foreign governments deride us with the neglect of our government, and what can we say in its defense? With shame and confusion we are subjected to the humiliating confession of the truth. We are informed that Congress at their last session passed an act to establish a mail by sea from the United States to Oregon, but the information of such an act being passed is all the benefit we have as yet derived from it.

But our political circumstance is too gloomy a subject for me to dwell longer upon, even if time and space would permit. And now, my dear sister, since the rehearsal of a few out of the many of our political misfortunes have put me somewhat in an ill humor, I hope to be forgiven if you should feel a little of its effects.

Are you aware that your letter dated January 31st, the first I ever received from you, and which now lays open before me, is not even embellished with your signature, and your name nowhere to be seen on the sheet? Now, I think such a nice, clean, and above all, such an affectionate letter, should not have been ashamed to bear the signature of its fair author, and the only excuse I can frame for the omission was the indisposition of which you complained when you wrote.

I return you an affectionate brother's thanks for the souvenir I received enclosed in your second letter, which although of small nominal value, I assure you is highly esteemed, and would be doubly so had the letters comprising the motto been wrought with your own fair hair.

You seemed to be pleased that I was not married, but I assure you that should I get married in this country, or should death (who is no respecter of persons) overtake me, my last will will testify my regard for you. Your affectionate letters have added much to my anxiety to visit Maine. I have not at present the least inclination to marry in this country. But I must first secure the title to my lands before I can visit the United States.

My health since I wrote last has been better than formerly.

The past winter has been the finest I ever saw; the finest quality of beef is now being killed from the natural pastures. Oregon promises a more abundant crop of wheat this year than was ever before known in this country.

I have sent my journal of mine residence in the Rocky

Mountains to New York for publication, and have instructed my agent at that place to forward you a copy of it when published.

Give my best wishes to Daniel, Lemuel and families, and tell them I cannot anticipate the contents of their letters enough to answer them before I receive them. Since the year 1834 I have received five letters from my relatives, viz, one from Daniel, one from Samuel, one from Eleanor, and two from yourself.

You thought I had better go to Maine and get a load of Kennebec girls and fetch out to Oregon. Such a cargo would doubtless find a ready market in Oregon, if the policy of insurance upon it were not purchased too dear, and I think no man in his right senses would ship such a cargo without having it insured, not only against the insults of Neptune, but the wantonness of Cupid.

Give my best compliments to Uncle Sam and Ursula, and tell the old gentleman I have known jokes accidentally turned into hard earnest. And tell those who are solicitous about gaining mother's consent on my behalf that it is not impossible that I may appear among them some day like Irving's Dutchman after twenty years' sleep.

Give my respects to old Mr. Boswell and family and all others who feel enough interested in me to inquire for me.

It is a great consolation to me to think that you live happy and contented. Notwithstanding my philosophy has taught me how happy three clams can live in a junk bottle, it teaches me that true happiness is contentment, and vice versa.

Give mother the love of an affectionate son and William that of a brother. Tell mother I should be extremely glad to grant her request to "come home," but it is impossible for me to do so at present without a sacrifice which, I dare say, she would not wish me to make; but do not despair of seeing me at no far distant period. I should have been in Hallowell before this, had the United States extended their jurisdiction and gave security to my property.

Another subject occurs to my memory which I had almost forgotten. Before I left Maine, grandfather sent to the family a recipe for making pills; if that recipe is in being I wish to obtain a copy of it, and shall consider it a great favor if you will forward it by the first opportunity.

You half expressed a wish to be with me to enjoy with me the evening hours. Could I harbour a wish that you should leave mother, the next one of all others would be that you were with me. Write every opportunity. If the mail goes into operation this year by way of Panama, we shall have a better opportunity for communication. I write Eleanor tomorrow in answer to her letter. My time is brief and the sheet full; I will therefore close this epistle by imploring the blessing of that Being in whom we live, move and have our being, now and forever. Adieu from your brother,

/Sgd/ Osborne Russell.

To Mrs. Eleanor Read, Lewiston, Maine (by the politeness of James Neall, Esq.)

Oregon, Polk County, April 4th, 1848.

Dear Sister:

I received the letters from Martha and yourself dated January 31st, '47, on the 18th day of September, last; your own experience will dictate to you the inexpressible delight which I felt on the receipt of them, better than my pen can describe it. A person by the name of Hanford brought these letters from the States to Oregon but I have never been able to see him of learn anything from your friend Haket. This is the first opportunity I have had of answering your letter; a party is now about to start across the mountains to the States, to which I entrust the care of a letter to yourself and one to Martha Ann.

I cannot answer my brother's letters until I receive them. It would afford me the greatest satisfaction to comply with your earnest request "to come home" and visit with you all, but it is a pleasure which reason dictates that I must forego at present, as my presence in Oregon is indispensably necessary, until the United States extend their jurisdiction over us, in order to acquire title to my lands and property. Nevertheless, I sincerely hope the time is not far distant, when my ardent desires to see my native land will be fulfilled.

It affords me consolation to know that you have a partner suited to your wishes. May your days glide smoothly in uninterrupted happiness and may you continue to dwell in the affections of your husband and favour of your God, and may Lemuel by a faithful discharge of the duties he owes to his family, to society, to his country and his God, continue to merit those affections.

We have had one of the most pleasant winters I ever experienced. The grass has been remarkably fine all winter, and the finest quality of beef is now killed from the natural pastures. Garden vegetables such as beets, onions, turnips, potatoes, and in fact nearly all roots, do best in this country to stand in the ground all winter, especially where the soil is inclined to be sandy, as we never have frost sufficient to injure them. The wheat promises an extraordinary crop this year; it is thought it will average twenty-five bushels to the acre throughout the country. It was generally put in the ground in autumn or the early part of winter, although winter wheat can be sown here in any month of the year. You who have never seen what is called a prairie country, can form but a faint idea of the beauty of its scenery. A diversity of oak-covered hills, cleared of underbrush as if by the hand of art, and plains covered with the most luxuriant verdure, intersected with small streams from the mountains, whose serpentine courses divide them into convenient farms, which are supplied with wood and timber from the narrow groves along their banks, or the oak groves on the intervening hills, constitute the face of this valley as viewed from my residence eastward, until the sight is lost in the smokey atmosphere thirty miles distant, or rests on the towering peaks of Mount Washington and Jefferson, with their snow-crowned heads,

That ofttimes pierce the onward fleeting mists,
Whose feet are washed by gentle summer showers,
Whilst Phoebus' rays play on their sparkling crests.

But, my dear sister, beautiful as this country is, that is, this portion of it (for I now speak only of the Willamete valley) my better reason would not prompt me to wish you were here at present, although the contemplation of the scenery around me often dictates the wish that not only you, but all the family were here. We have to undergo, the best of us, in this country, privations of which you are little acquainted, and which must always be expected in the settlement of a new country.

We are now engaged in an expensive Indian war which we have been unavoidably drawn into, but the theatre of action is 200 miles from this valley. The particulars of this war I have briefly described in Martha's letter.

My health is very good in comparison to what it has formerly been.

Give my best respects to your husband, and tell him that although we are not personally acquainted, yet a letter from him would be received as a favour. Give my love to your children and my respects to all inquiring friends.

Write every opportunity.

And now, that the God of heaven may bless you and yours, and his spirit guide you in the path of duty, direct [and] protect you from the snares and temptations which the flesh is subject to in this world, and bring you to everlasting happiness, is the sincere prayer of your affectionate brother,

/Sgd/ Osborne Russell

To Mrs. Eleanor Read, Lewiston, Maine (by the politeness of Mr. Kinney).

California (Gold Mines) Nov. 10, 1849.

Dear Sister:

You will probably be astonished when you see my locality at the date of this letter, as I think Maine, and even Hallowell, must by this time have had a touch of the gold fever.

I left Oregon last September for this country by land, and arrived here on the 25th of the same, and on the 20th October was attacked with the bilious fever, which lasted until winter. I remained in the mines during the winter and until now, and shall also spend this winter in the mines.

Owing to my ill health last winter I engaged in merchandising; in March commenced collecting gold with my own hands and continued working until the first of October, when I commenced business under the firm of Russell & Gilliam—provision store and boarding house—my partner, an old neighbor from Oregon, having his family here. We are doing a thriving business for this country. About 30,000 people have come across land to this country this season. The old miners, I think average from $12 to $16 per day, estimating gold at $6 per ounce.

Cities and towns are rising up among the hills and mountains in the gold region as if by the effect of magic.

The place where we are located is called Gallowstown. It is situated fifty-five miles east of the city of Sacramento, on the south side, within four miles of the American River. It takes the name from the fact of our having hung three men for murder last winter. Your brother sat as one of the judges pro tempore on the trial. Since that dreadful execution, this has been one of the most quiet communities I ever lived in.

Some people here are getting gold by the pound per day, and others not making more than their board, and I am informed it is the same throughout the mines, which are nearly 400 miles in length—confined entirely to the hills, mountain streams and ravines. The most I have ever dug in a day was $100, but have frequently obtained $40 to $60 per day.

The gold here in this place is coarse, from one-half dollar to six ounces in a piece, yet some is so fine that it can hardly be seen with the naked eye. But let this suffice for the gold diggings and let something else take its place.

I received a letter from Martha, dated September 24th, 1848, in which she informed me that she was to be married in December, and that is the only cause why she does not get an answer from me. Not that I have the least wish to prevent her from uniting with the man of her choice, but I must hear of her being certainly married, and to whom, before I shall know how to direct a letter to her, as this life is filled with uncertainties.

A gentleman from Thomaston, Maine, with whom I became acquainted this spring, stepping into the store today, told me he should start for Maine on the 12th and should pass through Lewiston, as he had some relatives living there. I also having a dear relative living there, determined at once to send her a letter, although she has not yet answered my last.

I am in good health, good spirits, and full of business at present, and it is now near eleven o'clock at night and I must yet write a few lines to Daniel before I sleep. When I shall see Maine I cannot tell, but expect to see it before long and fetch with me some of the California gold. But people value not gold here as they would in the United States. The sight of so much of it makes it familiar to them and depreciates its value. Silver coin seems like iron.

Give my best respects to Mr. Read and an uncle's love to your children, with compliments to all inquiring friends.

Send your letters to Sacramento City, California, by the first opportunity, and believe me to be your most affectionate brother,

/Sgd/ Osborne Russell.

The Coe Collection at Yale University Library contains another letter—apparently the last written by Russell to his family in Maine. Written from Placerville, California, on August 26, 1855, to his sister, Eleanor, soon after returning ill and discouraged from ten months in the Sierra Nevada Mountains, Russell's words appear to be little more than irrational ravings. Since most of the information conveyed—the causes of his estrangement with his family—is of no importance to history, the letter is omitted except for the conclusion of the postscript. In it Russell says:

". . . I have asked Martha 4 times if she ever received a package entitled a *Rocky Mountain Journal,* or rather *A Trappers Journal During Nine [Years] Residence in The Rocky Mountains,* by O. Russell, sent her privately by PSUS.

"Now cannot any of you tell me if she has or has not received it. That one I was offered one thousand dollars for last week but my reply was, 'my youngest sister has the copyright.'

O. Russell."

INDEX

Abernethy, George, xi

Absaroka Indians, *see* Crow Indians

Absaroka Range, 22, 159

"Account-Books of Fort Hall," xvi, 157, 164, 166, 170

Ague, 7, 67, 157

Aiken-lo-ruckkup (Bannock Chief), 36-37

Algonquin linguistic group, 161

Allen, A. J., 155

Allen, E. T., 163

Allen, William, 61, 64, 65, 66, 67, 69, 71, 72, 75, 77, 80

American Falls Reservoir, 156

American Fur Company, vi, vii, 3, 55, 157, 166, 167

Anderson, William Marshall, 166

Antelope, 3, 15, 47, 112, 122, 123; description of, 134-135

Antelope Island, 122, 172

Aricara Indians, 167

Arkansas River, 127, 128, 167

Ashley, William H., 49, 155, 158, 169

Astorians, 155, 156, 159

Atkinson, Rev. George H., viii, xii, xvi, xvii

Atlantic Creek, 163

Badger, 131

Bailey, Dr. William J., ix, x, xi, xviii

Bald Eagle, 69

Bancroft, Hubert Howe, xvii

Bannock Indians, 157; *see also* Bonnak Indians

Bannock Trail, 160

Baptiste, ——, 169

Battles and skirmishes, 8, 12, 16-17, 30-31, 32, 40, 48, 49, 52, 54, 55, 56, 59-60, 61, 86-89, 102, 161, 164, 165

Baudins Fork, *see* Bodair's Fork

Bear, 3, 51; black, 133; grizzly, 6-7, 9, 11, 47, 65, 66, 83-84, 124, 131-132

Bear Lake, *see* Snake Lake

Bear River, 3, 4, 9, 11, 13, 40, 41, 59, 112, 122, 123, 124, 125, 158

Bear River Range, 156

Beauvais Creek, *see* Bovy's Fork

Beaver, 10, 11, 20, 28, 31-33, 40, 44, 46-50, 55, 57, 60, 65, 66, 83-85, 90, 91, 94-96, 99-101, 108-110, 122, 125; construction by, 151-152; description and habits, 149-152; furs of, 71, 81, 112; medicine from, 105; scarcity of, vii, 27, 82, 112, 123; sickness from eating, 124-172; trapping of, 150

Beaverhead Creek, 33

"Beavers head," 162

Bechler Meadows, 170

Beckworth, Jim, 169

Beers, Alanson, xviii

Beer Springs, *see* Soda Springs

Belt Mountains, 163

Bellevue (Fort), 168

Biggs, Thomas, 79, 80

Big Lake, *see* Salt Lake

Big Hole Mountains, 159

Big Horn River, 25, 54, 55, 56, 57, 61, 70, 82, 83, 165, 168

Big Rosebud, 163

Big Salt Lake, 3; *see also* Salt Lake

Big Woody River, 172

Black Bear Lake, *see* Snake Lake

Blackfeet Indians: avoided by trappers, 38, 57, 68, 86, 93, 101; battles with trappers, 16-17, 30-31, 32, 49, 52, 56, 86-89, 102; character of, 161;